A TIGER IN HIS TIME

A TIGER IN HIS TIME

Hal Newhouser and the
Burden of Wartime Ball

DAVID M. JORDAN

Diamond Communications, Inc.
South Bend, Indiana

1990

A TIGER IN HIS TIME
Copyright © 1990 by Diamond Communications, Inc.

Manufactured in the United States of America

Diamond Communications, Inc.
Post Office Box 88
South Bend, Indiana 46624
(219) 287-5008
FAX (219) 287-5025

Library of Congress Cataloging-in-Publication Data

Jordan, David M., 1935–
    A tiger in his time : Hal Newhouser and the
burden of wartime ball
  /   David M. Jordan.
        p.   cm.
    Includes bibliographical references and index.
    ISBN 0-912083-49-2
    1. Newhouser, Hal, 1921–   . 2. Baseball
players – United States – Biography.   3. Detroit Tigers
(Baseball team)   4. Baseball – United States – History.
I. Title.
GV865.N48J67   1990
796.357'092 – dc20
[B]   90-43187
                                                    CIP

CONTENTS

To Laura

FOREWORD

This is the story of Hal Newhouser, a baseball pitcher of great skill and considerable accomplishment, but it is also necessarily the story of big league baseball as it was played during World War II. The two stories have to go together because Newhouser was arguably the most accomplished player of the wartime years and because his record is inevitably darkened by the shadow of wartime ball, the suspicion (indeed, a certainty in some minds) that wartime baseball was an ersatz game played by cripples, clowns, and children.

Baseball had enough problems during the war to lend credence to some of the suspicions, but there is a good bit of evidence on the other side, too—evidence that the game played during World War II was not really that much different from what was played before and after the great conflict.

Major league baseball in the mid-'40s, to set the scene, was played by 16 franchises in two leagues, with each club playing a 154-game schedule. The geographic configuration of the big leagues, unchanged since 1902, ran from Boston in the East to St. Louis in the West. The city of New York supported three teams, while Philadelphia, Boston, St. Louis, and Chicago each had two. Most games took place in the afternoon, although wartime conditions helped to foster the growth of night baseball, in those ball parks that were equipped with lights. Baseball was played on grass and dirt, and it was played outdoors. The players left their gloves on the field while their team was at bat, and the press photographers, with their big Speed Graphics, clustered back near the dugouts, ready to scurry out to any base where a close play might be developing. The ballplayers wore flannel uniforms, which appear a trifle baggy in pictures from the time, and they all had white skins. Even in the face of the manpower problems which the draft and defense factory work presented, there was little thought given, except by innovators like Bill Veeck and, later, Branch Rickey, to breaking down the barrier which had kept black men out of organized baseball since the 1880s.

The governance of the game was in the stern hands of Judge Kenesaw Mountain Landis, the white-haired autocrat who had been named commissioner in the aftermath of the Black Sox scandal of 1919. Landis, in these final years of his long tenure (he died after the 1944 World Series), was concerned primarily with keeping the game going through the war. The two league presidents were ex-newspaperman Ford Frick in the National League and the distinguished-looking Will Harridge in the American.

This, then, is the stage upon which Hal Newhouser's story unfolds, slowly and unevenly at first, as the young pitcher struggles to control himself and his pitches, but then triumphantly as the war ends and Newhouser drives his team to the championship. Then, of course, the story continues on for many years after the war, as times and conditions change, and so, inevitably, does Harold Newhouser.

This is not an authorized biography. I had Hal Newhouser's cooperation, to the extent of sitting down with me and my tape recorder for several hours, and later of answering some written questions I submitted to him.

He expressed initial skepticism about my project – he's not too happy with how his career has been treated by posterity – but he was willing to go along with me. My starting point was wonder that Newhouser was not in the Hall of Fame at Cooperstown, and I told him that, but he had no guarantee that my viewpoint would not change as I went along.

Whether or not Newhouser makes it into the Hall is now up to the Veterans Committee, which is empowered to elect two persons a year; the members of that committee seem to have their own agendas, and I have not heard of Newhouser's name being considered seriously in recent years. No matter. What I think this book demonstrates is that Hal Newhouser was one of the leading pitchers in baseball history, based on his record and on the judgment of those who saw him play, regardless of what happens in Cooperstown.

In the early years of his career, Newhouser was regarded by his teammates and opponents as a sorehead. With those pre-war Tiger teammates I was able to contact, there was reluctance to talk about Newhouser; Tuck Stainback said that to discuss Hal's relations with his mates would be "too personal," and he would not do it. The exception was Hank Greenberg, who admitted that he did not really get to know Newhouser until after the war, when they became close friends. Hal Newhouser, of course, was an immature kid, trying too hard, overreacting to adversity, having to grow up in the goldfish bowl of big league baseball. When he fell into the hands of Paul Richards, the wise old veteran who taught him how to control his volatile temper, Newhouser changed – as a pitcher and as a person.

From that time on, he is remembered as a gentleman. He still had a burning desire to win – one of the keys to his baseball success – but he sublimated that drive to the necessities of sportsmanship and kindness. Hal Newhouser did not smoke, drink, or chase women, and he is described by his contemporaries, of his playing days, his scouting career, and his banking years, as a man of competence and quality.

In telling this story, I had help from a number of other sources besides Newhouser. The National Baseball Library at the Hall of Fame in Cooperstown was an invaluable resource, and Tom Heitz and Lloyd Johnson, later executive director of the Society for American Baseball Research, were most helpful in my use of the library. The newspaper sections at the Library of Congress, the New York Public Library, and the Free Library of Philadelphia were very useful; George Brightbill and Pam Austin at the Photojournalism Collection of the Temple University Library helped with photos and news clippings. Other valuable assistance on photographs was rendered by Patricia Kelly of the National Baseball Library, Steven Gietschier of *The Sporting News*, and my daughter Diana Jordan. Some of my fellow members of the Society for American Baseball Research (SABR), like Eddie Gold of the *Chicago Sun-Times*, Jerry Malloy, Bob Garfinkle, and Barry Evans, had recollections of Newhouser which they shared with me. Many old ballplayers did the same; they are quoted throughout the text and are listed in the "Note on Sources" at the back. Particular thanks go to my friends Kit Crissey and Dennis Bingham for their helpful review and criticism of the manuscript and to Paul Adomites for his help and encouragement. I had brief contact with Dan Ewald, public relations director of the Tigers, who advised that the club had no plans to retire Newhouser's number "16." Janice Milam typed the manuscript and in the process learned more about baseball in the '40s and '50s than she ever dreamed she'd know. One other item: in press coverage of his early years, Hal's name was frequently misspelled "Newhauser." I have simply corrected this in quotations I have used rather than scattering through the text a multitude of "[sic]"s.

Finally, I want to thank my wife Barbara and my daughters Diana, Laura, and Sarah, for their cooperation and forebearance. Once they got over their initial surprise ("A baseball pitcher? Why a baseball pitcher?"), they became most enthusiastic in support of the project.

David M. Jordan
Jenkintown, Pennsylvania

1
HALFWAY THERE

The date was September 22, 1948, a cold and blustery Wednesday afternoon in Detroit, Michigan. A tall blond young man, slim and serious of mien, stood on the pitching mound in downtown Briggs Stadium, a large Old English letter "D" on the chest of his white uniform, the numerals "16" on his back, and went to work against the batters of the Philadelphia Athletics. He was Harold Newhouser, and he was perhaps the best pitcher in baseball at the time.

With two good pennant races pounding down to the wire, September 1948 was an exciting time. Cleveland, Boston, and the New York Yankees were fighting for the American League lead, while the Boston Braves and Brooklyn Dodgers contended in the National League. The world outside of baseball was exciting as well. The United States, throbbing with vitality and purpose in the years after World War II, led the free nations in opposition to Russian expansionism. On that day, September 22, the United States, Britain, and France addressed identical notes to the Kremlin, seeking to bring the burgeoning crisis over the status of Berlin to the negotiating table. The quadrennial presidential campaign was well underway; although its outcome was regarded as virtually settled, it still provided a good show. Governor Thomas E. Dewey of New York, the heavily-favored Republican candidate, spoke on that day in Albuquerque, New Mexico, delivering a dignified call for the unification of western Europe; Dewey's opponent, President Harry S Truman, appeared before a crowd in Oakland, California, denouncing the reactionary "mossbacks" of the GOP for strangling public power development in the West, while his listeners shouted, "Give 'em hell, Harry!" A number of newspapers carried the words of columnist George Sokolsky, urging the president to elevate his campaign from its low-toned, "vaudevillian" level, and conservative radio commentator Fulton Lewis, Jr., ridiculed Truman's efforts.

On the same day Hollywood gossip columnist Louella Parsons noted that actress Jane Wyman was a cinch for an Academy Award nomination for her portrayal of a deaf-mute in the film *Johnny Belinda*. It was this picture, though, Miss Parsons went on, that caused trouble between Wyman and her husband, actor Ronald Reagan, "because," he said, "Jane was Belinda at home and could never get herself out of the mood." America's jukeboxes that September were playing the music of Margaret Whiting, singing plaintively of "A Tree in the Meadow," and of a crooner named Jack Smith, whose hit record was "You Call Everybody Darling."

In the baseball game in Detroit, Newhouser stifled the bats of the Athletics by a score of 5-1. It was his 19th victory of the season and the 150th win of his major league career. Five months past his 27th birthday, Newhouser had reached the halfway point on the way to certified pitching immortality, the magic total of 300 lifetime victories. Few had gotten there at so young an age.

There were only 3,067 paying customers in the ball park that afternoon; the attendance was held down by the weather and by the unmistakable fact that the season which was approaching its end had not been a successful one for the Detroit ball club. The Tigers lost as often as they won, and they were 18 games behind league-leading Boston and Cleveland. Indeed, they were fixed in fifth place, nine games behind the A's. Two of their best players, outfielder Walter "Hoot" Evers and third baseman George Kell, were out of commission — Evers with pneumonia and Kell with a broken jaw. The team's pitching had been poor; one visiting Philadelphia writer commented that "Hal Newhouser is the only pitcher on the staff who has shown any form in recent weeks."

Newhouser, with the ragtag team that the 1948 Tigers had become, continued to demonstrate that he was one of the very best pitchers in the game. He was bidding for his fourth 20-win season in five years, and he alone, it seemed, was keeping the Detroit club from folding up in the last days of the season.

His teammates got off to a good start in the first inning that day, against the A's French-Canadian right-hander, Phil Marchildon; with two outs, two walks and a single loaded the bases and Eddie Mayo's hit to right scored a pair of runs. As it turned out, this would be enough for Newhouser, but the A's scored a lucky run and spoiled his shutout in the fifth inning. Second baseman Pete Suder singled to left, advanced to second on a sacrifice, to third on an infield out, and scored when Barney McCosky tapped a slow dribbler down the first-base line. Newhouser rushed over to cover the bag, but George Vico, the Detroit first baseman, lost his balance after picking up the ball and was unable to throw it to the pitcher. No other Athletics' baserunner would reach third base against Newhouser that day.

The Tigers scored three more runs in the bottom of the fifth against relief pitcher Charlie Harris, with a double by outfielder Pat Mullin the big blow, but they were just icing on Newhouser's cake. These were not the feeble Philadelphia Athletics of a few seasons earlier, chronic last-place finishers; these A's had been in contention for the pennant until a couple of weeks before, paced by solid hitters like McCosky, Ferris Fain, Eddie Joost, Elmer Valo, and Sam Chapman. Nevertheless, they went down quietly against the strong pitching of Newhouser, and when McCosky made the final out in the ninth inning, the Detroit lefthander had his milestone victory.

Watson Spoelstra, a Detroit baseball correspondent, celebrated the occasion in *The Sporting News*, writing: "Now right in the prime of his career, Hal presumably will get the opportunity to make it 300. This is a notable season for Newhouser. With a club that scarcely has been able to hold the .500 mark, he has been both a stopper and a big winner."

Newhouser tacked on two more victories before the end of the 1948 season, and the baseball experts got out their record books. They looked at the statistics of the Detroit lefthander – 152 wins at age 27, and an average of 23 wins a year for the last five seasons – and they projected him into the midst of the all-time top winners. The record for left-handed pitchers was 327 wins, held by Eddie Plank, who pitched for Connie Mack's Athletics from 1901 to 1914 and for St. Louis clubs in the Federal and American Leagues for three more seasons; Plank did not win his first game until he was 25 years old. (Of course, Plank was still pitching – and winning five games – at the age of 41.) Next in line for lefthanders was Robert Moses "Lefty" Grove, who won 300 for the A's and Red Sox between 1925 and 1941. Grove, too, was 25 when he reached the majors, but he also was 41 when he racked up his 300th and last triumph. This was exalted company for Newhouser to contemplate, but many observers of the game had little doubt that he would attain it. Lyall Smith, of the *Detroit Free Press*, wrote that "right now, the Tiger lefthander is on his way to all-time stardom" and predicted that "he will be flirting with the fabulous 300-victory mark for his major league career, a figure that will put his name in the baseball record books and in the Hall of Fame at the same time."

As things developed, Hal Newhouser did not approach the 300-win mark. He was afflicted by that bane of many fine pitchers, arm trouble, which took the zip from his fastball and too often confined him to the trainer's room. Although he pitched on for several seasons with an increasingly painful arm and shoulder, he had to struggle to reach his career total of 207 wins. As his fastball slowed down, as the victories became harder to come by, some of those same experts who had predicted his ascension to the 300-victory level started to denigrate what Newhouser *had* accomplished; the whispers began that Newhouser was really only a wartime pitcher and all his numbers were ersatz. Two of his big seasons, they said, came during the war when the real ballplayers were in the service; these critics chose to ignore the fact that Newhouser continued to win after the servicemen returned to the game. There are a number of pitchers in baseball's Hall of Fame whose records are inferior to Newhouser's but who are recognized as great pitchers before arm problems cut short their careers; this allowance seems never to be made for Harold Newhouser.

Is Newhouser an all-time great who should be enshrined in Cooperstown? After all, in the years following World War II, it was generally conceded by everyone around baseball that the two best pitchers in the game were Bob Feller and Newhouser. Confrontations between the two were eagerly-awaited classics, like the match-ups between Steve Carlton and Tom Seaver in the '70s. Or is Newhouser's record so tainted by his wartime achievements that he is deservedly consigned to the limbo reserved for pretty good pitchers who do not measure up to the status of "superstar"?

Newhouser's career requires examination so that we can try to come up with answers to these questions. If

Newhouser is not worthy, why should Ted Williams, admittedly one of the greatest hitters of all time, say, "I have always thought he should be considered seriously for the Baseball Hall of Fame"? Williams, long an intense student of the arts of hitting *and* pitching, has never been one to hand out meaningless accolades. Bill Dickey, the Yankees' Hall of Fame catcher, said, "I thought Newhouser was a hell of a pitcher. I know he was one of the toughest for me to hit." Ray Boone, who has seen many great pitchers in a long playing and scouting career, says of Hal, "I can't believe his being overlooked for the Hall of Fame." And George Kell, who played with Newhouser for seven seasons of *his* Hall of Fame career, and played against him for four others, before starting a broadcasting career that has kept him current with the game, writes, "I have long felt that Hal was one of the most underrated pitchers in all of baseball — and that his induction into the National Baseball Hall of Fame was long overdue."

On the other hand, one so-called baseball "historian" has written books about the American League, including a chapter on the 1940s, and the World Series, including a game-by-game account of the 1945 Series, without even mentioning Newhouser's name. Other more responsible analysts have acknowledged Newhouser's record but have then discounted it almost completely: it was World War II, you know, so those years cannot be counted.

What we will do here is look at Hal Newhouser's career, look at the impact of the war on baseball and on Newhouser, and try to determine where he should stand in baseball history.

2
THE PROSPECT

Harold Newhouser was born on May 20, 1921, in the city of Detroit, the son of Theodore and Emlie Macha Newhouser. Theodore, of German extraction, was an immigrant from Austria who earned a steady living as a wood patternmaker for the auto manufacturers. Emlie was of Czech descent, so Harold was blessed with a strong Middle European background. He was one of two boys in the Newhouser family, his brother Richard being almost four years older.

Detroit in the 1920s was the nation's fourth largest city, with a population of just about one million people. It was a gritty industrial city, prey to all the woes that early-20th-century American capitalism could inflict upon it. Detroit's economic life fluctuated, as it still does, with activity in the automobile industry. Indeed, at the time of Harold's birth, the city was just getting over its shock of the prior Christmas, when Henry Ford shut down his entire plant for six weeks. When he reopened, workers were hired at beginners' wages regardless of previous seniority, and 20,000 of the 70,000 laid off were not rehired at all. "A great business is really too big to be human," Ford said, and Detroit got his message.

Ford's announcement, seven years earlier, of $5-a-day wages for an eight-hour day, had spurred a great surge of people to Detroit. The city's population doubled between 1910 and 1920, and by 1921 Ford had produced more than five million cars. The 15-story General Motors Building was erected in the 1920s. Containing 20 million cubic feet of office space, the GM Building became the nucleus of a new business and entertainment center some four miles north of the downtown area.

Detroit, through the '20s, was the country's principal port of entry for bootleg liquor, due to its proximity to Canada. And it was proud of its native son Charles Lindbergh, whose mother still taught at Cass Tech in the city at the time of his famous flight. Lindbergh stopped over at Ford Airport in Detroit with his "Spirit of St. Louis" in May 1927, before flying east for his appointment with destiny and fame.

Detroit was a city of ethnic concentrations. Greeks and Belgians were clustered on the east side, and Poles were centered around Hamtramck, a separate municipality completely surrounded by Detroit. Serbs and Chinese and blacks had their own areas. The Newhousers lived in a blue-collar neighborhood in the northwestern part of the city, an area of predominantly German and Italian population, leavened with some English and Scottish folk as well.

Theodore Newhouser was a good provider for his family, although he was affected like everyone else by the ups and downs of the auto industry. "He as a wood pattern maker always had a job to put bread on the table," his son recalls. Theodore was a gym instructor in his spare time, and he made sure that his sons grew up strong and fit. They worked on the parallel bars and the rings and the other gymnastic paraphernalia, and Harold played football and ice hockey in pick-up games around the neighborhood. The young man had more than his share of childhood mishaps — a puncture of his stomach when he fell from a woodpile onto a nail, a badly-cut head

when hit by a brick, several cases of blood poisoning –
but they did not diminish his ardor for athletics.

Brother Richard took up baseball and was good enough
at it to sign a professional contract; he played several
seasons as an infielder in the Tigers and Red Sox farm
systems until his career was cut short by a pitch which
hit him in the head. Surprisingly, Harold did not start
playing ball until he was 13 or 14 years old. Then, he
said, "I played a little baseball on some of these scrub
teams, and that's how it all came about." The first semi-
organized team he played for was that of his own block.
"We had a block and we played the next block, and it
was one mile of blocks . . . probably about 20 streets in
there." Harold Newhouser played as a left-handed shortstop on his block team, "because nobody else could play
and I threw pretty good." A block team from some distance challenged Harold's team to a game, and afterward
the coach of the other team came over to Harold with
a proposition. He said he was organizing a Class E team
in the Detroit Baseball Federation and he would like to
have young Newhouser on his team.

The Detroit Federation operated a far-flung sandlot
baseball system around the city, and Class E was the lowest rung on its ladder – for boys 15 years old or younger.
It was not a fancy operation, especially at the Class E
level. "All we had were shirts," Newhouser said; "we didn't
have any shoes, we didn't have any baseball pants, we
just went out and played."

Young Harold joined the All-City Stars as a pitcher,
"and that's the first time I pitched." The coach had been
attracted to him by his arm, and he asked Harold, "Why
don't you see if you could pitch for us?" The results were
dramatic. Harold Newhouser found out that he could
pitch, a lot of kids who faced him found out that baseball sometimes was not much fun, and his team won all
nine games he pitched and the championship. Hal was

named Most Valuable Player on the Class E level, and he struck out most of the batters he faced. When a 15-year-old faces a pitcher throwing the ball faster than anything he's ever seen (and he's wild as well), the tendency is to swing the bat with the arms while backing away from the plate with all the rest of the body. It is hard to hit that way.

Most important to his future, the young lefthander knew, the first game he pitched at 15, that he was going to be a professional ballplayer. "I knew then," he said, "because I could throw pretty hard. As long as I got the ball over – I was a little bit wild – but when I got the ball over, why, I knew then that was gonna be my category."

The coach of the team that Newhouser beat in the Class E finals, a man named Al Wynn, recruited the young lefty for a team in the American Legion league for the next year. There was a complication, because under Legion rules Wynn's particular club could recruit players only out of one high school, Eastern High, while Newhouser would be going to Cooley High School, on the west side of town. This difficulty was overcome when Harold enrolled in Wilbur Wright Trade School to learn metalworking; the Legion teams were allowed to draw from the city's three trade schools without geographic constraints. There was an extra bonus for the young man; he had to have a B average to get into Wilbur Wright, so he was forced to work hard at his books to pull up his C and C-minus average.

Finally, with all of the preliminaries taken care of, Newhouser was able to pitch for the Roose-Vanker American Legion Post. His first season, the summer of 1937, when he was 16 years old, was sensational. His second was better. Hal Newhouser became simply the best player ever to play sandlot ball in Detroit; there are old-timers around the town today who will tell you that there have been none better in the years since.

In his first season young Newhouser won 15 games

and lost three. During the course of the year he struck out 24 batters in one game against Learned Post and pitched a no-hitter against Bushway Post. In the state tournament after the season, with Roose-Vanker representing the city of Detroit, Harold threw another no-hitter, this one a 1-0 victory over Kalamazoo in the quarter-finals. He was awarded the Kiki Cuyler Trophy as the Most Valuable Player in the state tourney.

During the 1937 American Legion season, Newhouser attracted the attention of a scout named Lou D'Annunzio, who worked for the Detroit Tigers. D'Annunzio reported his find to Aloysius J. "Wish" Egan, the head of scouting for the Detroit club, and Egan went to see the young lefthander for himself. What he saw he liked, and Egan soon became a fixture at Roose-Vanker games in which Hal was scheduled to pitch. Egan befriended the young man and introduced himself to the senior Newhousers as well.

Wish Egan was a legend in the Detroit area, a kindly old Irishman who combed the sandlots and high school diamonds of the city and signed the kids of greatest promise for the hometown team. Egan had been a pitcher of moderate ability; he played parts of three seasons for the Tigers and St. Louis Browns in the early years of the century, with uninspiring results. Later on, though, he found his true calling and became one of the earliest and most successful of scouts. Harold Newhouser soon became a major project for Wish Egan.

Lou D'Annunzio and Wish Egan were not the only people to take note of Newhouser's American Legion pitching. People at Wilbur Wright started to question why the young man was not playing for the school's team, and the baseball coach invited Harold out for a trial. The first day he showed up for practice, Hal hit one on the nose that rolled and rolled all the way to the end of the concrete-hard field. The coach's eyes widened, as he thought of all the extra-base hits that young Newhouser might represent, and he announced to his new recruit that he was now a rightfielder. Newhouser balked at this: "I'm a left-handed pitcher," he said; "I don't want to play the outfield." He never went back, and his high school baseball career ended right there.

Unfortunately, the baseball coach was also Newhouser's English teacher, and Harold's marks suddenly fell off in that class. Another English teacher, Bill Foy, who was to become a longtime friend of the young man, arranged to have Newhouser transferred to his class, and the grading problem disappeared. Foy just happened to be the basketball coach, and he was able to convince Harold to try out for the cage team. Harold did so, and his height and natural athletic ability took care of the rest. He wound up as Wilbur Wright's basketball captain.

When Newhouser resumed his pitching for Roose-Vanker in 1938, he was ready for a big year. He had reached his full height of six feet two, he packed 170 pounds on his slim frame, and his array of pitches was awesome on the Detroit sandlots. He had a sizzling fastball, one of the best curveballs ever seen in those parts, and much-improved control. After 10 games he had 10 complete-game wins, including four shutouts and a no-hitter, with 163 strikeouts. He had allowed only seven runs in those 10 games and an average of 3.4 hits per game. When Steve Gromek, a young shortstop from Hamtramck playing for the United Auto Workers team, managed to hit two line drives against Newhouser, the Cleveland scout watching the game was so impressed that he signed Gromek to a contract before he left the field.

The first controversy over how good Newhouser really was sprang up during the summer of 1938. John N. Sabo in the *Detroit Free Press* reported the argument among sandlot observers: "One side claims that Newhouser is the greatest young pitcher ever to perform on the Detroit sandlots. The opposition says that Newhouser is overrated, that he has compiled his great record at the expense of a lot of inexperienced youngsters." Those who challenged Hal's record said that the Legion league was composed of younger boys and that he was much bigger than the average 17-year-old. They said that his strikeout record could be attributed to overeager Legion batters swinging at a lot of balls they could not possibly hit, and they doubted that Newhouser could win even in Class B of the Detroit Federation. Even his critics, though, admitted that there was not "a sandlot manager in town who wouldn't jump at the chance to sign Mr. Newhouser."

Meanwhile, the object of all this attention just kept on winning. He helped Roose-Vanker wrap up the city title again and prepared for the state tournament. On August 5 the state round-robin opened, sharing the headlines with the news of Mickey Cochrane's replacement by Del Baker as manager of the Tigers. Roose-Vanker beat Big Rapids, 12–0, and Saginaw, 7–0, with Newhouser holding a Saginaw team which had won 15 out of 16 to just two hits, striking out 10, in six innings. The next day Newhouser threw a no-hitter at a Flint team which was unbeaten for the year up to that time. He fanned 14, and only two balls, both easy flies, were hit out of the infield.

On the following day Roose-Vanker played Flint again, this time for the state title. A 15-year-old righthander named Nick Popovich started for the team from Detroit and carried a 5–1 lead into the sixth inning before he weakened. With one run in, men on second and third, and none out, Newhouser was called in to pitch. He started poorly, allowing two runs to score on a wild pitch and an infield roller. The score was 5–4, but Flint was done, as Hal settled down and gave up nothing for the rest of the game. His teammates scored four more runs, and Roose-Vanker Post won the state championship with a 9–4 victory.

Several days later Hal and his mates went off to East Chicago, Indiana, for the regional American Legion tournament. Roose-Vanker drew a first-round bye and watched on August 13 as Cheviot, the Ohio state champion, edged East Chicago, 3-2. The next day Newhouser held Cheviot to four hits and struck out 17, winning the regional by a 10-0 score. It was noted that the young lefthander had now run up 40 scoreless innings in succession.

From there it was on to the sectional tourney at Princeton, Indiana. The first game, against Trenton, New Jersey, was "strictly a one-man show," reported the *Free Press*, "because Newhouser became the big attraction the minute he stepped to the mound." He gave the Jerseyans two hits, struck out 16, and blanked them 4-0, stretching his shutout streak to 49 innings. The *Free Press* reporter quoted spectators saying "they never had seen such pitching in the Junior Legion games." Two days later, on August 20, Roose-Vanker won the northeastern sectional championship with a 13-1 drubbing of Revere, Massachusetts. Newhouser pitched the first seven innings, giving up three hits and no runs, and getting 17 of his 21 outs on strikes. "There seems to be no stopping southpaw Harold Newhouser," reported the *Free Press*, as he extended his scoreless streak to 56 innings.

The national tournament was held in Charlotte, North Carolina, in 1938. It would match Newhouser and his team against a club from San Diego in a best-of-three elimination for the right to meet Spartanburg, North Carolina, in a final series. San Diego had a pitching star of its own in Chet Kehn, a righthander who would later appear with the Brooklyn Dodgers in 1942. The opener saw the two stars pitted against one another, but Newhouser prevailed by a 4-0 count, giving up three hits and fanning 10. The Detroit lefthander saved his scoreless streak with an alert play after San Diego catcher Stan Sharp hit a triple to deep center field. When the throw from the outfield was wide of third, the San Diego coach waved Sharp home. Newhouser, however, backed up the play and nailed the runner at the plate with a perfect throw. Kehn got the other two San Diego hits, but his team's 14-game winning streak came to an end. By this time the Legion games had the lead headlines in the Detroit sport sections; the *Free Press* banner read: "Newhouser Pitches 65th Straight Scoreless Inning."

The second game, on Saturday, August 27, went to San Diego by a score of 3–2, with Newhouser not pitching. It was only the second loss for Roose-Vanker in 32 games that season. In the rubber game on Monday the 29th, Newhouser's shutout string ended in the first inning when the leadoff man reached on a two-base error, went to third on Chet Kehn's sacrifice, and scored on Sharp's bad-hop single. Roose-Vanker tied the game at 1–1 in the seventh, but another unearned run in the eighth inning proved decisive. The Roose-Vanker third baseman made a two-base wild throw, and the runner moved to third on a passed ball and scored on Sharp's fly to right. When Kehn closed the door on the boys from Detroit, to eliminate them from the tourney, Hal Newhouser had his first loss of the season after 17 wins, despite giving up only three hits and striking out nine. Nevertheless, it was apparent that much more would be heard from the blond lefthander.

For some time the writers covering the Roose-Vanker games had been speculating that Newhouser would be signing with the Tigers. Because of a rule prohibiting signing American Legion players, speculation was all it could be until Harold's season ended in Charlotte. Charles P. Ward in the *Free Press* wrote on August 20, 1938, that Egan was "intent on steering the young man into the Tiger organization. The dope is that the seventeen-year-old youngster will report at Beaumont for the spring tryouts next year." Ward said Newhouser's "chief stock in trade is a fast-breaking curve, although he has a very good fast ball and good control for a pitcher of his persuasion." He figured that with Hal "coming up in a couple of years and young Virgil Trucks destined to make his bid for a berth next season, the Tiger fortunes should be improved shortly."

This was all well and good, but Newhouser had not signed with anyone yet. Egan had been following him closely for a couple of years and assumed that he had the inside track. He had young Harold work out at Briggs Stadium several times and had given him some pointers, including improving his grip for throwing a curveball. A Cleveland scout named Bill Bradley had also been following Newhouser, and on a couple of occasions he had arranged for Hal to pitch in exhibition games so he could see what the youngster looked like pitching against better hitters.

With the Legion restrictions removed, shortly after Harold returned home from North Carolina he received a visit at the house from Egan and Del Baker, the Tigers' new manager. Newhouser tells the story:

> When he [Egan] showed up at the house, we went into the dining room and he put down four $100 bills. And back in those days we were just getting out of the Depression and when we looked at the $400, it was not that my folks were destitute or anything . . . Well, $400 was $400, and they were smart. If it had been a check, it wouldn't have looked like anything, but being dollar bills, I had never seen anything like that. I didn't have any money. And a salary of $150 per month. That was the first job I ever had outside of selling newspapers and setting pins in a bowling alley . . . And so . . . he put down the money . . . and then Wish said, "Here's going to be your manager,

Del Baker, and he'll be on the ground floor with you." I liked Del, and I said, "all right," so we signed a contract.

As Egan and Baker left, Harold and his parents went out on the porch. Harold gave his parents three of the four $100 bills and kept the fourth to help him get through school, for books and transit fares to downtown Detroit. "And a little pocket money that I had never had before," he adds. As the Detroit officials turned the corner, the Newhousers suddenly saw a big Lincoln Continental coming down the street – an unusual automobile to see in that working-class neighborhood. The car pulled up in front of their house and two men got out – Bill Bradley, the Cleveland scout, and Cy Slapnicka, the Indians' general manager. Bradley introduced Hal and his parents to Slapnicka and then said, "Well, Hal, we're here to sign you to a contract with Cleveland." Before anyone could interject anything, he continued, "Here's $15,000, and here's the keys to the car for your dad." With a sick feeling in the pit of his stomach, Hal then said, "I'm sorry, but I just signed with Detroit."

Mrs. Newhouser turned on Bradley and said, "You never did call us or anything or show any interest." Bradley said, "That's why we had Hal pitching those exhibition games." Hal answered, "Yeah, but you showed no interest and you didn't say you were coming or anything and I had an opportunity to sign with Detroit."

Then Slapnicka said, "We can annul the contract; it's really not a contract." He suggested they come to Cleveland. "Bring your mother and come on over to Cleveland and we'll work you out and see what we can do for you."

So the Newhousers went to Cleveland. Harold said he was not so much interested in the money for himself: "The $15,000 was for the family; if they wanted to get a different home they could have it, and the car for Dad,

I just thought that was great." There was an attempt to get pictures of the new left-handed phenom, Newhouser, with Cleveland's 19-year-old pitching sensation, right-hander Bob Feller, but Feller was not in when they called at his hotel room, so the effort failed. The Newhousers stayed in Cleveland for a couple of days and then came back home without signing anything. Hal was "leery," he said, of signing another contract, because, although *he* was only 17, his parents *had* signed the Detroit contract.

When they returned to Detroit, Hal's mother called Egan and told him they had been offered $15,000 and an automobile by the Indians. "You hoodwinked my young son," she said.

Harold said, "Gee, Ma, don't do that, because I'm in their hands now. They can tell me what to do, and it may hurt my career."

Mrs. Newhouser said she was going to do it anyway, and she let Egan know what she thought. The Tigers did not change the contract, of course, but Egan assured her that, if Harold made the big leagues, "we'll take care of him." Nevertheless, the circumstances of his signing were to have an influence, subliminal at times, overt at others, on Hal Newhouser's early years as a Tiger.

3

LOUISIANA
AND TEXAS

It was not actually a contract with the Detroit ball club that Harold Newhouser signed for Wish Egan in the late summer of 1938. He bound himself to play for the Beaumont team, the Tigers' farm club in the Class AA Texas League. It was not the highest level in the Detroit minor league organization – that was Buffalo, in the International League – but Beaumont was well up the ladder. It was a couple of rungs too high for young Hal Newhouser's initiation into professional baseball.

A reporter named Harvey Patton, Jr., took note of Newhouser as he bade good-bye to his parents at the Union Depot in Detroit, "a worried and bewildered youngster, for the first time entering the professional baseball world to seek his fortune on a promising left arm." He left Detroit on March 5, 1939, and soon arrived in Texas for spring training with the Beaumont Exporters. During the six weeks he spent in Texas, Harold looked nervous and somewhat frightened. Though he impressed everyone with his raw talent, it became clear that he was having trouble adjusting to professional baseball; Tigers' officials decided the young man should start out at a lower level.

The day before the opening of the Texas League season, Jack Zeller, the Detroit general manager, took Newhouser aside and told him he was being sent to Alexandria in the Evangeline League. No one had given the young man an inkling of this move ahead of time, so he thought that he had made the Beaumont club. In fact, he had already been assigned a uniform for opening day. When he learned that the Evangeline League was Class D, organized ball's lowest level, Newhouser was furious. Zeller had arranged to have the young pitcher driven the 175 miles from Beaumont to Alexandria, Louisiana, and Harold sat in the back seat, fuming and silent the whole way, bitterly recalling the honeyed words of Wish Egan, the big headlines of his Legion triumphs, and Cy Slapnicka's Lincoln Continental. Arriving in Alexandria at two o'clock in the morning, the driver pulled up on a darkened street, pointed out a boardinghouse, and told the angry young man – now rather frightened – to go on up and knock on the door. Newhouser recalls the scene:

> I went up there – I was scared to death, and I never lived in a boardinghouse in all my life – so I went up and I knocked on the door and a great big heavy-set woman came out, half asleep, wanted to know what I wanted, and I said, "Well, I'm with the Alexandria Pilots and I just came in from Beaumont." She said, "Oh, yeah, you're the young boy they told me about. Come on in, we've got a room for you." So she took me into a room, no doors, nothing, and she said, "The washroom is down the hall, you can't make any noise, you can't bring anybody into the room." So I laid there from 2 o'clock until daylight, scared to death – I didn't know who was in that room. When it got daylight I just picked up my bag and walked out the door, and that was my first glimpse of what Alexandria looked like.

He found a man on the main street and asked, "which way is the ball park?" Given the direction, Newhouser walked a mile and a half to the park, found a gate open, and went inside. "There was a clubhouse down in left field and I walked down there and the door was open and that's where I slept. Because I felt that was my home. And then about 10 o'clock I woke up and I went over to see if anybody was in the office and they were and I reported."

Manager Art Shelan of the Pilots wasted no time putting his new lefthander to work. On April 18, Hal made his official professional debut, beating Lafayette, 5–2. He pitched a complete game, gave up only three hits (all in the last two innings), and struck out 13. That he was nervous is shown by his three walks, two hit-batsmen, two run-scoring wild pitches, and two fielding errors. But he won, and he was on his way. Al Zarilla, who was to play for 10 years in the American League with the Browns, Red Sox, and White Sox, was in center field that night for Lafayette; he was 0-for-3 against the young lefty. Later, Zarilla said of his efforts against Newhouser: "With the lights there, trying to hit him was like hitting in a clothes closet."

After his first rude introduction to Alexandria, Harold came to love the town. He called his time there "three of the finest months I ever spent in any town." The people, he said, "were just outstanding." He recalled the billboards on the outfield walls: "You hit this sign, you get a free meal; hit this sign, you get a free haircut. Pitchers, if you pitched a shutout you got this and that . . . " On a player's birthday, "they collected money for you in a hat all the way around, and that's how we lived. You know $150 doesn't last too long. And you had to pay for room and board and all that."

Alexandria was in almost the geographical center of the state of Louisiana, and it was the northernmost town in the Evangeline League. The other clubs in the league were spread around southwestern Louisiana – Lafayette, Jeanerette, New Iberia, Rayne, Abbeville, Lake Charles, and Opelousas. These were small towns, some of them really no more than hamlets, but this was the heyday of minor league baseball. There were no radio or television broadcasts of big league games from New York or St. Louis or Chicago, and the local ball club helped to give a place a sense of identity. The Evangeline League was Cajun country, backwoods bayou country, the home of the peckerheads and rednecks who had made Huey Long a national figure, and it was strange and wonderful to a wide-eyed kid from the big city of Detroit who had never seen an alligator or a pelican in his life.

"Oh, the roads were terrible, absolutely terrible," Newhouser recalls. "You worked out in the afternoon, put on your uniform and went to the next town and you played maybe 75 miles away, 100 miles away, played a game, come back two or three o'clock in the morning, take your shower and go home. Well, that to me was fun."

Though it was at the bottom of the minor league structure, the Evangeline League had some pretty fair ballplayers. Among those who played in it during 1939 were Edgar Busch, who later played for the A's; Ed Head, who pitched a no-hitter for Brooklyn in 1946; Ted Cieslak, who was with the Phillies in 1944; Zarilla; Joff Cross, later with the Cardinals; Dale Jones, who made it briefly with the Phils; Al Jurisich, who pitched four years for the Cards and Phillies; and Howie Pollet, who twice won 20 games for the Cardinals. When Newhouser went back to Beaumont, his place on the Pilots' roster was taken by Virgil Trucks. So the Evangeline was a good cut above the Detroit American Legion.

Harold Newhouser mastered his new challenge without too much difficulty. Working every fourth day, he pitched in 12 games and had an 8–4 record with an earned run average of 2.34. He struck out 107 in 96 innings, and the fans nicknamed him "Smoky Hal." In those same

96 innings, he walked only 29 hitters. On his 18th birthday, May 20, he almost pitched a no-hitter. With two
outs in the ninth, an Abbeville batter squibbed a ball
over the first baseman's head for the only hit of the
game off Newhouser. Two and a half weeks later, he was
recalled to Beaumont. Hal left Alexandria in good shape,
and the Pilots went on to win the league championship.
Things were a lot different, he would find, at Beaumont.
The Exporters were a bad team, dead last in the Texas
League, and the experience at Beaumont was not a happy
one for Hal Newhouser. He pitched pretty well, but it
certainly did not show up in his won-loss record. He won
five games and lost 14, though his earned run average
was a respectable enough 3.83. Hal pitched a couple of
one-hit games, but even that feat was not enough to
assure victory: he lost one of them when the opposing
pitcher held the Exporters hitless, and he won the other
only by 1–0 when Ned Harris stole home. Whatever it
took to lose the Exporters usually managed to accomplish, and many times Hal Newhouser was the victim
of their ineptitude.

It was a tough league. The Houston Buffs, a well-
stocked Cardinal farm club, won the season championship, with such future big leaguers as Harry Brecheen,
Ernie White, Johnny Hopp, Hal Epps, Murry Dickson,
Ted Wilks, and John Wyrostek. Other standouts in the
circuit were Lou Novikoff, the "Mad Russian" who won
the batting title with .368 for Tulsa, Bob Kennedy, Bob
Swift, Mule Haas, Don Kolloway, John Lucadello, and
Guy Curtright. The leading lights, such as they were,
on Al Vincent's Beaumont club were Pat Mullin, who
hit a passable .278, Murray Franklin, Dixie Howell, and
catcher Jack Tighe, who hit only .220 in the broiling heat
of a Texas summer.

The Texas League was made up of real cities – Dallas,
San Antonio, Shreveport, Oklahoma City, Fort Worth,
Tulsa, Houston, and Beaumont – and the greater dis-

tances necessitated train travel. That was a big difference from the Evangeline League and its buses, but the main thing Newhouser remembers from his Texas League days is the heat.

Some of the other clubs in the league had lights and played night games, but Beaumont played all its games in the afternoon. In the Beaumont park the sun always came right into the face of a left-handed pitcher. "Every time I'd go to throw," Newhouser said, "here's this scorching sun hitting me." The Exporters had red uniforms, half wool and half cotton, which just soaked up the heat. "It was worse than a furnace," Newhouser recalls. At times Tighe, the catcher, got so hot that he discarded his chest protector, wearing only the mask for protection.

The Texas League was blistering hot, at home and on the road. There were no visiting dressing rooms when the Exporters were away from home; the players dressed at their hotel. Newhouser recalls an arrangement the players had with the bellhops in most of the hotels: when the bellhops heard on the radio that the game was in the seventh inning, they were to put a 50-pound block of ice in the bathtub in the room (there were four players to a room), and in the ninth inning they were to fill the bathtub. By the time the players got back from the ball park there was cold water for a bath. "The guys that played got the first bath," Newhouser said ruefully; "and, of course, me being the pitcher I never got the bath – except the day I pitched." After the baths were finished, the players put their sheets in the water, wrung them out, and put them on the bed. Then they would put their uniforms on the four blades of the big wooden ceiling fan. One man would stand on the bed and get the fan swinging by hand – "then you'd flip on the switch and then we'd take the other sheet and we'd pull it over us and that's how we slept. That was our air conditioning. Now, that's hot."

One thing which Newhouser found odd was that no one, at either Alexandria or Beaumont, tried to teach him anything about pitching: "They just said here's the ball, and they taught me absolutely nothing." Years later, when Vincent, his Beaumont manager, was coaching at Detroit, Hal asked him about this. Vincent said he was given orders "not to do anything with Newhouser. Just leave him be. With his temperament and his way of doing things he'll work it out." Newhouser told Al Vincent, "Hey, that isn't the way to take a young kid at 17, and throw him to the wolves." The effects of this ill-considered directive, issued presumably by Jack Zeller, were felt by Newhouser and by the Tigers for years.

Nevertheless, at the end of Beaumont's season, Newhouser was called up to the parent club for September. H.G. Salsinger, the dean of Detroit baseball writers at the time, told of Zeller making a trip to Texas in early August to search for a left-handed pitcher. In Houston, he ran into Nick Cullop, a former big league outfielder who was playing out the string and coaching with the Buffs. "I'd like a good lefthander," Zeller said. "Do you know where I can get hold of one?"

"You've come to the right place if that's what you're looking for," Cullop replied. "There's the best lefthander down here that I've seen in 10 years or more."

Zeller's eyes widened. "What's his name?" he asked.

Cullop chortled as he answered: "His name is Newhouser. He pitches for Beaumont and you've probably heard of him."

What Zeller knew, in his office in Detroit, of course, was that young Harold was in the process of running up a long losing streak. When he talked to his own people at Beaumont, however, they confirmed Cullop's assessment; so Newhouser was recalled to the Tigers for September, when the major league rosters were opened up.

4
BIG LEAGUE ROOKIE

The same reporter who had seen Harold Newhouser off to Texas in the spring of 1939 observed his return in September: "No bewildered youngster was Newhouser at the Michigan Central Depot when he greeted his parents . . . on his return. The intervening months in the minor leagues have matured him . . ." Time, and perhaps the American League hitters, would tell about that. In any event, Hal returned to his hometown with some experience of pitching for a living, against hitters whose livelihood depended on their ability to hit *him*: he also had a much closer acquaintance with losing – courtesy of the Beaumont Exporters – than he had ever gotten in his sandlot days.

Zeller brought 13 players up from his minor league teams for September, but there was no guarantee that any of them would see much action. *The Sporting News* noted that: "High on the list of pitchers, in the affections of the Detroit public, is the name of Harold Newhouser." The Detroit public, though, did not make up the pitching rotation. Manager Del Baker felt that his team, sitting in fifth place, still had a chance to catch Chicago or Cleveland, the clubs just ahead of it, to finish in the first division and share a small bit of the World Series money. The pennant was long since decided – the

New York Yankees would ultimately win it by 17 games over second-place Boston—but with everyone playing out the string the Tigers might catch someone relaxing too much. So Baker did not use his youngsters very often. The 1939 Detroit Tigers had a small nucleus of the players who had won back-to-back pennants in 1934 and 1935 (and a World Series the latter year)—pitchers Tommy Bridges, the great curveballer, and Lynwood "Schoolboy" Rowe, who had been dogged by arm troubles in 1937 and 1938 but seemed to be coming back; steady outfielder Ervin "Pete" Fox, and three-fourths of their great infield, Hank Greenberg, Charlie Gehringer, and Billy Rogell, with only third baseman Marv Owen gone. But the Tigers had been on a steady downhill slide since 1935 — second, second, fourth, and now struggling to get back into the first division. They made a big trade in May, shipping six players, including starting pitchers Vern Kennedy and George Gill and promising young outfielder Chet Laabs, to St. Louis for the Browns' 20-game winner Bobo Newsom and three other players. It was a good deal—Newsom won 17 for Detroit which, added to his three wins for St. Louis, gave him 20 again, while Kennedy and Gill had terrible seasons for the woeful Brownies. Still, it was not enough to get the Tigers back into the first division, and, as the season wound down, it became clear that fourth place was out of reach. Baker decided to give his 18-year-old lefthander a start in the final series.

On Friday, September 29, 1939, Harold Newhouser made his first major league appearance in the second game of a doubleheader at Briggs Stadium. He started against Cleveland and lost the game, 3–0, to the Indians' lefthander Al Milnar. The game was called because of darkness after five innings, but the young Tiger was impressive. "Surprisingly," he said, "I wasn't a bit scared." He wanted to do well for his parents and his many friends who showed up, and he did. Newhouser gave up only

three hits – a double to Roy Weatherly and singles to
Odell Hale and Oscar Grimes – and he was hurt by Benny
McCoy's error behind him at shortstop. He walked four,
struck out four, and uncorked three wild pitches. After
the game, Oscar Vitt, the Cleveland manager, raved
about Newhouser. "I never saw this kid before," Vitt said,
"but I'd give $100,000 for his arm."

So, a very eventful 1939 season ended for Harold
Newhouser. It ended with his 14th straight loss, but his
record in Beaumont was largely discounted. The year
started in Alexandria, Louisiana, in Class D, and finished
in Detroit, Michigan, in the American League. A jump
like that represented a considerable accomplishment for
a young pitcher in a day when baseball players custom-
arily spent several years learning their trade in the minor
leagues.

With his year of professional ball behind him, Harold
went back to Wilbur Wright High School, where he was
still a student. Indeed, he had gone back to school as
soon as he returned from Texas, since he had missed
most of the spring semester. He kept in shape playing
basketball over the winter and prepared mentally for his
first major league spring training, the Tigers' camp in
Lakeland, Florida.

It was decided that Newhouser would ride south to
Florida with the Detroit traveling secretary, late in February 1940, so that he could stay as long as possible in
high school. It was a nervous world that winter and early
spring – indeed, the top song hit in the country that
March was Glenn Miller's "It's a Blue World" – with the
European war having broken out the previous September. After Germany and Russia crushed Poland, Europe
had settled down to what was called "the phony war,"
but with the coming of spring there was little doubt that
hard fighting would convulse the continent. America
watched – and waited.

In the meantime, the clubs of major league baseball

prepared for another season. At Lakeland, Baker looked for the combination that could propel his Tigers back into contention. One move had been decided: Rudy York, a big, slow-moving slugger, a three-year veteran who was part Cherokee Indian, would move from behind the plate, where he was a detriment, to first base, where he might not do too much harm. Greenberg had agreed to move to the outfield (Zeller helped induce this agreement by raising Hank's salary), and the move would keep York's big bat in the lineup; catching was well covered with George "Birdie" Tebbetts and Billy Sullivan, picked up in a trade from the Browns. The dependable Gehringer, now approaching 37 years of age, was still at second. At shortstop the Tigers had made another deal, trading the fading Billy Rogell to the Chicago Cubs for scrappy Dick Bartell, a longtime star in the National League. Mike Higgins would hold down third, and in the outfield Pete Fox and the rookie sensation of 1939, Barney McCosky, were to team up with Greenberg.

The big question mark for Detroit was pitching. As he looked over his staff, Baker saw almost all righthanders – Newsom, Rowe, Bridges, Dizzy Trout, Al Benton, Hal Manders, youngsters like John Gorsica and Fred Hutchinson. The Tigers had been shy of left-handed pitching in 1939, and the shortage had contributed to their lacklustre season. Archie McKain was a southpaw, and he was back, but he was primarily a relief pitcher. As he watched young Harold Newhouser, still several months short of his 19th birthday, Del Baker cooked up a plan to keep the lefty with the Tigers.

Early in March, *The Sporting News* reported that Baker had "cast an unofficial vote for Harold Newhouser." The manager was quoted as saying "the kid is a standout" with stuff sufficient to win in the majors. "All he needs is experience," Baker said, "and I have an idea he will get that this year with Detroit." Up to this point it had been generally assumed that Newhouser would

spend at least one more season in the minor leagues. He
was used frequently in spring exhibition games, and
speculation continued about Harold's chances of making the team. His major drawback was his wildness, but
on March 30 he pitched a brilliant seven-inning job
against the Kansas City Blues, a top Yankee farm club,
and his control was fine. Against a lineup containing
players such as Phil Rizzuto, Jerry Priddy, Joe Collins,
Billy Hitchcock, Frenchy Bordagaray, and Mike Kreevich,
Newhouser pitched a two-hitter and gave up only two
unearned runs. The next day the club broke camp and
headed north, dropping four pitchers from the roster as
it did so. Newhouser remained with the team.

On April 8, Newhouser pitched three scoreless innings
behind Newsom against the Knoxville Smokies of the
Southern Association. Charles Ward, of the *Detroit Free
Press*, noted that Newhouser had plenty of stuff and
good control: "when Harold has control he is a hard
young man to beat." After the game, Baker said, "I hesitate to say it, but it looks now as if the kid is going to
make it." With improved control, the manager said, "he
can win in the big league, and I don't care if he has had
only one year of professional experience. The kid has a
lot of stuff, perhaps even more than any of our other
pitchers.

"If Harold gets off to a good start," Baker went on,
"I'll toss him in indiscriminately, working him in his
regular turn. If he doesn't, I'll pick spots for him and
nurse him along, just as the Indians nursed Bob Feller
until he learned the ropes." He concluded: "I think the
kid has the makings of a good pitcher and I'm going to
give him every chance."

Curiously, the Detroit club continued its strange policy
of letting Newhouser learn to pitch on his own. That
veteran pitchers such as Newsom and Rowe and Bridges
did not go out of their way to help a youngster trying
to win a job from one of them was not that unusual; it

had long been accepted practice in baseball that veterans did not ease the way for rookies. But Baker, an old-time catcher with years of accumulated lore, and his coaches also left Newhouser alone, again presumably on orders from the front office. It was a peculiar situation: the Tigers were looking for a capable lefthander and thought Newhouser might be the man, but, as he recalled, "they just said here's the ball and they taught me absolutely nothing."

On April 14, Harold pitched three good innings against Cincinnati, in his final exhibition appearance, and clinched a spot on the season-opening roster. On the 19th, the *Free Press* carried a column by Charles P. Ward on Newhouser's superstitions – or lack of them. That a regular columnist for one of the two Detroit dailies devoted a column to young Newhouser indicated as much as anything else that the young man was considered to have arrived.

As the season got underway, Baker looked for an appropriate opportunity to use his young lefthander. On April 20, he said he planned to use either Rowe or "the kid" the next day, depending on the weather (Rowe was not comfortable in cold weather), and the next day he announced that Newhouser would pitch at Cleveland on the 22nd, but when Feller was named as the Indians' starter, Baker backtracked: "It would be asking too much of a boy to send him out to beat a pitcher like Feller. I guess we will have to save Harold for another spot."

The manager was anxious to give his young lefthander some work, because further decisions had to be made. "We know that Newhouser has enough stuff to win in the American League," Baker said. "The only question is whether he will have the control. If he can get that ball over the plate with something on it, he is staying with us from now on." John Sabo wrote in the *Free Press* on April 24 that Detroit's pitching future lay in the hands of two 18-year-olds, Newhouser and righthander

Dick Conger, from Los Angeles. It was very doubtful, though, that both youngsters could be carried on the Tigers' roster.

On April 27, Hal Newhouser made his first start of the season, against the Indians at Briggs Stadium. Cleveland shortstop Lou Boudreau led off by hitting Newhouser's third pitch of the game out of the park. Roy Weatherly and Ben Chapman followed with singles, and the rookie pitcher looked very shaky. But Hal Trosky lined into a double play, and Chapman, dancing and feinting off first in an attempt to rattle the pitcher, soon found himself picked off by Newhouser. A reporter wrote of the young pitcher: "One would have gathered that he was Walter Johnson or Lefty Grove, so calmly did he do his chores. Not only did he pitch with poise but with great showmanship." This reporter marveled at the transformation of what he called "a bashful, backward boy off the ball field." Newhouser went the distance but unfortunately never did find the key to pitching to Boudreau. The shortstop had two home runs and a run-producing single as the Indians won, 4–2. Still, it was a fine outing. Baker said, "I thought the kid pitched a swell game. We just couldn't get runs for him." A day later Dick Conger was optioned to Beaumont.

In his next outing, May 2, Harold Newhouser won his first major league game. Aided by a two-run home run by Rudy York and a big triple by McCosky, Hal beat the Senators, 5–3, at Washington, giving up only six hits. He had to weather ninth-inning trouble, when Rick Ferrell walked with one out. Johnny Welaj forced Ferrell at second but scored on a double by George Case. The game ended, however, when McCosky caught Buddy Lewis' line drive. After 13 losses at Beaumont and two with the Tigers, Newhouser had finally won a game. "I never thought it would be over," the young pitcher said after the game. "I never thought I would win a game . . .

Bartell kept telling me that such things had to end, but when you're 19 years old I guess time seems longer." Del Baker smiled and said, "It looks like we've at last come up with a starting lefthander."

Five days later Baker started Newhouser, still a couple of weeks shy of his 19th birthday, against the world champion Yankees at New York's Yankee Stadium. It was a pretty fair lineup that the young lefthander faced: Frank Crosetti, Red Rolfe, Charlie Keller, Joe DiMaggio, Bill Dickey, Joe Gordon, George Selkirk, Babe Dahlgren, and pitcher Steve Sundra. Newhouser was unfazed; he beat the Yanks, 4–2, and, as one Detroit writer put it, "mowed the Yankees down as if they had been a group of sandlotters." In the ninth inning he developed a blister on a finger of his pitching hand; Tebbetts called Baker out to look at it, and the manager decided to take Newhouser out. The young pitcher was incensed, and Baker had to remove him almost forcibly from the mound. Al Benton came in and finished off the New Yorkers.

When Newhouser entered the Tiger clubhouse after the game, Bobo Newsom threw his arm around the young man and shouted, "Congratulations, Bo! You got it!" He turned to the other players: "Gents! You have the supreme honor of being acquainted with a real pitcher."

Wish Egan was ecstatic after the victory over the mighty Yankees: "I knew the kid had it," he crowed. "I knew it all the time. But it never was proved until today."

Because of the blister on his finger, Newhouser's next start was delayed until a week later, when he faced the Senators in Detroit. The week between the young man's starts was an eventful one in the larger world outside baseball. On May 10 Hitler opened his offensive in western Europe, sending his superbly-prepared troops in lightning strikes through Belgium, Luxembourg, and the Netherlands, and Neville Chamberlain gave way as prime minister of Britain, to be replaced by Winston Churchill.

The American League carried on business as usual, but thoughtful baseball men were well aware that the appalling events overseas might someday have a heavy impact upon the United States – and its games.

Newhouser's start against the Washington club on May 14 was not as successful as his two earlier efforts. Veteran knuckleball pitcher Emil "Dutch" Leonard outpitched him as the Nats won, 4–2. Harold was touched for 10 hits in seven innings, but he still pitched tenaciously enough to keep his team in the game. On the 22nd, though, he was knocked out early by the Yankees, who scored five runs on seven hits in three innings against Newhouser, as they cruised to an 8–2 victory. Another start on May 28 resulted in another third-inning departure for Newhouser and no decision.

Baker was trying to find a fourth starting pitcher to go with Newsom, Bridges, and Rowe. He was experimenting with Trout, Gorsica, and Newhouser; he even contemplated starting Al Benton, though he preferred to use Benton as his key man in the bullpen. Although the Tigers were running third in the early going, losing almost as often as they won, Baker could see that his team had a shot at winning it all. The Yankees were not pulling away from the rest of the league, and Cleveland, though it looked powerful, did not seem able to put everything together. The York/Greenberg switch was working out well, with both sluggers producing as hoped; Gehringer, Higgins, Fox, McCosky, and Tebbetts were all hitting, and Bartell hit some and held the infield together. But another reliable starter seemed essential. Newhouser's first three games had pushed Baker's hopes sky high, but his next three games brought the manager crashing down to the reality represented by a raw rookie who was just 19 years old, no matter how much potential he had. "When You Wish Upon a Star," from the movie *Pinocchio*, was one of the country's hit songs that May, and it seems that wishing on a star was just what

Del Baker was doing. He told one reporter that Newhouser was easy to handle: "I just toss him into a game and if he gets beaten I just toss him back into another one . . . He isn't afraid of anybody."

Early in June, the manager had Newhouser in the bullpen, but a perfect two innings in relief by young Harold in Philadelphia raised Baker's hopes again. On June 7, he started Newhouser in the oddly-shaped Fenway Park in Boston, and Hal responded with a complete-game, 7-1 victory. Although he walked seven, he struck out six, including the great Jimmy Foxx twice. Newhouser's record was even at three wins and three losses.

A week later Hal went the route as he stifled the Senators back home in Detroit, beating Walt Masterson by a 10-1 score and holding the visitors to just five hits. On June 20, Chubby Dean of the A's beat him, 6-4, with Harold departing the game in the sixth inning.

By mid-June the Tigers were starting to talk pennant. Both Newhouser and Gorsica were pitching fairly well, enough to take up the slack on the staff for the three main men. On the 25th, Newhouser took on the Red Sox again, a heavy-hitting lineup that included Dom DiMaggio, Doc Cramer, Lou Finney, Jimmy Foxx, Jim Tabor, Bobby Doerr, and Joe Cronin. The Detroit lefty held this group, which included three future Hall of Famers, to four hits and beat the Sox, 6-1.

On June 30, Harold lost to the Browns at St. Louis 7-6, but he pitched the full 11 innings it took to decide the game. His record was now 5-5. Still, the Tigers went into July in first place, and the club which looked like their chief obstacle, Cleveland, was in some disarray. On June 13 a delegation of disgruntled Indian players went to the office of club president Alva Bradley and asked him to fire manager Oscar Vitt, who was, they claimed, too hard on them, too sarcastic, too nasty. Bradley sent the players on their way and Vitt kept his job as manager, but the 1940 Indian team was soon labeled the

"Cleveland Crybabies," and they heard jeering and derision around the league for the rest of the season. It was a talented team, with strong hitters like Boudreau, Hal Trosky, Jeff Heath, Roy Weatherly, and Ben Chapman, and such pitchers as Feller, Johnny Allen, Mel Harder, and Al Smith. But they had brought upon themselves an extra burden, one which would make it just a little bit harder to win.

Newhouser started one game of the July 4th doubleheader against the Indians, pitching eight strong innings in a game which Detroit eventually lost, 2–1, in overtime. Harold gave up just one run and four hits in his tenure, fanning six. When the league broke for the annual All-Star Game on July 9, the Tigers trailed the Indians by just one game; they moved to bolster their pitching by recalling the much-heralded Fred Hutchinson from Buffalo.

On the 11th, as the pennant race resumed, Newhouser had a bad game at Griffith Stadium in Washington, lasting only two innings in a 7–3 loss to the Senators. He came back four days later at Shibe Park in Philadelphia and beat the A's, 9–8. The young lefty was touched for nine hits in five innings, but his teammates piled up eight runs in the fourth inning and the lead held up. It was, however, not a particularly good outing for the youngster. Del Baker's gloom deepened a couple of days later when his pitching ace, Bobo Newsom, who had won 13 games in a row, fractured his thumb on a throw from first baseman Rudy York.

Newhouser's next two starts were winners. He beat the Yankees at Yankee Stadium, 3–1, on the 20th of July, going the route once again against the world champions, and on the 25th he beat the Senators and Dutch Leonard, 5–2, though reliever Archie McKain pitched the last couple of innings to save it. Just when it appeared that he was in a good groove, though, Harold was hit hard by the Yankees and lost to them on July 30 by an 8–6 score.

He gave up 10 hits and was knocked out in the seventh, and his record fell to eight wins and seven defeats. Birdie Tebbetts tried to explain why the young pitcher was so erratic. Talking to a bunch of reporters one afternoon before a game, the Tigers' catcher said that Newhouser was "the best young pitcher in the major leagues today." Newhouser, he said, had the stuff: "You haven't seen a better fast ball . . . this year and you haven't seen many better curves." Challenged as to why then the young man had lost six games, Tebbetts said that was because of "his youth and his inexperience." He said that Newhouser lacked complete confidence in his delivery, but he would gain that in another year or two. As it was now, when his control was a bit off, he would hold back on his pitches and the batters would hit him. "When he gets experience, and with experience he's bound to get better control," Tebbetts went on, "he'll keep pouring the fast one in there, confident that he'll get the corners in an inning or two, and he will. He won't be afraid of walking them. And he won't walk many." Tebbetts concluded by predicting that Newhouser would "be at the top within two years and I'd be much surprised if he isn't there next year."

As August started the Tigers held on to first place, but it was a precarious grip. And August was not a good month for Baker and his charges, as his shaky pitching became a little more wobbly. Schoolboy Rowe's mother was sick, forcing him to leave the team for a while, and Newsom, his thumb better, suffered from a bad cold. On top of these problems, Hal Newhouser developed a sore arm.

He pitched August 4 but lost to the Red Sox, 7-3, at Briggs Stadium. He gave up seven hits, struck out only two, and left in the fifth inning, his pitching arm hurting. Harold was passed over for his next two starting assignments because of his achy left arm. All it really needed was some rest, and it was soon healthy again.

When Newhouser said he felt better, Baker had no hesitancy in throwing him into perhaps the biggest game of the year to that time.

On August 12, the Tigers and Indians opened a series at Cleveland's League Park, tied for first place. Cleveland led with its ace, Bob Feller, and the Tigers countered with young Newhouser. Feller, in his book several years later, described Hal as "still a frail, nervous youngster of 19. Hal didn't have much luck that year," he wrote, "but the signs of future greatness were on him. He was very fast and he came in with the ball from a wicked angle." Unfortunately, the fans in League Park had to pay close attention to see much of Hal that day, for the Indians knocked him out with a three-run first inning, on their way to an 8–5 victory, Feller's 20th win of the year. Cleveland took over first place, and Baker decided to send his young lefthander to the bullpen. With one astonishing exception, the Tiger manager relied mainly on his veterans the rest of the way.

Newhouser's role was basically that of a mop-up man for several weeks, as the Tigers struggled to stay alive. In addition, once school started, Harold was back in the mornings for classes at Wilbur Wright. On September 2, Detroit lost a doubleheader to the Chicago White Sox and fell three and one-half games behind Cleveland and tied with New York. The following day the White Sox routed Hutchinson in the first inning and then chewed up Newhouser in a dismal relief effort as they topped Detroit, 10–2. It was the low point for the Tigers.

The next day they embarked on a three-game sweep of the Indians, behind the pitching of Rowe, Benton, and Newsom. When Detroit then took two from the Browns, they led the Indians by half a game and the Yankees by a whole one.

Hal Newhouser had a moderately good outing against Washington on September 15 and then won a crucial game in relief against the Indians at home on the 20th.

A raucous and unruly crowd turned out at Briggs Stadium for the start of the big series with Cleveland; the fans taunted the visitors with baby bottles dangling on strings over the Indians' dugout and the usual jeers of "Crybabies." Newhouser pitched one scoreless inning and was the pitcher of record as the Tigers pounded Feller in relief for five runs in the eighth inning to win it, 6–5. Harold pitched two excellent innings in the finale of the Cleveland series two days later, and Detroit led Cleveland by a full game on September 23 after taking two out of three from the Tribe. The Indian players had been shaken by the ferocity of the Detroit fans, who pelted them with eggs and vegetables and screamed and hooted at them. The Yankees were three and a half games back and running out of time.

The Indians then split two games with St. Louis, while the Tigers were beating Chicago twice, to eliminate New York from the race. The Tigers went to Cleveland to close the season, leading by two with three games left, needing just one win to clinch the pennant. Baker knew that Oscar Vitt would have to throw Feller in the first game – the Indians could not afford to lose any – and he was disinclined to use up one of his top pitchers, Newsom, Bridges or Rowe, against the Cleveland ace. He called his non-pitchers together in the hotel when they got to Cleveland and let them make the choice of a starter for the first game. There were votes for Newhouser and for Hutchinson, but the consensus was Floyd Giebell, a righthander recently recalled from Buffalo, about whom the Indians presumably knew little. The Tigers hoped that the 30-year-old Giebell would not get rattled. Newhouser, of course, had not started a game since August 12, so it is not surprising that he was not selected. Baker told young Hal that he wanted him ready in the bullpen throughout the game, so that the moment Giebell got in trouble he could be relieved.

It was a tumultuous game. The Cleveland fans, retaliating for the events in Detroit, several times showered the visiting players with garbage; Tiger catcher Birdie Tebbetts was knocked cold in the bullpen when someone dropped a basket of empty bottles and fruit on him. Giebell repeatedly escaped from trouble, and Feller was excellent. Unfortunately for the Cleveland faithful, one of the three hits the Tigers managed was a fourth-inning home run by York with Gehringer on base, and Giebell somehow made the 2–0 lead hold up. Floyd Giebell never won another major league baseball game, but he won the pennant for the Detroit Tigers on September 27, 1940. Hal Newhouser had a long afternoon in the bullpen.

Newhouser pitched two good innings in relief in the last game of the season two days later, and then his year was about over. Although he was on Detroit's post-season roster, Baker told him not to expect to get into any games in the World Series against Cincinnati because he was too young. "I didn't agree with him," Newhouser said, "but he was the boss." As it developed, he saw no game action. In one way, though, the World Series was a unique experience for young Harold: "I was going to school in the morning and going out to the World Series in the afternoon." Not just to watch it, but as one of the 25 Detroit eligibles. "My classmates," he said, "couldn't believe it."

The Tigers and Reds divided the first four games, with Newsom and Bridges each hurling a winner. Detroit took a 3–2 lead in the Series when Bobo Newsom pitched a three-hit shutout to win Game Five, but the Reds came back to win the last two games in Cincinnati to take the crown. It was a disappointing end to the season, but, considering the Tigers' fifth-place finish of the year before, 1940 was a highly successful campaign for the people and players of Detroit.

It was a most significant year for Harold Newhouser at 19. He won and lost nine games, and his earned run average of 4.86 left a lot of room for improvement. He had some excellent games and he had some bad ones. He made a major contribution early in the season, when Del Baker was desperate for pitching help and Hal provided it. He was less of a factor after the arm strain of early August, but almost everyone who saw him was impressed with his potential. *Baseball Magazine* featured Newhouser and Johnny Gorsica in an article called, "Two Tiger Terrors and Both Rookies"; inexplicably, the story, by Detroit sportswriter Charles P. Ward, said both young pitchers were righthanders, even though the picture accompanying it clearly showed Newhouser throwing with his left hand. Regardless, Hal was a comer, and Detroit fans and players and the Tiger organization expected great things from him.

5
A SEASON WASTED

On September 16, 1940, President Franklin D. Roosevelt signed the Selective Service Act of 1940, instituting the first peacetime draft in American history. At about the same time, Adolf Hitler, already in control of most of central and western Europe, stepped up the assault of his Luftwaffe upon England. "Wolf packs" of German U-boats swarmed across the shipping lanes of the Atlantic. And, on September 27, the Japanese Empire signed the Tripartite Pact with Germany and Italy. The "Axis" was born, and the United States saw potential enemies across both the Atlantic and the Pacific.

It was not long before the new state of world affairs made its effect felt in the closed community of baseball. The Tigers' Hank Greenberg won his second American League Most Valuable Player award in 1940. Greenberg hit .340 and led the league with 150 runs batted in, 41 home runs, and 50 doubles, all while playing left field for the first time in his career. If anyone represented the heart of the Tiger ball club, it was big Hank, who turned 30 on New Year's Day 1941. He was a great baseball player and a young man of dignity and character. When the mid-November Selective Service lottery was conducted, with low-numbered registrants to be among the first called, Greenberg had one of the lowest numbers, along with pitcher Hugh Mulcahy of the Philadelphia Phillies, who was in fact to be the first player drafted. The officials of the Detroit ball club worried through the winter about the status of their prize slugger, but it seemed obvious that Greenberg was going to be lost to them – at least for the one year of service required by the new law.

Greenberg's impending induction cast a pall over the Tigers' 1941 spring training. At the end of camp Del Baker said he had never seen so much bad baseball as he had that spring. "The explanation for the lacklustre exhibitions is not difficult," he told a writer. "Chaotic world conditions are responsible. The type of baseball this spring is a reflection of a confusing present and an uncertain future." With so much else to worry about, the Tigers – and other players – were having difficulty concentrating on baseball.

But Baker's job was to get his team ready, and he worked hard at it. He was handicapped by a ridiculous rule the American League had adopted a year earlier, forbidding a pennant winner from making any straight player trades with any other club in the league. Aimed obviously at the Yankees, the rule's effect was to place the Detroit roster in a straitjacket. Baker shuffled his existing players around to try to make up for the anticipated loss of Greenberg. And, aware of his pitching problems of the year before, he took 20 pitchers to camp in Lakeland, although this turned out to be a mistake; none of them got enough work.

Del Baker's enthusiasm for Harold Newhouser's left-handed pitching was at a high level. "Newhouser will be one of the top pitchers of the year and for years to come," he told Salsinger. "He's a great left-hander about to arrive." He said that Hal had more confidence and more experience, and these things would help him immensely.

As spring training ended and the clubs prepared to open the season, the experts looked into their crystal balls and decided that Cincinnati and Cleveland should be favored to win their respective league titles. They saw the Yankees finishing second in the American League and projected the Tigers for third place. It was plain that Detroit's offense would suffer if Greenberg departed; improved pitching would have to take up the slack if the champions were to repeat.

As one of those pitchers counted on for improvement, Hal Newhouser made his first start of the new season on April 23 at Briggs Stadium. His teammates got him a lot of runs and he beat the White Sox, 13-5, pitching the whole game. The only disquieting note was six walks, four of which turned into Chicago runs.

Five days later, Newhouser lost at Cleveland, working six innings in a 7-2 defeat. Salsinger wrote in the *Detroit News* that "Newhouser had more stuff yesterday than he probably ever showed before. He struck out nine batters in six innings but he matched each strikeout with a base on balls and tossed in a wild pitch that cost a run. He had stuff, and plenty of it, but he could not make it count at the right time."

On May 3, Newhouser won his second game, beating the Athletics, 4-3. His control was better, and he pitched seven fine innings. In the eighth, though, he yielded successive singles to Bob Johnson, Sam Chapman, and Dick Siebert, so Baker quickly brought in Benton to save the game.

Three days later the blow fell on the Tigers: Hank Greenberg was inducted, and a major part of their offense went off to war. Rookie Ned Harris was installed in left field, and Pat Mullin was called up from Buffalo; no one believed that they could come close to Greenberg's production. On May 7 the club ceremoniously raised the 1940 pennant, but symbolically the Tigers then lost to Washington in a ragged and listless game.

On the 10th Newhouser pitched seven innings at Comiskey Park in Chicago but was not involved in the decision in a 4–3 loss. Again, his control was bad (nine walks), and he was victimized by bad fielding by his teammates. The next day Detroit released Dick Bartell, who was hitting just .167 and had lost his shortstop job to Frank Croucher. The club kept on losing. On May 15, still looking for some punch, the Tigers bought outfielder Rip Radcliff from the Browns.

That day, Newhouser beat the A's, 10–2, at Shibe Park, the first Detroit victory since Greenberg's departure. The Tigers pounded pitcher Phil Marchildon: Mullin had four hits, Harris had two doubles and a single, and Bruce Campbell had three hits. Newhouser walked five, and H. G. Salsinger wrote that he "had comparatively fine control."

On May 20, his 20th birthday, Harold received a set of red pajamas from his mother and a 4–2 defeat from the Red Sox at Boston. Again his control hurt him; he walked five batters and three of them scored. In his next appearance, Newhouser lost to Thornton Lee and the White Sox, 7–3, at Detroit. He took a 2–0 lead into the seventh but quickly lost his control, his stuff, his lead, and his ball game.

On Memorial Day, Harold was knocked out by the St. Louis Browns in the second inning, though his mates rallied to win by a 10–6 score. "Newhouser," the *News* wrote, "lacked stuff and control." At the first milepost of the season, 1941 was not shaping up as a big year for either Hal Newhouser or the Tigers. The club was in sixth place, playing at about a .500 pace, and the young lefthander had a record of 3–3 and an obvious control problem. Another problem that was becoming obvious was Newhouser's tendency to lose his temper when things went awry. He tried to explain it away as anger at himself, but his teammates and opponents did not buy that.

Catcher Billy Sullivan recalls, "I have seen Hal turn a withering glare toward Charley Gehringer and upbraid

him for making a critical error when Hal was pitching."
To the Tigers, for whom Gehringer had been a solid and
dependable star since 1926, Sullivan said, "that was like
blaspheming God."

Lamar "Skeeter" Newsome, an infielder with the Red
Sox, said Newhouser had everything a big league pitcher
could have, "except control of himself." When Newhouser
was young, Newsome said, he was "always *very* angry
on the mound [and] we took advantage of that . . . He
would charge toward our bench at times, yelling as loud
as possible."

Newsome's teammate, Ted Williams, recalled the young
Newhouser in 1941: "He was wild at first, and a fiery
guy. You would hit one off him and it was like you had
taken his blood. He'd give you that rotten stare. He didn't
think anybody was supposed to hit Newhouser."

What few recognized, of course, was that Harold Newhouser was an immature young man with a fierce desire
to win, who had received very little instruction on how
to pitch in the major leagues or on how to conduct himself. As his tantrums on the field multiplied — whether
it was glaring at a teammate who had booted a grounder
or shouting at the opposing players or firing his glove
into the dugout as he came off the field — the other Tiger
players gave him little support or comfort. A 20-year-
old pitcher who lost as often as he won, who "showed
up" his teammates, as they supposed, and who had a bad
temper was not going to be a very popular player.

June was not any better for the young lefthander or
for the ball club. On June 1, Hal pitched the ninth inning of each game of a doubleheader and he managed to
lose the second one. He walked leadoff hitter Dominic
DiMaggio, and when no one covered third on Lou Finney's sacrifice bunt, DiMaggio took the extra base. He
then scored the winning run on a long fly by Williams.

Four days later, Newhouser had a 4–2 victory in his
grasp as he entered the ninth inning against New York.

With one out, though, he walked Red Rolfe, and Tommy Henrich's home run to right tied the score. Newhouser retired Joe DiMaggio, but when he walked catcher Buddy Rosar, Baker took him out of the game.

On Sunday the 8th, Hal pitched two undistinguished relief innings in a 9–3 loss to the Senators, giving up a hit and three walks.

On June 10, Ford Frick, president of the National League, announced that his league would let all servicemen in uniform into games free; this mirrored a policy adopted earlier by President Will Harridge of the American League. Military uniforms were becoming a part of the American scene, and baseball recognized the fact.

Newhouser got another start on June 15, in Washington, but it was not a resounding success. His record fell to three wins and five losses as he absorbed a 7–5 defeat. He gave up seven hits and four bases on balls in a six-inning stint. After another bad relief outing in Boston, Hal started on June 22 in New York. His work over six innings was fairly good, but he did not figure in the decision, a 5–4 loss to the Yankees. This, incidentally, was the 35th game of Joe DiMaggio's 56-game hitting streak; he had one hit off Newhouser.

Another relief appearance in Philadelphia preceded a start back home against the Browns on the 29th. Harold beat Bobby Muncrief with eight strong innings for a 3–1 triumph. Al Benton pitched the ninth, and it *was* against the Brownies (or "the Little Brownies," as they were called by some Detroit sportswriters), but still it was a win and it gave some hope. Harold's record was now 4–5, but *The Sporting News*, reviewing the Tiger pitching woes, wrote, "Delmar Baker's spring faith in Harold Newhouser has not been rewarded."

Newhouser won the second game of the July 4 doubleheader against the White Sox, 10–6, although the *News* said he should have been charged with no more than one run. The major miscreant was the 38-year-old Gehringer,

who butchered two balls which led to four runs, though
they were called hits. Late in the game, for the first time
ever, Gehringer was taken out for defensive reasons.

After a relief appearance against St. Louis, Harold
started against Philadelphia and was knocked out in the
seventh inning. Jack Knott held the Tigers to five hits
and won, 5–4.

Newhouser's next game was a start against Red Ruffing and the Yankees. Hal carried a one-run lead into
the sixth, but his luck turned sour when a DiMaggio
fly ball eluded Barney McCosky for a triple. Joe Gordon walked, and Rosar singled home DiMaggio to tie
the score. When Keller walked to load the bases, Baker
brought in Rowe to pitch. The big righthander threw
seven pitches to five batters and got only one out. The
end result was a 6–2 Newhouser loss, dropping Hal's
record to 5–7.

Five days later, Newhouser carried a 5–2 lead into the
ninth inning at Griffith Stadium in Washington. He
walked Jim Bloodworth and Jake Early, then struck out
Buddy Myer and retired George Case on a soft fly ball.
Roger Cramer singled for a run, and then Buddy Lewis
walked to load the bases. Cecil Travis singled, and when
the ball rolled through the legs of outfielder Tuck Stainback, Lewis came all the way around from first with the
winning run. It was, said the *Detroit News*, "indeed an
inelegant finish." Hal Newhouser was not happy.

Five days later, though, he beat the Yankees in New
York by a 6–3 score. He pitched six strong innings, giving up the three runs on home runs by Rolfe and DiMaggio, and Rowe wrapped it up with three scoreless relief
innings. Hal Newhouser's record was 6–8 as July ended,
and he felt that perhaps a strong conclusion to the season lay ahead. The Yankees, by this time, were way ahead
of the rest of the league, and the Tigers were flounder-
ing in sixth place. Their main trouble was a lack of offense, with Radcliff, McCosky, and Higgins the only

ones hitting for much of an average and York the only big home run producer. Attendance at Briggs Stadium was way down from 1940; the Detroit fans were not much attracted to this pale imitation of the prior year's champion.

Perhaps the biggest news generated by the Tigers in 1941, other than the departure of Hank Greenberg, was the signing, on June 21, of a handsome young outfielder from the University of Michigan. For signing with Detroit, Dick Wakefield received the sum of $52,000 and a car; he was the first of the big "bonus babies." Unfortunately, the hoopla surrounding Wakefield's signing did not help Newhouser's disposition; it was all too easy for him to remember those four $100 bills from Wish Egan and the late arrival of Cy Slapnicka. One of America's top song hits of the summer was Sammy Kaye's rendition of "Daddy"; Walter Briggs of the Tigers had indeed been a "daddy" to Dick Wakefield, but he had not been similarly generous thus far with Harold Newhouser. Another problem was that Wakefield, who spent very little time in the minors before playing for the Tigers, was a none too enthusiastic outfielder, and his frequent defensive lapses infuriated Newhouser.

August was not a bad month for Newhouser. He started out with a 6–3 win at Fenway Park, staggering through eight innings as he allowed 11 hits and six walks. He fought the Red Sox in the clutch, though, and he held on to his lead. Six days later Newhouser evened his record at 8–8 with his first big league shutout, a six-hitter against the Browns, with only two walks.

On the 14th, Hal lost to Johnny Humphries of the White Sox, 3–0, but he gave up only one base on balls in seven innings. Five days later, Newhouser beat the Yankees again, going the distance in a 12–3 win. This game was not a thing of beauty, with Harold issuing 10 bases on balls, but he won it.

The next two Newhouser starts were not good ones;

he left in the fifth inning against Washington and in the first against the Red Sox. The Tigers won both games, so Hal's record stayed at 9–9 as August ended.

September was a washout for the young lefty. He was driven out in the first inning of a start against the Browns, pitched into the seventh inning in a no-decision game that Cleveland eventually won, and then lost his final two appearances of the season. On the 12th, he lost at Yankee Stadium, 8–2, leaving in the fourth inning, and three days later the Senators knocked Newhouser out in the second inning, pinning an 8–5 loss on him.

Baker did not use Newhouser again for the balance of the season, so Harold wound up 1941 with a 9–11 won-and-lost record. The jury was still out on the young pitcher as he finished his second complete season in the American League. He should have spent both those seasons in the minor leagues, probably, or at least one of them, learning more about his craft. He was still very young, he had a fine fastball, and he had an exceptional curve. He had certainly not received much help, offensively or defensively, from his teammates. And the Tigers still had not done much of anything to help Newhouser learn to pitch. There was an occasional word or two from Tebbetts, but there was no program of manager or coaches imparting to the young man any of the tricks of the trade. They simply handed him the ball and sent him to the mound, to learn, in effect, by bitter experience. Harold had clearly not improved much in his second season: his earned run average of 4.79 was just fractionally better than the 4.86 of 1940, and he had given up an average of 7.13 walks per nine innings, compared to 5.13 the year before. The poor control, of course, was a function of both mental and mechanical shortcomings. Newhouser was a workhorse; his 173 innings pitched was second on the staff and an increase of 40 over the prior season. But his frequent temper tantrums were not a good sign.

As the season ended, with the Tigers tied for fourth place with Cleveland but four games below the .500 level and 26 games behind the Yankees, the hope that 1942 would see Greenberg's return began to seem more remote. War clouds were gathering in Asia and the Pacific, as the United States sought to curb the expansion of Japan, and America was already fighting an undeclared war with German submarines in the North Atlantic. As more and more of America's young men entered the service, a song called "Till Reveille," played by Wayne King's band, climbed to the top of the music charts. No one really anticipated Pearl Harbor, but the probability of war against the Axis powers in the near future was clearly quite strong. There was little doubt, too, that war in the 1940s would involve everyone in the nation — soldiers, sailors, civilians, young and old, ballplayers and spectators.

6
NO SUPPORT
FOR NEWHOUSER

On December 20, 1941, Harold Newhouser got married. He wed Beryl Margaret Steele, a pretty brunette who had been his girlfriend "ever since we first met." Beryl, born in Canada but raised a Detroiter, would, it was hoped, help to settle down the temperamental young pitcher.

Two weeks earlier, of course, the Japanese had bombed Pearl Harbor, Germany and Italy had declared war on the United States, and the country found itself in a world war. The steady run of disasters and defeats which followed Pearl Harbor—there were names like Wake Island, Guam, Singapore, Bataan, Corregidor—made it obvious that it would be a long and bitter war which would demand the commitment of the entire nation.

Baseball was expected to join in that commitment. The rulers of baseball, from Commissioner Kenesaw Mountain Landis to the league presidents Frick and Harridge and the 16 club owners, announced that they were fully prepared to make their contribution to the war effort. What no one knew, of course, was what the nature and extent of that contribution was to be.

For some the answer came promptly. Hank Greenberg had been discharged from the army on December 5, but when the Japanese attacked two days later, Greenberg immediately re-enlisted. "I'm going back in," Greenberg said. "We are in trouble and there is only one thing to do—return to service . . . I am going back of my own accord. Baseball is out the window as far as I'm concerned. I don't know if I'll ever return to baseball." Feller, the Cleveland pitching ace, enlisted in the navy on December 9, as newsreel cameras rolled for the edification and inspiration of the American people. Within the next several weeks the armed forces inducted, among others, Sam Chapman of the A's, Buddy Lewis and Cecil Travis of the Senators, Fred Hutchinson of Detroit, and Johnny Sturm of the Yankees. These were men who had had low draft numbers; many more would soon be following them.

In World War I, Secretary of War Newton D. Baker had indicated that baseball was a non-essential activity and in his famous "Work or Fight" edict had brought about the curtailment of the 1918 season. Baseball men wondered anxiously if something of the same sort was in store for them with a new war. *The Sporting News*, right after Pearl Harbor, said baseball was ready to shut down if the president required it, although the paper quickly emphasized the value of sports in general and baseball in particular in building morale and true Americanism.

Baseball, though, had been doing a little discreet lobbying. Clark Griffith, the veteran owner of the Washington Senators, and Robert E. Hannegan, a Democratic politician and a St. Louis baseball fan of long standing, talked with the president and then suggested to Judge Landis that he write a note to Roosevelt, asking what the wartime role of organized baseball should be. Landis, who loathed the president, did so, and Roosevelt replied on January 15, 1942, with his famous "green light" letter:

I honestly feel that it would be best for the country to keep baseball going. There will be fewer people unemployed and everybody will work longer hours and harder than ever before. And that means that they ought to have a chance for recreation and for taking their minds off their work even more than before.

Baseball provides a recreation which does not last over two hours or two hours and a half, and which can be got for very little cost. And, incidentally, I hope that night games can be extended because it gives an opportunity to the day shift to see a game occasionally.

With that go-ahead from on high, baseball's executives started planning for the operation of the game under wartime conditions. The first essential, of course, was to make clear from the start baseball's patriotic dedication to the war effort. Warren Giles, general manager of the Cincinnati franchise, wrote a letter in January 1942 to all of the players on his team, urging that all who were eligible for military service should join up. "We would rather finish last, or not operate at all, and take the attending financial loss and have all our players who should enter the service enter the service," Giles wrote, "than win the pennant, World's Series and make a great profit with even one player of military age who could not justify his reason for not being in the service." The Phillies inserted a notice in their scorecard that "under no circumstances do we wish you to attend our games if your presence at Shibe Park means your absence from vital war work."

The second priority was players. Through the winter there was a steady trickle of baseball players into the military, men such as Mickey Harris and Earl Johnson of the Red Sox, Harry Lavagetto of Brooklyn, Al Brancato and Benny McCoy of the Athletics, Pat Mullin of the Tigers, Joe Grace and Johnny Berardino of the Browns, Don Padgett of the Cardinals, and Bill Posedel of the Braves. The draft would obviously be a continuing drain, but the minor leagues, still vast and abundant with manpower, would furnish replacements – at least until the minors themselves were decimated by the demands of the war. Sooner or later, it was recognized, baseball might be forced to fill its rosters with physical rejects as well as players too old or too young for the draft. The 1942 season, it was assumed, would not be that time.

Spring training got under way at the usual time and in the usual places, although people now were singing songs like "The White Cliffs of Dover," a sentimental ballad which decried the effects of the war upon civilians, and "Deep in the Heart of Texas," a snappy hand-clapper which demonstrated the proper American get-up-and-go spirit. The Tigers opened in Lakeland, with Del Baker complaining about the lack of team speed. With Mullin gone, he said, only Barney McCosky seemed capable of stealing a base.

H. G. Salsinger followed up by pointing out that, "being slow, the infielders clog up the Detroit defense as well as the offense." He said that Rudy York had to play 10 feet closer to the bag than any other first baseman in the league and the Tigers made fewer double plays than any other club. These were defects which Hal Newhouser had already noted, of course, but he was not expected to be happy about their continuance.

Jack Zeller assembled his Tigers (and the Beaumont players who were training with them in Lakeland) and told them: "Your first duty is to your country. You owe everything you have to her. If you're needed go gladly and give all you've got." He then told the press that he was irked at the club's 10 salary holdouts, to whom he had given an ultimatum to sign at his offer or find another line of work. He intimated that refusing to sign at the club's figure was unpatriotic. One of those holdouts was Buck Newsom, who balked at taking a major salary cut simply because his record had fallen from 21–5 in 1940 to 12–20 in 1941. After prolonged haggling and long-distance sniping in the newspapers, Zeller sold Newsom to Washington for $40,000. Zeller also dispatched Billy Sullivan to Brooklyn when the catcher scorned his contract offer.

Hal Newhouser opened the exhibition season with a terrible game against the Cardinals, walking seven and giving up six hits in four innings. After that, though, he was very effective in outings against Washington, the Yankees, and the Indians. Still, whatever feelings of optimism about his young lefthander may have been felt by Del Baker were kept under wraps by the Detroit manager, who had harbored too many unrealistic expectations in prior years.

The gentlemen of the press, too, were not about to let Newhouser raise their hopes again. Salsinger, in a preview of the season, wrote that Newhouser had "shown nothing to create optimism. Newhouser has been wild as ever . . ." But then Salsinger was feeling glum. In the same article he wrote that three things seemed certain: 1) the Yankees would win the American League pennant, 2) Brooklyn would win in the National, and 3) "the 154-game schedule will not be completed." Whether the season would be played out, he said, depended on attendance and gate receipts. "Few baseball men believe that the 1942 season will extend beyond Labor Day"; many thought it would end before then. "Automobile, tire and gasoline restrictions will wreck out-of-town attendance. Many more players will be in Army or Navy uniforms before September. Lack of playing talent and lack of cash customers will close the ball parks. It's about as sure as anything can be in these muddled times that the 1942 schedule will be curtailed and no plans made for 1943."

After this lugubrious pronouncement, 39,000 fans paid their way into Briggs Stadium for Opening Day. Unfortunately, the Tigers and Al Benton lost to Cleveland, 5–2, so perhaps a good number of those in attendance did not come back.

Newhouser started the season in the bullpen and pitched very well. He pitched a hitless inning in each of two losses to the White Sox, saved a win for Charlie Fuchs over the Browns, and threw two more effective innings at the Red Sox. As May started he pitched well in two more relief roles against the Yankees and A's, and on May 4 he came in to relieve Fuchs against Philadelphia in the ninth inning with the bases loaded, a two-run lead, and two out. Again he got his man to save the game.

On May 6, Harold got his first start of the year in Washington; unfortunately it came in Buck Newsom's first game against the Tigers, and ol' Bobo, looking to get even with his former employer, was sharp. Roger Cramer got a triple for Detroit, but that was the only hit the Tigers got as Newsom won, 7–0. Newhouser's control was not good in the seven innings he worked.

A week later, Newhouser hooked up with Newsom again, back in Detroit. Young Hal was the one who had it on this day, as he cruised to a 6–2 win on a three-hitter. Roberto Estalella's two-run homer was the only damage done to Newhouser, who fanned seven and walked only one.

As the baseball season moved into high gear, Americans settled down with their war. Castle Films advertised a home movie of the bombing of Manila ("Fires! Explosions! Lawless war in all its barbaric cruelty!") for $1.75; Australians welcomed the arrival of the first American troops, who promptly turned the antipodean nation into a "49th state"; actress Joan Crawford sprained her back jitterbugging in the filming of *He Kissed the Bride*; OPA's Leon Henderson explained the "straitjacket of a controlled economy" for the duration, and a new rationing system went into effect on sugar, with price ceilings on all sorts of consumer goods. The George Burns and

Gracie Allen Show, sponsored by Swan soap, was one of the big favorites on radio; in the movies, people flocked to see Alfred Hitchcock's *Saboteur*, starring Robert Cummings, with its famous climax as the Nazi saboteur falls to his death from the torch of the Statue of Liberty. *Life* magazine ran an article on cotton's new fashionability as the war made it the only fabric widely available; the article gave *Life* a chance to show pretty girls wearing cotton clothes and bathing suits. On May 27, Reinhard Heydrich – "Heydrich the Hangman," the S.S. boss of Bohemia and Moravia – was killed by two assailants on the outskirts of Prague; the Nazis then wiped out the town of Lidice and massacred thousands across Czechoslovakia. The unsuccessful struggle against German U-boats off the east coast of the U.S. resulted in gasoline rationing, entitling most motorists to three gallons per week, in 17 eastern states. And, as the draft boards continued their inroads, popular music reflected absence and its effect; the top songs in May included Russ Morgan's "Somebody Else is Taking My Place" and Glenn Miller's "Don't Sit Under the Apple Tree."

Johnny Rigney, Herman Franks, Frankie Pytlak, Bama Rowell, John Lucadello, Morrie Arnovich, Ed Pellagrini, Frank Hoerst, and Jack Wallaesa were among the players who had been taken into the service as the month of May moved along.

On the 19th, Hal Newhouser pitched his second straight complete-game victory, beating the Red Sox, 5-2. The Boston roster seemed to be holding up against the inroads of war; in the lineup for the Sox that day were Dom DiMaggio, Johnny Pesky, Pete Fox, Ted Williams, Bobby Doerr, Jimmy Foxx, and Jim Tabor. In his next appearance, Newhouser went the distance again but lost to St. Louis, 3-2. The winning run scored in the ninth when Newhouser picked up a sacrifice bunt and threw wildly to third.

Hal pitched one-third of an inning in relief on June 4,

aiding in a win over the A's by 8–7. Two days later he started and lost a game with the Senators, 11–3, giving up nine hits in six innings. The next day Newhouser was back in the bullpen, but his two scoreless innings helped Virgil Trucks beat the Nats, 6–4.

On June 16, Newhouser started against New York but lasted only until the fourth inning. He gave up only one hit, but he walked six and lost, 5–3. With his record now 2–4, he was surprised to learn that the American League managers had named him as a pitcher on the All-Star team. It was a pretty fair pitching staff that was picked for the July 6 game at the Polo Grounds in New York, with Tex Hughson of Boston, Edgar Smith of the White Sox, Jim Bagby from Cleveland, Newhouser and Benton of the Tigers, Ernie Bonham, Spud Chandler, and Red Ruffing of the Yanks, and Sid Hudson for Washington. Smith, a good pitcher with a bad team, had a 1–11 record at the time of selection and was the only White Sox representative; all the others were picked on merit, indicating that the league managers thought rather highly of Harold Newhouser.

The Detroit executives were quite concerned about Newhouser at this time, for he became eligible for induction into the service. In fact, he did not wait for his draft board but volunteered for the Army Air Corps. The plan was for him to be sworn in right on the mound at Briggs Stadium. Baker had thought he would have Harold for the whole season and recognized that the loss of the lefthander would sorely overburden his pitching staff. As it developed, however, the army doctors turned Newhouser down because of a heart problem, which they called "a leaky heart," probably some kind of a murmur.

Three more times over the next couple of years Newhouser was rejected by military doctors. His own physician advised him that baseball might place too severe a strain on his heart. But Harold was determined to keep pitching and told the doctor so. In that case, he was told, it was essential that he take care of himself. He did not smoke or drink, but now he was directed to get plenty of sleep, eat often but not heavily, and avoid getting tired. Hal was celebrated as one of the champion eaters in baseball – Dizzy Trout told a tale of watching Newhouser eat a whole five-pound roast, and Hal allegedly won a bet from Dick Bartell in 1940 by wolfing down 14 steak sandwiches, three barbecued chicken sandwiches, and two quarts of ice cream without getting up from the table – but now it was necessary to change his habits. He ate small meals six or seven times a day and tried to leave the table still a little hungry. He averaged 11 hours of sleep and rested whenever he felt tired. He took iron pills six times a day, and he checked in regularly with his doctor. After several years, it became evident that Newhouser's regimen was actually strengthening his heart.

Back again with the ball club, Hal pitched eight good innings against Washington but was not involved in the decision. He then went the distance to beat the A's, 3–2, on a three-hitter. Newhouser took a no-hitter into the seventh before the first Philadelphia hit, but two hits and a walk tied the score in the eighth. In the ninth, though, Don Ross hit for Newhouser and singled home the winning run.

June 1942 saw "the kiss heard 'round the world," Shirley Temple's first screen kiss, and the 16th birthday party of Princess Elizabeth of England, who reviewed her regiment of the Grenadier Guards for the occasion. It saw President Roosevelt award the Medal of Honor to General Jimmy Doolittle for his April 18 bombing raid on Tokyo and Greer Garson star as a "plain and ordinary" British housewife in the film *Mrs. Miniver*. B. F. Goodrich advertised its tires, "Built for Main Street ... But they made good on the Burma Road." And Americans celebrated the victory, early in the month, of the Battle of Midway. New names which became familiar across the land were General Joseph Stilwell, Admiral William F. "Bull" Halsey, and Mrs. Oveta Culp Hobby, head of the WAACs.

The Tigers were sitting in third place as June ended, well behind the Yankees, who seemed not to miss a beat with their powerful lineup of DiMaggio, Keller, Henrich, Gordon, Dickey, and the rest. Detroit's hitting was weak and its fielding was not much better, and all this placed a great burden upon the pitching staff.

There was a little extra drama connected with Newhouser's next start. As the *News* wrote, "Nowhere in the major leagues was the selection of Hal Newhouser for the All-Star team criticized more bitterly than in Cleveland," where they felt that both Mel Harder and Al Smith were more worthy candidates. When Virgil Trucks became ill, Newhouser was named to start in his place at Cleveland's vast Municipal Stadium on the night of July 3, to "show his critics whether or not he deserved the nomination." He came up with a gem, a three-hit victory by the score of 5-1. He gave up a double to Jim Hegan in the fifth and two more hits in the ninth, when the Indians scored their run, in the meantime striking out 10 batters.

Newhouser then traveled to New York for the All-Star Game on July 6, watching from the bench as Spud Chandler and Al Benton muffled the National League bats. The next day the victorious American Leaguers played a specially-recruited team of Service All-Stars in Cleveland before 62,094 paying customers. Again Newhouser sat on the bench as his teammates won, 5-0, over the military, managed by Mickey Cochrane, and featuring such stars as Feller (who was knocked out in the second inning), Pat Mullin, Johnny Rigney, Sam Chapman, Don Padgett, Cecil Travis, Joe Grace, and Frankie Pytlak.

Resuming the regular season, Newhouser pitched a classic against the Red Sox at Fenway Park on July 9, only to lose, 2-1, in 11 innings on his teammates' misplays. One reporter wrote that Newhouser "lost the game through no fault of his own . . . but . . . made the Red Sox, leading the league in batting, look almost pitiful at bat." His curve, fastball, and change of pace were all working to perfection, and only one of the six hits picked up by the Sox was a solid shot; other hits were scored on balls misplayed by York, second baseman Jim Bloodworth, and shortstop Billy Hitchcock. The winning run scored in the 11th on Joe Cronin's short fly to left; Don Ross failed to throw home after catching the ball, which the *News* reporter called "a baseball crime."

The writer summed up: "It's no secret among the Red Sox that Newhouser has outstanding stuff and from top to bottom, including Joe Cronin, Ted Williams and Bobby Doerr, the Hose acclaim Newhouser a sure candidate for summa cum laude honors in the pitching circle."

Three days later, Newhouser saw his record fall to 4–6. He pitched six strong innings in relief at New York before losing, 3–1, to the Yankees on Buddy Hassett's two-run homer in the 13th inning. On July 17, Harold pitched a complete game at Washington but lost, 3–0, to Bobo Newsom. Newhouser held the Nats hitless for seven innings but lost it in the eighth. And a week later he lost another one to Washington, 5–3, despite yielding only five hits; in this one nine bases on balls kept him in trouble throughout, and Johnny Sullivan's bases-clearing double in the sixth did him in.

So July saw a string of fairly well-pitched games go into the loss column; it was a frustrating month for Harold Newhouser. It was a month of oily, fouled sands on the Jersey beaches from the heavy toll of oil tankers taken by the U-boats, a month of Rommel's victory at Tobruk, the "Stage Door Canteen" in New York City, the Jeep, and new personalities such as Donald M. Nelson, head of the War Production Board, and a general from Kansas named Dwight Eisenhower. People sang "I've Got Spurs that Jingle, Jangle, Jingle" with Kay Kyser's band and read a book by Franz Werfel entitled *The Song of Bernadette*.

After a no-decision start against Boston, Hal Newhouser lost a heartbreaker at Chicago on August 5. Lefty Thornton Lee blanked the Tigers, and rookie Don Kolloway stole home for the only run of a 1-0 game. The Tigers soon after lost shortstop Billy Hitchcock, second baseman Charlie Gehringer, and catcher Birdie Tebbetts to the military as they gradually sank into the second division. On the 9th Newhouser ended the Tigers' five-game losing streak (as well as his personal losing string of the same length) with a 9-3 victory over the Browns. His record now stood at 5-9, and it improved a notch when he shut out Cleveland on five hits three days later, 2-0.

On the 16th, Newhouser beat the White Sox and their ace Ted Lyons, 3-2, in 11 innings to make his won-loss record 7-9. A week later, however, the Browns beat him, 2-1, before a Briggs Stadium crowd of 50,758, Detroit's benefit for the Army & Navy Relief Fund. His Tiger mates were unable to do much with the knuckleball pitching of Johnny Niggeling, and both St. Louis runs scored in the seventh on a double error by big Rudy York. And on the last day of the month, Newhouser's wildness hurt him in a 7-1 loss to the Yankees.

August saw the successful landing of the Marines on Guadalcanal in the Solomons and the disastrous landing of 6,000 Canadian and American Rangers on the French Channel coast at Dieppe. Arturo Toscanini led the NBC Symphony Orchestra in a broadcast playing of Dmitri Shostakovich's Seventh Symphony, written during the siege of Leningrad in 1941. And Brooklyn's Branch Rickey spoke optimistically about baseball's prospects in 1943: "The game should and will continue. Thousands look to it for diversion . . . The game has done a wonderful job of co-operation so far and the fans appreciate it." Rickey warned that "profits must be subordinated in these grave times," a warning which no doubt brought smiles to the faces of those players who had ever negotiated contracts with Rickey, and he predicted that "the majors have not yet felt the full impact of what will come in the drain on manpower."

Another prediction of problems to come was a sensational article in the August 17 issue of *Life* magazine, entitled "DETROIT IS DYNAMITE." The article began: "The news from Detroit is bad this summer. Few people across the country realize how bad it is. Wildcat strikes and sitdowns, material shortages and poor planning at the top have cut into Detroit's production of war weapons." The article detailed the labor unrest, racial and religious hatred, and low morale with which the city was bedeviled. "More than half of its population of nearly two million came to Detroit in the last 20 years. They have no great love for their city and they give their loyalty to their own group, creed or union." Substandard housing was the sorest problem in the city, along with the conflicts between 200,000 newly-arrived southern whites and 150,000 blacks. "The people of Detroit are confused, embittered and distracted," and demagogues of various persuasions played upon this confusion. "It is time," *Life* said, "for the rest of the country to sit up and take notice. For Detroit can either blow up Hitler or it can blow up the U.S." The country did not yet sit up and take notice, but that time was coming.

On September 3, Newhouser lost his 12th game of the year, a 2-0 loss to the Red Sox in which he pitched well once again but got little support from his teammates. A week later, though, Hal came back and beat Boston and its pitching ace Tex Hughson by a 5-4 score. The next day, as the A's were beating the Tigers, pitcher Dizzy Trout grabbed a heckling spectator and had to be restrained from punching the man; Trout received a five-day suspension.

On the 13th Newhouser came in to pitch relief in a

game against Washington which Rudy York had just tied with a home run. In the Senators' ninth, Sullivan singled and Ellis Clary walked before Newhouser struck out Early Wynn. Both runners moved up on a passed ball and Case was intentionally walked. Stan Spence hit a bouncer to York, who fumbled it for one run, and two more runs scored when Bruce Campbell's grounder also went through the first baseman. The reaction of the Tigers' pitcher, already nicknamed "Junior" by the sportswriters because of his immaturity and tantrums, can be imagined. His season came to an inglorious close with two games in which he pitched to a total of six batters and retired none: he lost, 5-1, to the pennant-winning Yankees, giving up three hits and a walk before departing in the first inning, and several days later pitched to two batters, walking both, in the ninth inning of a game with Cleveland.

The Tigers finished 1942 in fifth place with a 73-81 record; they were 30 games behind New York. Hal Newhouser ended with a record of 8-14, and it looked as if 1942 had been a major reverse for him. A closer look at his record, though, indicated just how bad his support had been. His earned run average was an excellent 2.45, a great improvement over the year before. He reduced his walks from 137 to 114, while pitching 10 more innings than in 1941. And he led the entire American League in the most strikeouts per nine innings and the fewest hits per nine innings. Unfortunately, these latter statistics were not compiled at the time, so that it is mainly in retrospect that it is possible to see just how well Newhouser pitched in 1942. Earned run averages were not published until after the season, so even that indicator of Newhouser's improvement was easy to overlook. Everyone at the time just looked at that 8 and 14.

7
GREAT START, BAD FINISH

As the troubled year of 1942 came to an end, Americans, looking to some far-off day after the war, were singing "When the Lights Go On Again" or dreaming of a "White Christmas," the smash hit by Irving Berlin from the movie *Holiday Inn*. The war itself was clearly far from its end; December '42 saw the continuance of fierce fighting on Guadalcanal and New Guinea, and Allied offensives in North Africa simply served to emphasize how far the British and Americans were from getting at Hitler in his home country.

Baseball struggled to come to grips with the war. Organized baseball had contributed some 1,400 players, major leaguers and minor leaguers, to the armed services as well as more than a million dollars to military relief funds. Fans threw foul balls back onto the field, with the clubs turning these balls over to military recreation programs. With the "green light" from President Roosevelt, baseball had gotten through a season which many so-called experts felt was doomed to failure and curtailment. Now, heading into 1943, it had to do it all over again — with more players gone, more restrictions, and more apparently insurmountable problems.

On January 5, 1943, the 16 major league club owners held a special meeting in Chicago with Judge Landis, who had just come in from Washington. They agreed to continue with a full 154-game schedule, although the season opener was to be set back eight days to April 21. The big bombshell was Landis' announcement that spring training must be conducted north of the Potomac and Ohio rivers and east of the Mississippi, except for the two St. Louis clubs, which could train in Missouri. "Transportation during spring training will be held to a minimum," said Landis, "and after spring training there will be need for utmost cooperation on the part of the various clubs to cut man mileage as much as possible."

It developed that these restrictions were not imposed by the government but were volunteered by the commissioner. Joseph B. Eastman, director of the Office of Defense Transportation, had simply suggested that baseball consider means of reducing its transportation needs. Landis came up with the new spring training routine and a schedule change by which each team would make only three visits to opposing cities instead of four.

Baseball received much favorable publicity for its new travel plans, but the game's most crucial problem was, of course, the draft. Shortly after the start of the war Congress amended the law to provide for the drafting of men between the ages of 20 and 45. This was just the start, though, for the implementation of the draft law was left basically up to the Selective Service System, under the command of General Lewis B. Hershey, and local draft boards around the country. Each local board had its own particular problems; a board with a large pool of available manpower might have much different ideas of what were "essential occupations contributing to the war effort" than one with only a few draft-age men available. Single men and those without dependents were supposed to go ahead of married men with or without children, but again much depended on the individual draft board. Late in 1942, the law was changed again, this time to permit the induction of young men age 18 and 19. Still, the ever-increasing needs of the military were not met, and Selective Service regulations and interpretations made the able-bodied man of draft age who was not in some eligible category an increasingly rare specimen. By the time 1943 came to an end, one of the top songs on the music charts was a lament by singer Kitty Kallen, about the men left at home, that "They're Either Too Young or Too Old."

Pete Reiser, the brilliant young star of the Brooklyn Dodgers, entered the army on January 13, and Joe Di-Maggio announced that he was planning to enlist. The next day, Leo Durocher, the 38-year-old manager of the Dodgers, was notified to report for a draft physical, and Branch Rickey was forced to think about finding a new manager. (Eventually a perforated eardrum kept Durocher out of the service.)

In mid-February the Giants' Johnny Mize was called, and the Cardinals ran an ad in *The Sporting News*, saying they had openings on their minor league teams for free agents with previous professional experience. The minors, which had had 41 leagues in operation in 1941, were down to nine for the 1943 season: the International, American Association, Pacific Coast, Southern Association, Eastern, Piedmont, Interstate, Appalachian, and Pony leagues. The historic Texas League was the largest of the minors to disband for the duration.

Baseball intended to persevere. Veteran slugger Joe Medwick told the Associated Press, "You know, these old timers — fellows who won't be called to the service — will surprise you. Baseball may be a little below past standards but I don't think it will be enough to hurt the game."

As the 16 big league clubs scrambled for spring training locations in the north, the new manager of the Detroit Tigers talked to the press. Del Baker had been released after the 1942 season, and 52-year-old Steve O'Neill was named to replace him. O'Neill, one of four ballplaying brothers from the Pennsylvania hard-coal region, was an old-time catcher who had managed the Cleveland Indians for three seasons in the late '30s. He felt good about his new job. "It's great to come back," he said. "We'll be all right; I know a lot about the Tigers – both the ones who have been with the club for years and the ones we'll try out for the first time in the spring." He hoped for improvement from McCosky and York, he looked for great things from rookies Dick Wakefield and Frank "Stubby" Overmire, and "the pitching," he said, "with Hal White, Hal Newhouser, Virgil Trucks and the others, ought to be all right."

A couple of weeks later Zeller signed a catcher named Paul Richards, who had played bits and pieces of four seasons in the early '30s with three teams and had just been released after four years as player-manager of the Atlanta Crackers in the Southern Association. He had never been much of a hitter, but he was a good catcher and could help to make up for the glaring loss of Tebbetts.

Richards would be reporting, with the rest of the Tigers, to Evansville, Indiana. Indiana turned out to be a favorite state for the northern spring training, with the Pirates in Muncie, the Reds in Bloomington, the Indians in Lafayette, and both the Cubs and the White Sox in French Lick, which they found flooded when they arrived. Other exotic locales were Asbury Park (the Yankees), Wilmington, Delaware (the A's), Medford, Massachusetts (the Red Sox, guests of Tufts College), and Bear Mountain and West Point, New York (where the Dodgers used the facilities of the U.S. Military Academy when the cadets were done with them). Photographers delighted in setting up gag shots such as one at the Giants' camp at Lakewood, New Jersey, with pitchers Cliff Melton, Van Lingle Mungo, and Carl Hubbell in baseball uniforms plus scarves and earmuffs warming their feet over a fire, and one showing three A's players dumping snow on the head of pitcher Luman Harris.

The Sporting News ran a headline reading "MAJORS GET OUT LONG UNDERWEAR FOR TRAINING TRIPS," and it was recognized that many workouts, particularly in the early days after the mid-March start, would take place indoors. The Detroit club did not have that consolation, for there was no fieldhouse or other indoor accommodation available for the Tigers. They worked outdoors or not at all. O'Neill and his men did have, in Bosse Field, one of the best minor league parks in the country at their disposal, and, as it turned out, Evansville produced almost perfect weather for them.

Newhouser and Dizzy Trout were the first Tigers to show up at Evansville, along with manager O'Neill; when the full squad had arrived there were only 22 players on hand. "It was evident," one reporter noted dryly, "that paring the personnel would be one of the lesser problems of Steve O'Neill." After a couple of weeks the manager realized he had too many exhibition games scheduled, and he started trying to cancel some of them. His small pitching staff was overworked, particularly after Hal White sprained his back. On April 3, Newhouser finished a workout against the Cubs and immediately boarded a train for Detroit, having been ordered home by his draft board for another physical. Hal Manders went home for his physical at the same time, leaving O'Neill with six pitchers. Manders was soon in the service, but Newhouser, to O'Neill's great relief, returned shortly, having been turned down by the army once again.

A new Selective Service regulation placed men who had children born before the start of the war in a deferred status, Class 3-A. Ford Frick said the new rule would permit baseball to play out the year. Admitting to much prior uncertainty about continuing play after Labor Day or even July 4, Frick said, "now it seems virtually assured that we can play out the season." His statement did not assuage Steve O'Neill's pain the next day when Barney McCosky left camp to go into Naval Aviation.

Still, H.G. Salsinger noted, "the squad that leaves Evansville next Wednesday will be as well conditioned as any that ever came out of Florida." Hard work and decent weather had brought about that happy result. Salsinger felt compelled, however, to issue his annual warning of dire expectations. "Baseball, in its present form, is doomed," he wrote. "It is doubtful if the major leagues will play their full 1943 schedules. It is certain that there will be no baseball after this year until the war ends." Detroit fans could be pardoned for singing, with Helen Forrest and the Harry James band, "It Seems to Me I've Heard That Song Before." Connie Mack, the patriarch of the Athletics, took a more realistic approach when he said, "as for baseball in general in 1943, we don't know what we will run into, but we're hoping for the best." The Cardinals and the Yankees were pennant favorites as the season openers neared. Steve O'Neill pegged six pitchers as potential starters – Bridges, Gorsica, Newhouser, Trucks, Trout, and White – with Roy Henshaw and Stubby Overmire in the bullpen. He still did not know who his catcher would be, but he hoped that Richards could hit enough to be useful.

The season opened, and baseball suddenly had a new problem it never dreamed of: a ball that went "splat" when it was hit. Earlier, *The Sporting News* had reported hopefully the adoption of "a wartime baseball which . . . will bring back the fat batting averages of 1939." Faced with a rubber shortage, the Spalding Company, which made the balls for the big leagues, had come up with a core of granulated cork, enveloped in two layers of "balata," a gum-like substance used for the covering of golf balls. "Tighter winding of the ball," it was said, "will improve resiliency."

This new, livelier baseball turned out to be a mirage. Four games were played on Opening Day, and all four of them saw shutouts pitched, with two of them 1–0 games. "Baseball was pushed back into the dead-ball era with the opening of the major league season," wrote Salsinger, and Steve O'Neill exclaimed, "Why, the ball is deader than the one in use when I was playing." Eleven of the first 29 games played produced shutouts, and the uproar over the "balata" ball became deafening. Scientists at Cooper Union in New York tested the "balata" ball and found that it had an average of 25.9% less bounce than the 1942 ball. The Spalding people tried to say the new ball had not yet had a proper trial, but they were eventually forced to recall what was out there, substitute leftover '42 balls temporarily, and come up with baseballs that had a little more life to them than the ill-fated "balata" balls. By May 9 the "balata" ball was a thing of the past.

There were other war-imposed problems that baseball had with its equipment. Catchers' shinguards had to be hoarded because the supply of them dried up. The material used to make them was converted to ration tokens, billions of which (red or blue) were punched out for use by the shopping housewives of America. High quality wool yarn was no longer available for baseballs, and cork from Spain for the centers of balls became hard to find. Kangaroo hide, the leather used for baseball shoes, was no longer being shipped from Australia, and the steel used in spikes for those shoes became scarce as well. High-quality leather for gloves and wool for sweatshirts and uniforms were also severely limited in availability. Bat manufacturers, of course, had always stockpiled quantities of ash for seasoning, so they had enough good wood on hand to carry them through for the duration, especially with the sharply curtailed number of hitters needing bats. With all of these problems, the leaders of the game were committed to improvising, scratching, and scrimping to keep things going.

Hal Newhouser made his season debut on April 25 with one inning in relief in a loss at Cleveland. He made his first start five days later at Briggs Stadium. It was

48 degrees with a wind of 21 miles per hour, and there were only 300 people in the stands. When it began to rain and snow in the second inning, the umpires called it off.

After a second relief job, Newhouser got another start on May 6, hooking up in a duel with Denny Galehouse of the Browns before 618 spectators at Sportsman's Park. With one out in the ninth, George McQuinn tripled to left-center, only the fifth hit off of Newhouser. Pinch hitter Don Heffner then put down a good squeeze bunt, with McQuinn off with the pitch, and Newhouser had a heartbreaking 1-0 defeat.

A week later Newhouser started again and again came up empty. He pitched eight innings against the A's at Detroit but left for a pinch hitter with the score tied at 1-1. The Tigers lost it in 13 innings, 2-1. The only run scored on Newhouser came across on a balk, with Mr. Mack's men collecting only three hits against the lefthander.

Finally, on May 21, Hal won his first game of the year. Even then he had to pitch 13 innings to beat the Red Sox and Tex Hughson, 2-1, with Doc Cramer doubling home the winning run after an error. Salsinger noted, "It is doubtful if any pitcher has pitched better ball than Newhouser and it is also doubtful if any other pitcher has had less offensive support." In the 33 innings that Newhouser had pitched, the Tigers had scored only three runs; "whenever Newhouser pitched the Detroit attack, not a good one at its best, died almost completely." It looked like a repeat of the 1942 season for the lefthander.

Six days later Newhouser beat the Yankees in New York, going all the way in a 3-2 victory over Atley Donald. Rudy York hit a three-run homer in the fourth, and then Gordon's two-run shot in the bottom of the inning made it close. But Newhouser shut the door on the defending champs, allowing only four hits and striking out 14.

The Tigers went to Boston from New York. O'Neill

sent Newhouser and White on to Philadelphia, their next pitching stop, ahead of the rest of the team, so they could get a good night's sleep. Unfortunately, with the crowded state of wartime rail travel, the two pitchers were unable to get seats on the train and stood all the way from Boston to Philadelphia.

On May 31, 23,833 fans turned out for a doubleheader at Shibe Park, and Newhouser showed that he was none the worse for wear from his long train ride. He completely dominated the Athletics in the first game, winning 7–0 and holding the home team to two scattered singles, by Dick Siebert and Hal Wagner. His masterpiece in Philadelphia completed the best month of pitching Hal Newhouser had ever had in the major leagues. His record was 3–1 and his earned run average was 0.90. There was now "evidence," as Ward wrote in the *Free Press,* "to support the suspicion that he is developing into a real big-league hurler." The writer noted that Newhouser "is the type that acquires critics easily. He is high strung and he has a very low boiling point . . . Newhouser's critics have said that he was too temperamental to become a good pitcher." But, Ward wrote, "something seems to have happened to Junior this season. Perhaps the influence of the gentle Steve O'Neill has had its effect on him. Perhaps he has matured."

In any event, he was winning and he was pitching well. Veteran Philadelphia reporter Ed Pollock watched Newhouser and said the lefthander "has a good chance of being rated eventually among the great southpaws of all time." Better control and a more deliberate delivery seemed to Pollock to account for the improvement in the young pitcher. Time would tell, of course, whether he had really turned the corner. After the game, Pollock asked Connie Mack, "How can you beat a pitcher like that?" The ancient manager of the A's reflected and then said, "The way he pitched today no club could beat him. But he can be beaten if things don't go the way he wants them and he gets a little upset."

The end of May and the Memorial Day holiday is a good time to take a look at baseball's season and the country in the second year of its war. Baseball, it seemed, was hanging on. The Tigers were 16–16 at the end of May, in fifth place, but only three games behind first-place New York. Attendance had been disappointing around the major leagues, but there were several factors that could account for that. The deadening effects of the "balata" ball, a lot of really bad weather, particularly in the Midwest – the Tigers and Yankees had an entire four-game series washed out – and the slower-than-usual development of baseball interest caused by the brief and less-ballyhooed northern training season all helped to hold down attendance in the early going; but as the weather warmed up and dried out, the crowds picked up. On the day one month after the start of the season when all clubs were required to cut their rosters to 25 men, there was very little of the usual activity; most clubs were already at or below the limit. The Tigers were carrying only 22 players. But no teams had yet run into difficulty in fielding a lineup, and there were quite a few pre-war stars still playing.

And who was playing ball in the big leagues at this time? We can look at the boxscores for May 31, 1943, and get some idea of what the major leagues looked like, a year and a half after the start of the war.

The Red Sox took two from the Browns at Fenway Park that day, the first game a 2–1, five-hitter by Tex Hughson in 13 innings. Harvard man Tony Lupien played first for the Sox, and the rest of the infield consisted of Bobby Doerr, Eddie Lake, and Jim Tabor. Lake had been a utility infielder for the Cardinals before the war, but his big league career would continue through 1950. The hard-drinking Tabor had been a consistent slugger for

Boston since 1939. In the outfield, Joe Cronin's team was using ex-Tiger Pete Fox, 41-year-old Al Simmons, and young Leon Culberson. The catching was shared by rookie Roy Partee and veteran Johnny Peacock, in his seventh year with the Sox. After Hughson's gem in the opener, Boston used Oscar Judd, a lefthander from London, Ontario, and two old-timers, 40-year-old Mike Ryba and 34-year-old Mace Brown, who had won a bunch of games for Pittsburgh in the '30s. The St. Louis lineup featured McQuinn, Heffner, rookie Floyd Baker, and the fading Harlond Clift in the infield, Vern Stephens (the regular shortstop), Chet Laabs, and Mike Chartak in the outfield, Rick Ferrell and Frankie Hayes behind the plate, and knuckleballer Johnny Niggeling, George Caster, Paul Dean (Dizzy's brother, in his only start for the Browns), Bob Muncrief, and Steve Sundra on the mound. Although the Browns finished sixth, they had a fairly solid lineup, with many of the names featured in the next year's pennant race.

The other Boston team, Casey Stengel's Braves, split a twin bill at Pittsburgh. Centerfielder Tommy Holmes picked up five hits and rightfielder Chuck Workman hit a home run. Jim Tobin, a big knuckleballer in his seventh big league season, won the opener, 6–1. Among the other Brave players were infielders John McCarthy, Connie Ryan, weak-hitting Whitey Wietelmann, and Eddie Joost, outfielder Elmer "Butch" Nieman (a Kansan who played three wartime seasons in Boston and then disappeared from the majors), and catchers Phil Masi and Clyde Kluttz. The Pirates got a shutout from pitcher Bob Klinger to achieve the split, after using rookies Bill Brandt and Harry Shuman and veterans Lloyd Dietz, John Lanning, and Max Butcher in the opener. On the field for the Bucs were infielders Elbie Fletcher, Pete Coscarart, Huck Geary, Frankie Gustine, and Bob Elliott, with Jim Russell, Vince DiMaggio, and Johnny Barrett in the outfield. Al Lopez and Bill Baker handled the catching. Geary and Barrett were wartime players, but the others had lengthy and productive careers.

At Yankee Stadium, 31,892 people showed up to watch Joe McCarthy's boys divide a doubleheader with the White Sox. The Yanks used Nick Etten (over in a trade from the Phillies), Joe Gordon, Snuffy Stirnweiss, and hot rookie Billy Johnson in the infield, Charlie Keller, Roy "Stormy" Weatherly, and Johnny Lindell in the outfield, and Rollie Hemsley and Bill Dickey behind the plate. Keller and Gordon hit round-trippers, while Dickey went 5-for-5 in the second game, with a double and a triple. Atley Donald, Johnny Murphy, and Marius Russo pitched the first game, while Bill Zuber won the second, with relief help from Jim Turner. These may not have been the Bronx Bombers of old, but there were still a number of high-quality professionals wearing Yankee pinstripes.

The Chisox, managed by Jimmy Dykes, featured infielders Joe Kuhel (with a home run in each game), Don Kolloway, Luke Appling (the eventual '43 batting champion), and Jim Grant, whose brief big league career covered just 146 games. Veteran Wally Moses and rookie Thurman Tucker, who played through 1950, held down two of the outfield posts, and 30-year-old rookie Guy Curtright manned the other. Curtright had put in nine years in the minors, five of them at Henderson in the East Texas League, had hit consistently well, but had been unable to make the big time until 1943. He hit fairly well for three years with the White Sox, held on briefly into the '46 season, and then returned to the minors. Mike Tresh and Tom Turner caught the doubleheader for the Sox, while Edgar Smith, Orval Grove, John Humphries, and relief specialist Gordon Maltzberger pitched.

The world champion Cards won the opener of their doubleheader against Brooklyn, 7-0, as Billy Southworth's big righthander Mort Cooper pitched a one-hitter, giving up only a fifth-inning double to Billy Herman. In the nightcap, though, Fat Freddie Fitzsimmons worked seven innings of a 1–0 win for the Dodgers, with Max Macon and Curt Davis pitching behind him. The Cardinal lineup still looked fairly potent, and of course the Cards won their second straight pennant in 1943. They had Ray Sanders, rookie Lou Klein, Jimmy Brown, Marty Marion, and Debs Garms in the infield, with an injured Whitey Kurowski waiting in the wings, and Johnny Hopp, Harry Walker, and Stanley Frank Musial across the outfield. Walker Cooper and Ken O'Dea handled the catching, and lefty Harry Brecheen was the hardluck loser in the second game. Durocher's Dodgers ran out a batting order of Augie Galan, Arky Vaughan, Dixie Walker, Dolf Camilli, Billy Herman, Mickey Owen, Joe Medwick, and Boyd Bartley. There are some heavy hitters (including three Hall of Famers) in that lineup, even though on this day it produced just one run in 18 innings against Cooper and Brecheen.

The Cubs and Phillies divided a doubleheader at Chicago. Danny Murtaugh, Babe Dahlgren, and Danny Litwhiler hit homers for the Phils, under the leadership of new manager Bucky Harris. Other starters for Harris were Ron Northey, the well-traveled Jimmy Wasdell, Earl Naylor, light-hitting Glen Stewart, the solid Pinky May, and catchers Tom Padden, back to the majors for the first time since 1937, and Mickey Livingston. Naylor was so anemic a hitter that he had tried to make it as a pitcher the year before (unsuccessfully; 0–5 with a 6.12 earned run average). Johnny Podgajny, a bespectacled young pitcher from Chester, Pennsylvania, nearing the close of a brief and undistinguished career, threw a complete-game victory in the opener, while Charlie Fuchs and Newell Kimball lost the second. The Cubs used an infield of Phil Cavarretta, Eddie Stanky, Lennie Merullo, and Stan Hack, with Harry "Peanuts" Lowrey, Bill Nicholson, and Lou Novikoff, "the Mad Russian," one of the great minor league players but a bust in the majors, in the outfield. Veteran Al Todd and Sal Hernandez caught for Chicago, while Kewpie Dick Barrett and Ray Prim started the two games.

In any discussion of "wartime players," Dick Barrett must be considered a classic of the type. Born in 1907 in Montoursville, Pennsylvania, Barrett was a little round man who threw right-handed and pitched in the minor leagues from 1925 to 1933. Purchased by the A's, he won four and lost four with a 5.79 ERA in 15 games. Connie Mack was unimpressed and sold him to the Boston Braves. Barrett pitched briefly and ineffectively for Boston in 1934 and was then shipped out to Albany. In 1935 he landed in Seattle, in the Pacific Coast League, and he pitched for the Rainiers for eight years, winning more than 20 games seven times. After his second season, he was drafted by the Reds but was returned to Seattle in spring training. When he won 27 in 1942, the Cubs drafted him and he started the next season in Chicago. On June 27, however, the Cubs announced that they were returning him and his 0–4 record to Seattle. Obviously, spending the rest of his career in the Coast League had lost its appeal for Kewpie Dick, so he refused to report. On July 6, then, general manager Jim Gallagher arranged for Barrett's sale to the Phillies, who were always in the market for a pitcher who could be had cheaply. For the rest of the '43 season, Kewpie Dick won 10, lost nine, and became a big favorite in Philadelphia. In 1944 he went 12–18 for the Phils and followed that with 7–20 in 1945, his final year in the majors. It should be recognized that those were very bad Phillie teams. Barrett was then 39 years old and there was not much thought of keeping him around for post-war play. But he had given the Phillies almost 600 innings during the war. It was clear that he had learned how to pitch in his lengthy minor league career, and his prime years were spent in Seattle. A "wartime player"? Yes, Kewpie Dick Barrett was that, but he was also a professional who knew how to play the game.

At Washington that May 31, the Senators and Indians split their doubleheader. The Senators' Alejandro Carrasquel won the first game in relief over Cleveland's Pete Center, while Center got credit for the second game with Carrasquel losing it. The Senators had George Case, Stan Spence, Mickey Vernon, Bob Johnson, Jerry Priddy, and Jake Early in their lineup, with Dutch Leonard and Early Wynn as their starting pitchers, while the Indians, under player-manager Boudreau, used Oris Hockett (who had washed out of a couple of pre-war trials with Brooklyn), Ken Keltner, Jeff Heath, Ray Mack, Roy Cullenbine, and Buddy Rosar. Otto Denning played the two games at first base for the Tribe, as he neared the end of a brief big league career.

The lineup which manager Mel Ott of the Giants presented at Cincinnati featured a number of well-known players in the latter stages of their careers, men such as Dick Bartell, Billy Jurges, Gus Mancuso, Ernie Lombardi, and Ott himself, a few like Buster Maynard, Babe Barna, and Joe Orengo, whose careers were brief and unimpressive, a solid journeyman named Mickey Witek, a future star named Sid Gordon, and a minor league hotshot who was destined to disappoint in the big time, outfielder Johnny Rucker. The Reds had an infield which was solid in three spots, with Frank McCormick, Lonny Frey, and Eddie Miller, along with veteran minor leaguer Steve Mesner at third base. In the outfield, manager Bill McKechnie used Eric Tipton, Gee Walker, Max Marshall, and Estel Crabtree (whose principal claim to fame was his birth in Crabtree, Ohio). Veteran Ray Mueller and Al Lakeman were his catchers and Elmer Riddle, Ed Heusser, and Ray Starr the pitchers.

Finally, the last games were the pair at Shibe Park between the A's and the Tigers, with Newhouser and A's flutterball pitcher Roger Wolff picking up the victories. Mister Mack's team started Siebert, Pete Suder, Irv Hall, and Eddie Mayo in the infield, Cuban slugger Bobby Estalella, ex-Tiger star Jojo White, and young Elmer Valo in the outfield, and Hal Wagner behind the plate. The A's had started off well, but ahead of them was a record-tying 20-game losing streak which doomed them to a last-place finish. The batting order for Detroit was Joe Hoover, Doc Cramer, Wakefield, Higgins, Ned Harris, York, Jimmy Bloodworth, and Paul Richards or Ed Parsons behind the plate. Hoover had come up to the Tigers after five years with Hollywood in the Coast League; he was a marginal player who did not stay in the majors after the war.

This brief review of the big league scene — a snapshot of the game on a particular day in the springtime — indicates that baseball in early 1943 was undergoing only a very moderate decline from pre-war standards. Perhaps there were worse times to come — H.G. Salsinger certainly thought so — but things were not yet too bad in terms of baseball manpower.

In the fighting overseas, there were signs of encouragement. May saw the successful completion of the North African campaign and the capture of a quarter million Axis soldiers in Tunisia. In the Atlantic, a complex of anti-submarine measures turned the tide on the U-boat menace, and what had been a major threat to the Allies was thereafter simply an annoyance. In the Pacific theatre the Japanese were being slowly pushed back in the Solomons and along the northern coast of New Guinea.

On the home front President Roosevelt named James F. Byrnes director of the Office of War Mobilization, with authority to unify and coordinate the production and procurement of materials for both military and civilian needs. A test of the government's authority and determination was provoked by the United Mine Workers of

John L. Lewis, who went out on a nationwide strike against the coal mine operators. Republicans were said to be looking with favor on the presidential hopes for 1944 of Ohio's Governor John W. Bricker, who, it was said, looked more like a president than anyone the GOP had had since Warren G. Harding. A colt named Count Fleet won both the Kentucky Derby and the Preakness and was aiming at a Triple Crown with the Belmont Stakes coming up in early June. Tyrone Power completed his last film before entering the service, a submarine epic called *Crash Dive* with Anne Baxter, and a judge in San Francisco sentenced bandleader Gene Krupa to 90 days in jail and a $500 fine for possession of marijuana cigarettes. Bestselling books included *The Robe,* a biblical novel by Lloyd Douglas, and *One World* by Wendell Willkie. And in Detroit, playing at the Broadway Capitol was the film *Casablanca,* while the Cecil B. DeMille epic, *Reap the Wild Wind,* with Paulette Goddard, Ray Milland, and John Wayne, was at the Palms State.

The Tigers moved on to Washington, and Hal Newhouser's brief winning streak ended at Griffith Stadium on June 5 with a 6–3 loss to Early Wynn. Newhouser left for a pinch hitter in the sixth with the score 3–0, and the Tigers did not score until the game was out of hand.

On the 9th the team returned to Detroit for a twilight game with the White Sox, starting at 6 P.M. A good crowd of 14,793 showed up, but the Chicagoans won, 3–1. As Salsinger wrote, "Harold Newhouser's luck is no better in the cool of the evening than in the heat of the afternoon." Newhouser went the distance, but his mates did little damage to Chicago's Johnny Humphries and were unable to overcome the three runs which scored when Rudy York dropped an easy pop fly in the first inning. Two more errors by York and four balls which second baseman Don Ross failed to get kept Newhouser busy, but he was able to prevent any further scoring.

Four days later Newhouser was used in relief against the White Sox, coming in to get the last two outs in the ninth to save a 3-2 win for Virgil Trucks. On June 17, his Tiger mates were up to their old tricks again as Newhouser lost another heartbreaker by a 3-2 count at Cleveland. Hal had a 2-0 shutout going into the ninth, when Buddy Rosar and Mickey Rocco singled. Ray Mack hit a ball that went right through Higgins at third, and, after one out, pinch hitter Gene Desautels hit a perfect double-play ball to shortstop Joe Hoover. Hoover booted it, and the Indians were alive. A moment later Lou Boudreau singled to right and the winning run scored.

Two days later O'Neill called upon Newhouser again when the Browns knocked Bridges and White out and tied the score in the ninth. Harold was equal to the task and stifled the Brownies with one hit over three and two-thirds innings. Finally, in the 12th, St. Louis pitcher George Caster walked the bases loaded before Roger Cramer drove in the winning run. Newhouser's record was now even at 4-4. A headline in the *News* the next day read: TIGERS' PITCHING QUANDARY: AFTER NEWHOUSER WHO?"

The following Sunday evening the long-feared explosion in Detroit took place. Earlier in the month there had been a nasty strike in the Packard plant, where white workers walked out rather than work alongside blacks on the assembly line – an "issue," one reporter wrote, that "seemed big enough to the workers to bring a vital war plant to a halt." Racial hatred had been simmering in Detroit's neighborhoods for several years, and there had been a number of nasty incidents, particularly in the schools. There had been a lot of talk around town that trouble, when it came, would most likely come in the summertime and start at Belle Isle, the island in the Detroit River where Detroiters were accustomed to going for relaxation and recreation. And so it turned out: at the end of a hot and sultry Sunday on the eve of summer, there was much pushing and shoving between young whites and blacks on a crowded bridge leading from Belle Isle back into the city. This quickly developed into physical conflict, and before the authorities could find out what was happening, the violence had spilled onto Jefferson Avenue and downtown, and from there it spread throughout the city. It was senseless and mindless and brutal, from a black kicked to death because he had the ill fortune to find himself on a street with a gang of rampaging white youths, to a white man pummeled after his car stalled in a black neighborhood. Blacks were pulled off of street cars and beaten, autos were overturned and set ablaze, and stores were broken into and cleaned out. "Here," a reporter wrote, "was the spectacle of a city at war with itself when a nation is fighting for its life." The violence and looting and rioting continued for more than 24 hours before U.S. Army troops, ordered into Detroit by President Roosevelt, finally brought matters under control. Thirty-four people had been killed, 23 of them blacks, close to a thousand were injured, 1,800 were arrested, and there was property damage in the millions of dollars. Detroit had learned that there could be a fearful price to pay for unrestrained hatred, demagoguery, and bigotry.

The Tigers were not scheduled to play on the following day, Monday the 21st, and Jack Zeller canceled the scheduled game with Cleveland on June 22, as martial law continued. The Detroit players kept to their homes or apartments and looked on with wonder as the city erupted around them. None of the players were quoted publicly on the riots or the causes of them; they just wanted to play ball and keep a low profile. Some 40 percent of the Tiger players, it might be noted, were southerners and none, of course, were black.

On June 23, before 5,210 paying customers and 300 Michigan state troopers on hand to preserve order, the Tigers and Indians played a doubleheader, one game be-

ing the makeup of the one postponed the day before. Hal
Newhouser pitched the first game, and, as C.P. Ward put
it, "as he has done on most occasions this season, Newhouser turned in a masterful pitching performance." He
won this one, 3-1, giving up only five hits, two by Oris
Hockett and three by Ken Keltner. He should have had
a shutout, but shortstop Hoover kicked in an unearned
run in the ninth. In the second game, Prince Henry Oana,
a Hawaiian with some spurious claims to royalty and
who had a brief trial as a Phillies' outfielder some nine
years earlier, made his debut as a Tiger pitcher after being purchased from Milwaukee earlier in the week. He
lost, 9-6.

Newhouser's record now stood at 5-4, but Charles
Ward, writing in the *Free Press* on June 25 about nomi-
nees for the All-Star Game, said flatly that Harold was
"now recognized as the best lefthander in the league."

On June 27, Newhouser lost, 6-3, to Bobby Muncrief
and the Browns, his fifth loss. Once again, Tiger errors
helped to do in the lefthander. On the 30th, he closed
out the month with three and two-thirds scoreless innings in a 3-3, 12-inning tie with Boston. Five strikeouts
added to his league-leading total.

June 1943 was a month in which a British Overseas
Airways plane went down en route to Lisbon, killing 13
passengers, including actor Leslie Howard; in which Judge
Landis sold radio rights for the 1943 All-Star Game to
the Gillette Safety Razor Company for $25,000; in which
racial fighting broke out in Los Angeles between servicemen and Mexican-American youths wearing zoot
suits; and in which the OPA announced that the current
shoe ration stamp had to last civilians through October
31. In the movie *Five Graves to Cairo*, Franchot Tone
licked Field Marshal Rommel and his Afrika Korps, while
Roddy McDowell showed the love of a boy and his horse
in *My Friend Flicka*.

July started off well for Newhouser, as well as for the

Tigers, running third behind the Senators and the league-leading Yankees. The three most pleasant surprises for Steve O'Neill to that point had been the solid hitting of Dick Wakefield, the catching of Paul Richards, and of course the excellent work of Hal Newhouser. On July 3, the Tigers swept a doubleheader from the Yankees at Briggs Stadium. Newhouser, lacking his usual stuff, battled desperately to win the opener, 6-5, in 11 innings. Hooking up with Yankee ace Spud Chandler, the Detroit lefty allowed two runs in the second inning and three more in the eighth. The Tigers came back to tie it with three in the bottom of the ninth, and Newhouser blanked the champions until Rudy York's home run won it for Detroit in the 11th.

Several days later Newhouser had a much easier time against the Senators. With solid support from his teammates, Harold beat Washington, 9-1, scattering five hits. He struck out eight, and the Senators hit only seven balls out of the infield.

On July 11, Newhouser lost a game in relief to the Athletics, 4-3, when he yielded a triple to Pete Suder and a single to Elmer Valo in the ninth. After that he departed for Philadelphia and the All-Star Game, for he had been named to the American League team for the second year in succession. Newhouser took a won-loss record of 7-6 with him, the league lead in strikeouts with 92, and high regard as one of the league's bright young pitching stars.

The All-Star Game was played on July 13 before 31,938 at Shibe Park. It was the first All-Star Game played at night, and it featured an unusual experiment by the American League manager, Joe McCarthy of New York. In the 10 earlier All-Star Games, the American League had won seven times; National Leaguers claimed that this meant nothing as to superiority between the leagues but simply reflected the presence of too many Yankees on the American League squads. For 1943 McCarthy resolved to quiet such talk by keeping all six of his Yankees on the bench and playing only players from the other seven teams. He started the Senators' knuckleballer, Dutch Leonard, against the Cardinals' Mort Cooper. Leonard gave up an early run, but a three-run homer by Bobby Doerr in the second inning put the Americans ahead to stay. Another run in the third made it a 4-1 game when Leonard left after his three-inning stint, and young Hal Newhouser came on in the fourth. Newhouser pitched three innings, giving up three hits and no runs, and, as veteran writer Fred Lieb put it in *The Sporting News*, "did the best pitching for his side." Harold had a bit of trouble in the sixth, when Stan Musial hit an opposite-field double down the left-field line and Brooklyn's Augie Galan walked. But Newhouser coaxed Babe Dahlgren of the Phillies to hit into a double play, and big Ernie Lombardi of the Giants flied out. The appreciative crowd gave the young Detroit pitcher a warm ovation as he finished his work. Boston's Tex Hughson gave up two late National League runs, but they were not enough to prevent a 5-3 American League victory. Not a single Yankee name made it into the boxscore.

Unfortunately, after the All-Star Game everything started going wrong for Hal Newhouser. The second half of the season was a nightmare of errors, bases on balls, bad pitching, temperamental outbursts, and losses. All the problems that, in May and June, seemed to be behind Newhouser came back to vex him all over again.

His first outing after the break was in Chicago on July 17. Carrying a one-hitter into the sixth inning, Newhouser suddenly lost effectiveness and was touched for five runs in two innings; the White Sox won, 5-2. Four days later, at Washington, the Tigers got Newhouser an early 5-0 lead, but things started to fall apart in the third inning, when Dick Wakefield let George Case's single with a man on get between his legs; the fleet Case came all the way around to make it 5-2. The Nats picked up another run but still trailed, 5-3, in the ninth. Alex Kampouris singled, Jake Early walked, and pinch hitter Ellis Clary doubled, driving in one run. Gorsica relieved Newhouser, and Case promptly singled to bring home the tying and winning runs.

After a poor showing in relief in the final game of the Washington series, Newhouser missed a start in Boston because of some soreness in his arm. When the Tigers got to New York, O'Neill decided to send his young left-hander home to Detroit to give his pitching arm some rest. Because of difficulties in travel arrangements, however, Newhouser stayed with the team and O'Neill used him in the second game of a doubleheader with the Yankees on August 3. It was a mistake, as the Yankees pounded him for five runs in less than three innings, lowering his record to 7-9.

After taking diathermy treatments at Henry Ford Hospital, Newhouser felt that he was up to pitching again. He started against the White Sox on August 7 and again was knocked out in the third inning of a 7-4 loss.

A week later, Harold struck out 11 Senators but still lost, 7-4, when his teammates concentrated three of their five errors in the visitors' three-run ninth inning. On the 20th, Newhouser led the Red Sox, 2-1, with one out in the seventh when he walked Roy Partee and Leon Culberson. After getting the second out, he got Joe Cronin to hit a fly ball to left field. Wakefield misplayed the ball and it fell safely for a double as two runs scored. In the following inning, errors by Bloodworth and Higgins led to another Boston run. The Red Sox went on to win, 4-3, Newhouser's record fell to 7-12, and in the clubhouse after the game the pitcher complained bitterly that "that $50,000 beauty blew another one for me."

In a morning game on August 23, a two-run homer by Joe Gordon was all that Newhouser gave up to the

Yankees, but it was enough to produce another loss as the Tigers were unable to touch New York pitcher Bill Zuber. Four days later, Newhouser pitched well at St. Louis but lost to the Browns' Denny Galehouse, 3–1. The season which had looked so bright in May and June was now a shambles for Newhouser; his ninth loss in a row made his record for the year 7–14. Dan Daniel of the *New York World-Telegram* said Newhouser was "among the more pronounced disappointments in the pitching ranks of the major leagues." Dale Stafford of the *Free Press,* answering a reader's query as to why Newhouser couldn't win, said that lack of batting and fielding support was hurting him. "Seasoned players," he went on, "know that the breaks even up and accept hard-luck defeats philosophically. Newhouser will probably develop the same outlook and won't be guilty of tearing up his uniform and breaking pop bottles which he did after a particularly heartbreaking setback in Washington."

September started out better; Newhouser ended his losing steak with a win over the Browns, 8–5. He pitched eight very good innings but fell apart in the ninth; Stubby Overmire came in and closed out the game. In his next start, Harold walked five White Sox in two innings and was lifted, in a game the Tigers eventually won. Three days later came another loss, to Cleveland, as Newhouser was taken out in the fourth inning after allowing four runs, five hits, and seven walks. On September 18, he lost again to the Indians, though he stayed around for six innings; "Newhouser's well known wildness did not assert itself until the third inning," wrote a local reporter, "but thereafter the youthful lefthander repeatedly put himself in trouble."

A couple of decent relief efforts followed, but in his last start of the season, on September 28 in Fenway Park, Newhouser lost to the Red Sox, 6–1. It was a game typical of the second half of his season: the pitcher was not very effective, failing to last the third inning, and bad fielding – Higgins and York were the culprits this time – aggravated his problems.

Newhouser's seasonal record finished at a dismal eight wins and 17 defeats. His earned run average of 3.04 was not bad, but his 111 bases on balls led the league. (He was second in the league in strikeouts). The weight of Newhouser's lost second half was one of the main things that dragged the Tigers down to a fifth-place finish, despite a surprising 20-win season by Dizzy Trout and home run and RBI titles for Rudy York. In addition to the poor control which led to walks and mislocated pitches, Newhouser continued to hurt himself with his bad temper. The tantrums contributed to the control problems and alienated his teammates. H. G. Salsinger summarized the season for "Junior" Newhouser: "It is inconceivable that a pitcher who started out as brilliantly as Newhouser could become such a failure. From the most effective pitcher in the league he became one of the most ineffective. Some of the games were tossed away for him but in the majority he was beaten because of lack of stuff, lack of control, or lack of judgment."

Newhouser himself looked back on those times and said, "It was just eating me up. I became confused; I didn't know how to pitch." Things were so bad that the young man seriously considered what he would do if he were out of baseball. He had an off-season job with Chrysler, which also offered him a drafting course at the Chrysler Institute of Technology. "I figured [drafting] was going to be my work," he said. "Because I didn't know how long I was going to stay in baseball. Not with the record I had." Harold Newhouser's baseball career was at a crisis point.

8
TO THE TOP

Cleveland had a big right-handed pitcher named Jim Bagby. He was the son of another Jim Bagby, who won 122 games for the Indians over seven seasons back in the late teens and early '20s, including 31 games for the pennant winner of 1920. Jim, Jr., had won 17 games for the Indians in both 1942 and 1943, and he led the league in innings pitched the latter season. The only problem with Jim Bagby, who was a tough, hard man, was that he despised Lou Boudreau, the Tribe manager, and had publicly demanded that the Indians trade him. Jack Zeller saw the Indians' problem as an opportunity to solve a situation the Tigers were growing tired of coping with; he offered to trade Hal Newhouser to Cleveland for Jim Bagby. After four seasons, Zeller was tired of Newhouser, tired of the tantalizing flashes of brilliance, tired of the bases on balls, tired of the childish displays of temper. Let the Indians cope with the erratic left-hander, Zeller felt, while the Detroit club picked up a proven consistent winner. He was confident that there would be no adverse public reaction to the trade, because the Detroit fans, too, had become disenchanted with the young lefthander.

The Cleveland front office required little convincing to agree to the deal, and Zeller said he needed only to clear it with Walter O. Briggs, the Detroit clubowner. At this point, though, the trade fell apart, because Briggs refused to sanction it. There is some cloudiness over who it was that actually shot the deal down, Walter Briggs himself or Steve O'Neill, who was then on a USO tour in the South Pacific; in any event, the swap was killed and Hal Newhouser remained a Tiger.

Newhouser, of course, heard all the rumors about a trade, and he felt that he would welcome such a move. He had decided that, as he put it, "pitching for your hometown team is not any fun"; the trade, he believed, would be good both for himself and for the Detroit club. Then he heard nothing more about it. He, Trout, Ned Harris, and Roy Cullenbine of the Indians made up a bowling team over that winter, participating in various charity events. One evening they were bowling in Cleveland, so Newhouser called up O'Neill, who lived there, and asked him to come out to the bowling alley. Between frames O'Neill and Newhouser talked about the young pitcher's future. First, Newhouser said the trade to the Indians was a good idea, but O'Neill told him there would be no trade. Then O'Neill asked, "Why can't you win?"

"Well, number one," Newhouser responded, "you're pitching me every sixth day, fifth day, seventh day, and then I'd lay off for a week or a week and a half. I can't pitch like that."

"So what do you want to do?" the manager asked.

"Pitch me every fourth day. If you're not going to trade me, pitch me every fourth day."

"Well, I'll tell you what I'll do," O'Neill said. "I'll pitch you every fourth day until you prove to me that you can't. And I'll tell you another thing. When you get down to spring training, you train on your own."

Newhouser recognized that O'Neill was challenging him, but he welcomed the challenge. "Then I knew exactly what direction I was going in," Newhouser recalls. "I've got to know where I stand so I know what to do."

On December 30, local writer Sam Greene wrote a full column in *The Sporting News* on the enigma of the young pitcher, citing "rumors . . . that Newhouser was a disturbing force in the morale of the Tigers." He explained that "Newhouser is a hard loser, and his reaction to defeat sometimes takes the form of rebuke to his fellows whom he believes, in part, responsible." After mentioning several incidents, Greene acknowledged that they "did not endear Newhouser to the Tigers" and that O'Neill certainly did not condone them. "At the same time," he said, "the Detroit manager holds that the lefthander's fury is the product of his youthful flame and a desire to win." These were qualities which were needed on his team, and O'Neill felt that Newhouser's youthful drive to win could "be controlled and converted into an asset."

Attempting to harness his young pitcher's passion for winning was a potentially rewarding job for Steve O'Neill; other parts of his managerial function would be more unpleasant. Already by early January, he had lost Wakefield, White, Bloodworth, and Tommy Bridges to the service; replacements for these players and others who might be called would have to be found on the existing roster, on the waiver wire, or among available minor leaguers.

In late January, J. G. Taylor Spink, who considered himself a quasi-official voice of baseball as the editor of *The Sporting News*, wrote to the president, asking that baseball be declared an essential industry and its players accordingly exempted from the draft. Spink was guilty of overreaching; his letter produced a reply on February 1, 1944, from Steve Early, Roosevelt's press secretary, stating that FDR "would prefer to leave the matter from now on for determination under the regulations laid down under the Selective Service Act and the regulations governing the manpower situation generally." Baseball would get no special breaks; it would survive, or not, in 1944 with 4-Fs, callow youths, and overage veterans.

As February slid into March, Americans hummed the Ella Mae Morse song, "Shoo-Shoo Baby," or the nonsense ditty, "Mairzy Doats," and the ballplayers who were still on the scene got ready for their second northern training camp. Hal Newhouser, as he often did, reported a week early to the Tigers' base at Evansville, Indiana. As spring training started, O'Neill had hopes for his team for 1944. Dizzy Trout, his 20-game winner, was classified 4-F, as were Newhouser, Overmire, and Rufe Gentry. Detroit had signed an outfielder named Charlie Hostetler, who had long years of minor league experience and was, at age 40, unlikely to be drafted. Veteran outfielder Roger "Doc" Cramer was also beyond the probable draft age, and a smattering of 4-Fs through the roster would presumably be around all season. The New York Yankees had lost Charlie Keller, Billy Johnson, Bill Dickey, and Joe Gordon to the service since their '43 World Series victory, so the league looked more balanced.

Everyone had relatively small squads, with the continuing manpower problems; the St. Louis Browns had only 17 players around at the end of the first week of camp. Interestingly, though, the Browns had 13 4-Fs and two discharged veterans; the nucleus of their team — George McQuinn, Vernon Stephens, Nelson Potter, Jack Kramer, Don Gutteridge, and a few others — would be around all year. But no one thought too much about the Browns.

At Evansville, Newhouser worked hard on getting into shape. He also spent a lot of time with the veteran Paul Richards, trying to figure out what he could do to become a winner. Richards was one of those who had been disappointed with Newhouser in 1943; "Hal acted like a spoiled kid. This was brought about because of frustration and a burning ambition to do well."

But the veteran catcher was determined to straighten out the young pitcher. He took stock of Newhouser's principal assets — a great fastball and curve, a smooth and fluid delivery, a fierce will to win – and worked on maximizing them. First, there were technical adjustments. Richards spotted the fact that Newhouser's wrist was a little floppy in his delivery, so that was tightened up. He also noted that Hal's pitches inside moved further inside while pitches to the outside part of the plate tended to run further outside. Richards figured that the problem was an inconsistency in the way Newhouser released the ball. "When . . . he began releasing the ball consistently in one way," Richards said, "his control dramatically improved."

Next, they worked on Newhouser's change-up. As Richards pointed out, "his great delivery made it possible for him to develop a super change of pace." Richards showed him how to throw it; the main thing to concentrate on was a delivery which looked exactly like the fastball. Richards drilled him in the pitch, and he soon was able to throw a perfectly-disguised change of pace and to throw it for strikes. "Hal now had three effective pitches," Richards said, "a 90-plus mile fastball, a biting curve, and an undetectable change of pace. With all of this together with exceptional control, he had to be a great pitcher." They also worked to develop a slider, the newly-popular breaking pitch that had a later break and a flatter trajectory than a standard curveball.

George Case, the Washington speedster, claimed that it was the off-speed pitch that made Newhouser the great pitcher he became. "This made his fastball, which was a good one, that much more effective," Case said. Roy Partee, the Red Sox catcher, called Newhouser's change of pace "tantalizing."

While working on Newhouser's mechanics, Paul Richards also worked on his disposition. The catcher knew that Newhouser was actively disliked by most of his teammates, who were fed up with the biting remarks, the disgusted glare after an error, the tantrums, that had been characteristic of the young lefthander over his four years in the American League. Yet Richards recognized that Newhouser was basically a shy and pleasant young man and that his tantrums, which looked bad, were mainly directed at himself, fueled by his enormous desire to win. Richards told Harold that the anger was counter-productive: because they feared another explosion, his teammates tensed up behind him, as a result of which they made misplays which produced his tantrums; then Newhouser, his adrenaline working overtime, would press too hard or overthrow, and he would lose control, resulting in walks or extra-base hits. The secret, Richards told him, was to take it easy, take the bad with the good, and treat his mates as if they were just as interested in winning as he was. A pat on the back would be more effective in relaxing a teammate who had just misplayed a ball than a sullen stare or a sarcastic remark.

Newhouser took the message to heart. He knew that he would not be pitching in the major leagues for long losing 17 games a year, but pitching was what he wanted to do for a living. Making a living was more important to him now, too, because in February 1943 he and Beryl had had a baby daughter, and there was another mouth to be fed. So Harold Newhouser, a four-year major league veteran but still not yet 23 years old, made a conscious effort to curb his temper. He became more businesslike on the mound, more sociable in the clubhouse, and more affable with teammates and reporters alike. The hardest part at first was placing a rein upon his temper, but he noticed that, when he began to get hot on the mound, Richards would stall around behind the plate, perhaps fiddle with his glove or his shin guards, until the young pitcher could get control of himself and cool down. It was not long before people started to take note of the change in Newhouser.

Herb Pennock, farm director of the Red Sox and formerly a prominent left-handed pitcher himself, was asked that spring why Newhouser could not win at least 15 games a season. "I think he will when he finds himself," Pennock said. "I've seen other pitchers with lots of stuff who couldn't win consistently. They were lacking in a little something – control or proper pitching tempera-ment . . . Some fellows like Newhouser are around for several seasons without getting a winning average. Then suddenly they get what they need and they're winners. That's what I expect Newhouser to do."

On March 26, Dale Stafford in the *Free Press* reported the rumor out of Evansville that Newhouser "has a changed attitude and, as a result, is due to become a winner at last." Stafford went on to say he hoped that analysis was correct because Newhouser "needs a new attitude almost as badly as your average citizen does a Grade-1 right rear tire." The writer described Newhouser's past prob-lems, the fact that he should have stayed longer in the minor leagues, and the signs of his possible redemption. "Newhouser has a long career ahead in baseball, and eventually he will find himself." It would be nice if 1944 was the year, Stafford said, "but we'll believe it when it happens." The pitcher himself read this column in an Evansville hotel lobby and became furious – until it sud-denly occurred to him that perhaps Stafford was right.

In the meantime, the Tigers and 15 other clubs were preparing for the 1944 season. In contrast to 1943, when the northern spring training camps were blessed with unusually mild weather, March and April 1944 were full of rain, hail, snow, sleet, and freezing temperatures. Nevertheless, the major leagues prepared to open the season the third week of April. Before they did, H.G. Sals-inger made his usual pre-season assessment of the state of the game: "The Army and Navy want Congress to pass a bill forcing 4-Fs into essential jobs or non-combatant work battalions and if such a bill is passed it will remove so many players from the major league rosters that baseball can scarcely continue . . . the ball parks will probably have to be closed." But on April 15, Steve Early,

FDR's press secretary, said, "I know the President is pleased to see baseball continuing."

Just before the season opened, Dan Daniel of the *New York World-Telegram* predicted the pennant races for *The Sporting News*. For the American League he figured a finish of the Yankees, Washington, Chicago, Cleveland, the Red Sox, Browns, Tigers, and Athletics. But Daniel knew that these were guesses; with the continuing man-power drain, with players coming and going all season, form would be a very elusive object.

As if to prove that in most positive fashion, the St. Louis Browns, under manager Luke Sewell, started off the season with a record nine consecutive wins. Now, no one expected the Browns to win anything—the St. Louis American League franchise was the only one in either league never to have won a pennant—but their winning streak certainly captured public attention.

The first three wins of the St. Louis string were over the Tigers. Jack Kramer, a returned veteran, outpitched Trout on opening day for a 2-1 win, and the next day Steve Sundra, who would soon be leaving for military duty, defeated Gentry by a 3-1 score. Newhouser started the third game and lost, 8-5, to Sig Jakucki, a big, hard-drinking righthander back in the big leagues for the first time since 1936. The Detroit pitcher gave up two runs in the first inning and was knocked out in the third by a Vern Stephens double following two bases on balls. Hal's defenders had little to say to those who snorted, "same old Newhouser."

The next day Harold worked two-thirds of an inning in relief in a loss to Cleveland, but two days later the Tigers won a doubleheader from the Indians, Trout winning the opener and Newhouser winning the nightcap, 4-3, with three excellent relief innings behind Gentry.

After a couple of days of rain, O'Neill received a double-barrelled shot of adrenalin on April 27. Rudy York was classified 4-F on the basis of an old knee injury, and

Harold Newhouser gave the skipper a gem of a perfor-
mance. He hooked up in a torrid pitcher's battle with
Thornton Lee, the White Sox southpaw, and won it, 2–0,
in the 12th inning, when singles by Don Ross and Mike
Higgins were followed by a two-run double by Bob Swift.
Newhouser yielded only four hits in the game, which the
News called "the best pitching exhibition of any Tiger
this season."

Two days later, though, Newhouser lost in relief to the
Indians in the 12th inning, when Mickey Rocco's lazy
fly dropped untouched behind third for a run-scoring
double. An interesting feature of this game was the
appearance of catcher Jimmy McDonnell for the Indians;
McDonnell, who got three hits that day (none against
Newhouser), had played right field for Hal's Roose-Vanker
Post team back in 1938. This was also the day that
O'Neill installed Hoover at shortstop and moved Eddie
Mayo to second base, having decided that veteran Don
Heffner was no longer up to the demands of playing in
a major league infield. The other noteworthy event of
April 29 was the Browns' first loss of the season.

April 1944 was a time when Americans on the home
front sang songs like "Besame Mucho," with Jimmy
Dorsey's orchestra, and watched Betty Hutton in *The
Miracle of Morgan's Creek* and Ray Milland and Ginger
Rogers in *Lady in the Dark*. They drank Schlitz beer,
with "just the kiss of the hops," used Trushay hand lotion, seasoned their Spam with Snider's Old Fashioned
Chili Sauce ("we put a Victory Garden in every bottle!"),
and followed the adventures of Elsie the Borden Cow.
Overseas, General Mark Clark's troops were banging
away at the Gustav Line in Italy, while in the Pacific
the Marines were digesting their conquest of Kwajalein
and preparing to invade the Marianas. The long-awaited
invasion of Hitler's Europe was much talked of, but it
had yet to take place.

On May 2, Newhouser picked up his third victory with

a 4–3 win at Sportsman's Park. The Browns tied the score at three in the fifth, but Newhouser bore down and limited St. Louis to two hits the rest of the way. Chuck Hostetler tripled in the seventh inning and scored the winning run on York's sacrifice fly.

After a couple more Detroit losses to the Browns, plunging the Tigers to last place, Steve O'Neill sent four players to Buffalo and warned the rest of his men that they had better start putting things together quickly. York, Higgins, and Cramer were all mired in a hitting slump, and without production from those three there was simply not enough punch on the rest of the team. In addition, the Tigers as usual were deficient in running speed; Jimmy Outlaw, Hostetler, Hoover, and Cramer were the only ones with even average speed. All of these problems were making it very tough on the Detroit pitching.

The club moved from St. Louis back home to face Chicago, but the losses continued. Overmire was unable to hold a 2–0 lead in the ninth and lost, 4–2, and on May 7 the White Sox won a doubleheader. The opener was started by Newhouser, who held Chicago scoreless through six innings but gave up two runs in the seventh after an error by Higgins. Two more runs against Gentry in the eighth, after Newhouser was lifted for a pinch hitter, made the final, 4–1, as the Tigers did little with Chicago pitcher Bill Dietrich. After Gorsica lost the nightcap, 4–2, the *Free Press* headlined its story: "PITCHERS SHOULD SUE TIGERS FOR NON-SUPPORT."

After splitting the first two games at Yankee Stadium, the Tigers took the third game, 10–4, rapping out 17 hits for Newhouser, as Hal became the first lefthander to beat New York all season. Higgins, Hostetler, and Swift had three hits each, and Newhouser drove in a run himself with a successful squeeze bunt.

The Tigers then took two out of three at Boston, before their hitting died again in Philadelphia, where they split four games with the A's. In the second game of the series, Newhouser took a two-hitter and a 3-1 lead into the ninth but was unable to get through that last inning. Mr. Mack's men tied it at 3-3 and pushed over the winner against Gorsica in the 10th.

Moving on to Washington, the Tigers swept four from the Senators, behind Gorsica, Overmire, Trout, and Newhouser. Hal's win, his fifth against three defeats, was a 7-1 five-hitter, with six strikeouts and only one walk. As the long eastern trip ended with 10 wins in 14 games, the Tigers could rejoice in their climb to fourth place, only four games behind the league-leading Yankees.

Meanwhile, in a little-noticed announcement, Vice President Bill DeWitt of the Browns told the press that outfielder Chet Laabs, who had not yet been able to play in 1944, was shifting jobs from a Detroit war plant to one in St. Louis; Laabs would henceforth be able to play night games and Saturday and Sunday games in St. Louis as well as make weekend trips to Chicago, Cleveland, and Detroit.

The Tigers, home again, promptly lost three in a row to the Athletics, to make their home record for the season an abysmal 1-12. On May 27, though, when they needed it most, they got a superb pitching job from Hal Newhouser, who beat Philadelphia, 2-1, in 12 tough innings. Russ Christopher of the A's was almost as good, but he lost in the 12th when Higgins walked, went to third on a single by Outlaw, and scored on an infield groundout by Richards.

After the Tigers took two of three from the Senators, they welcomed the Yankees to town. A crowd of 37,685 turned out for a Memorial Day doubleheader, and they went home happy as the home team took two from the champions. Trout won the opener, 2-1, while Newhouser beat Bill Zuber, 4-1, in the closer. Some sloppy play by the Yanks helped the Tigers score their runs, and Newhouser was masterful as he scattered seven hits, walked only one, and struck out six. Harold's seventh win moved his team into a tie for third place with the Senators and A's.

May 1944 was a month in which the names in the news included MacArthur, Montgomery, Admiral Ernest King, and General Carl "Tooey" Spaatz. *Life* magazine went to Shirley Temple's 16th birthday party and reported coyly that Shirley's breasts had developed in the two years since she had last appeared before the public. Secretary of the Navy Frank Knox died and was buried at Arlington National Cemetery, and Lockheed announced that it had produced its 5,000th P-38 Lightning fighter at its plant in Burbank, California. Meanwhile, General Dwight Eisenhower prepared his mighty force in southern England for its impending strike across the Channel.

June opened with the Tigers taking their fourth in a row from the Yankees, a 4–3 win in 16 innings. Newhouser entered in relief of Trout in the ninth inning and shut out the New Yorkers the rest of the way, scattering five hits. Don Ross doubled home the winning run in the 16th. Newhouser's record reached 8–3, with five wins in a row. Dale Stafford wrote in the *Free Press* that "Newhouser's victories are mounting in proportion to the control he has gained over his temper."

On June 5, the Allies captured Rome from the Germans, and the next day was D-Day, with American, British, and Canadian troops landing on the shores of Normandy. The people of the Allied nations collectively held their breath until it was clear that an unshakeable beachhead had been secured. Hitler's hold on the continent of Europe was beginning to loosen. Meanwhile the soldiers who had waded ashore on Utah and Omaha beaches, as well as those slogging their way up the Italian peninsula, were singing the song "Lilli Marlene," generally considered the best song to come out of the war, a curiosity in that it was originally a German song which had been "captured" by the British at El Alamein and was now being taken over by Eisenhower's GIs.

Back in the states, the pennant races continued, even though they were overshadowed by the momentous happenings in Europe. On June 7, 17,180 people turned out at Comiskey Park in Chicago to see the White Sox, winners of six in a row, and the Tigers. Hal Newhouser pitched for Detroit and, though he seemed to have good stuff, his control was bad. Nine walks in six innings kept him in constant trouble, and twice he walked in runs with the bases loaded. Orval Grove held the Tigers in check, and the result was a 3-1 win for the Sox.

Newhouser pitched briefly in relief on both the 11th and 12th of June and then came back to start the second game of the June 14 doubleheader at Cleveland. After Rufe Gentry blanked the Indians in the first game, Newhouser beat the Tribe, 11-3, in the nightcap to pull the Tigers within two and one-half games of the first-place Browns. The Red Sox were one and a half ahead of O'Neill's team.

Trout lost to the Indians the next day, however, and the following two days saw the Browns' Bob Muncrief and Sig Jakucki shut down the Tigers by 14-1 and 5-0 scores. On Sunday the 18th, a crowd of 27,917 turned out at Briggs Stadium to see if their heroes could stop the sudden skid and climb back into the race. Steve O'Neill sent Hal Newhouser out for the first game against the Brownies' ace, Jack Kramer, and Newhouser did the job for him. The Tigers won, 7-3, as Hal held St. Louis to six hits, and Eddie Mayo's bases-loaded single in the seventh brought the Tigers from behind. The victory for Newhouser made him the first 10-game winner of the season in the American League. Dizzy Trout won the second game in relief to cap a much-needed sweep of the league leaders.

The increasing evidence of Newhouser's turnaround

produced a spate of articles, in Detroit and beyond, explaining the lefty's new success. Hal credited the change to three things – the newly-acquired slider, better control of his pitches, and better control of himself. He gave full credit to Richards on all three counts. He acknowledged the tantrums of yesteryear: "Sure, I blew up. I stormed around when I lost. I squawked that the breaks and errors were costing me games. It didn't do any good." Richards, he said, convinced him that "in the long run the breaks will even up if you hang in there and do your best." Harold told one reporter: "Maybe I'm steadier because of my additional duties as a husband. You know, I am now the father of a six-months daughter and maybe the little one has given me a different viewpoint."

The week after the sweep of the Browns was a dismal one for the Tigers. They lost two out of three to Cleveland and then lost four in a row at St. Louis. The last two were in a Sunday doubleheader on the 25th, when the Browns beat both Trout and Newhouser, who was wild in a 5-2 loss to Al Hollingsworth.

The Tigers were off until Wednesday, when they lost their fifth in a row, to the Senators in Washington, 4-1. The next night, just as it looked as if the club was about to fall right out of the race, Harold Newhouser once more came to the rescue. With the formidable Early Wynn the starter against him, Newhouser gave the Senators two scattered singles, walked none, struck out nine, and was absolutely dominant in a 4-0 victory.

Overseas, as June passed into July, Eisenhower's army took Cherbourg but stalled in the hedgerows of Normandy, and Merrill's Marauders struggled in the jungles of Burma. On the home front, Robert Walker and Donna Reed starred in the hit movie, *See Here, Private Hargrove*, ads for Gaby Greaseless Suntan Lotion proclaimed the miracles it was performing "under blazing tropical skies . . . at bathing beaches . . . [and] in Victory Gardens," and the Republicans in Chicago nominated Governor Thomas E. Dewey of New York for president.

On July 2, the office of American League president Will Harridge announced the league's team for the All-Star Game scheduled for July 11 at Forbes Field, Pittsburgh. It included four Tigers – Rudy York, Paul Trout, Pinky Higgins, and Hal Newhouser, named for the third consecutive year. That day, too, Watson Spoelstra wrote in the *Free Press* that "barring a disastrous slump, lanky Hal Newhouser should be an easy twenty-game winner." He attributed the big change in Newhouser's fortunes to "improvement in control," citing statistics to show that the young pitcher had cut his base on balls ratio just about in half.

The Detroit club opened July by splitting a doubleheader at Philadelphia and then headed for Boston for a July 4 twinbill at Fenway. For the holiday doubleheader 24,195 fans turned out, but their enjoyment was dulled in the first game when Newhouser squelched the Sox, 4-3. An eighth inning home run by Higgins tied the score, and Richards singled in the winner in the ninth. This gave Newhouser a record of 12-5.

The Tigers took one of the three remaining games in the Boston series (Dizzy Trout's 10th win) and then moved on to New York. Ernie Bonham of the Yankees beat Stubby Overmire, 3-1, in the first game, but the next day Newhouser held the New Yorkers to four hits, beating them for the fourth time in 1944. On July 9, though, the Yankees beat Detroit twice, with Boom-Boom Beck and Rufe Gentry taking the losses. The Tigers were happy to come to the All-Star break, with a chance to regroup.

They did receive one piece of good news while they were in New York; on July 7 the Navy Department announced that it was releasing Dick Wakefield. The young outfielder had completed pre-flight training, but only half of his class was kept for air service. Wakefield was given an honorable discharge but with the stipulation that he could soon be drafted. He opted to rejoin the Tigers for as long as he was available.

The All-Star Game was not a great success for Newhouser. The National League players, so long bedraggled losers in the interleague classics, pounded out 12 hits and a 7-1 triumph. They got four runs off Boston's Tex Hughson in the fourth and resumed the attack when Newhouser came in to pitch in the seventh. After Phil Cavarretta singled, Stanley Musial sacrificed him to second and the Cardinals' Walker Cooper beat out an infield hit. Newhouser retired Brooklyn's Dixie Walker on a popup, but Whitey Kurowski scored two runs with a double into the left-field corner. In the eighth inning Newhouser was touched for an unearned run after Frankie Hayes, the catcher, missed the third strike on Marty Marion.

On July 13 the pennant chase resumed, and Wakefield returned to the Tigers. He started in the outfield and picked up two hits as Dizzy Trout beat the White Sox, 9-1. The next day Wakefield hit a home run and single as Overmire blanked the Sox. On the 15th Newhouser lost to the White Sox and Gordie Maltzberger, 5-4, but the Tigers won the second game of that day's doubleheader on another Wakefield home run.

The next day the Tigers split another doubleheader with Chicago, and, after a day off, Newhouser won his 14th game with a splendid three-inning relief job against Washington. A clutch hit in the 11th by Jimmy Outlaw won the game, 6-5. At this point the Detroit club was still in sixth place, seven and one-half games behind the league-leading Browns, but the addition of Dick Wakefield's bat to the lineup, combined with the strong pitching of Newhouser and Trout, infused the Tigers with new spirit. *The Sporting News* lauded Newhouser, "pitching in and out of turn for a team that has traveled in spurts and slumps all season," and said that "on his left arm Detroit rests in large measure its hope to challenge for the championship."

On July 19, Stubby Overmire beat the Senators' Dutch Leonard, 2-1, and on the 20th the Tigers won again, 7-6, with Newhouser shutting off a Washington rally with one inning of relief. Dick Wakefield's third homer sparked the Tiger offense.

The big headlines on that day, of course, were for the ouster of Hideki Tojo and his cabinet in Japan, the failed assassination attempt on Hitler, and the Democrats' nomination of FDR for a fourth term, to be followed the next day by the selection of Missouri senator Harry S Truman for vice president.

On the 21st the Tigers won their fourth straight one-run game over Ossie Bluege's Nats, as Trout beat Wynn, 6-5. The A's came to town next, and Hal Newhouser beat them, 4-3, for his 15th win. He pitched the whole game and was in constant trouble, giving up 13 hits. But he was tough enough in the pinch, and Rudy York's home run in the sixth put the Tigers ahead. With a lead in the last three innings, Hal Newhouser was hard to beat, and he proved it on this day when he did not have his best stuff. Ward wrote in the *Free Press* that "Newhouser had no right to win," but he was wrong; good pitchers win even when their pitches are not going right.

On the 23rd, the A's took both ends of a doubleheader, as Gorsica and Overmire came to grief. The next day, though, Trout pitched a beauty and got things straightened around with a 1-0 win over Bobo Newsom.

Over the next four days, however, O'Neill's club had all sorts of problems with the Red Sox, salvaging only a tie out of four games with Boston. Gentry, Overmire, and Trout lost, while Newhouser's game was a frustrating 1-1 tie called on account of rain and darkness in the eighth inning. Newhouser gave only four hits to the Bosox, but a baserunning blunder by Chuck Hostetler, who was tagged out when he neglected to slide into the plate, cost Hal the win.

The Yankees followed Boston into Briggs Stadium, and Trout beat them in relief on Saturday the 29th for his 15th win. The next day, 47,936 fans showed up for a doubleheader and were alternately depressed and elated as the two teams split. Hank Borowy beat Overmire, 10-2, in the opener, but Newhouser won the nightcap, 13-7. Harold had a 13-0 lead after seven innings and eased up noticeably at the end as the Bronx Bombers scored four in the eighth and three more in the ninth. Newhouser's record was now a sparkling 16-6. As August began, however, the Tigers were still in fifth place, nine games back. The Browns enjoyed a four and a half game lead over Boston.

As the baseball races heated up in August (at least in the American League; the Cardinals were never threatened in the senior circuit), Americans at home made yearning, wistful songs their favorites, songs like "Long Ago and Far Away" by Helen Forrest and Dick Haymes and "Amor" by the new singing star, Andy Russell. In Europe, the hope engendered at the beginning of the month with the U.S. Army's breakout at St. Lô gave way to disappointment some three weeks later when the trapped bulk of the German army escaped through the Falaise gap. On the 25th Paris was liberated by American and Free French troops, and most of France was soon free of Nazi occupation. In the Pacific Tinian and Guam were taken, and MacArthur planned his return to the Philippines.

The Tigers beat the Yankees on August 1 and then had three days off before Newhouser pitched a Saturday night game at Comiskey Park before 17,257 fans. White Sox third baseman Ralph Hodgin booted one to start the ninth, leading the way to two Detroit runs and a 5-3 win for Newhouser, whose record went to 17-6.

The next day Paul Trout matched Hal with his own

17th win as the Tigers took two from the Sox. The Detroit club then left on its last eastern trip of the year. The odds-makers at this time installed the front-running Brownies as an 11–5 choice to win the pennant, followed by New York at 5–1, Boston at 8–1, and the Tigers 15–1. Boston's chances suffered a serious setback on August 9 when manager Joe Cronin learned that his ace righthander, 18-game winner Cecil "Tex" Hughson, was to leave momentarily for induction into the navy.

The Tigers started the eastern swing by sweeping four games at Washington. Newhouser won the first one, out-pitching Early Wynn, 4–2, with a four-hitter, and Trout, Overmire, and Gentry followed with victories.

Moving on to Philadelphia, O'Neill's men split a twin-bill with the A's on August 13. Don Black beat New-houser, 6–1, in the opener (making Hal's seasonal record 18–7), but Trout won his 19th game with a shutout in the nightcap. Gorsica, in the throes of a long losing streak, lost to the Mackmen on Monday, but Newhouser came through the next day with another excellent relief effort. Hal came in with the score tied, 2–2, in the eighth, men on second and third, and two out. After an intentional walk to load the bases, he retired Bill McGhee to end the threat and gave up only two hits over the next three innings. Eddie Mayo's sacrifice fly in the 11th scored Joe Orengo with the winning run, and Newhouser had win number 19.

The next day Rufe Gentry beat the Red Sox in Fenway Park, 4–2, on a three-run homer by Rudy York. This win moved the Tigers to within a half game of second-place Boston, though they were still well behind the Browns. Another tie caused by a rainout followed, so on the 18th the two teams played a doubleheader. In the first game Hal Newhouser stifled the Red Sox, beating Dick Newsome by a 3–0 score. This game was Hal's 20th win of the season, marking the first time he had achieved this level and making him the first 20-game winner in the majors for 1944. The win also put Detroit in second place, although Gorsica's 7-4 loss in the second game dropped them behind the Sox again, still seven games behind St. Louis.

The *Detroit News* saluted Newhouser's achievement: "Steve O'Neill put him on a steady work diet in '44 and he thrived, working every fourth day and often with only one or two days' rest to start or relieve." And Dan Daniel, of the *New York World-Telegram*, wrote that behind Newhouser's "amazing improvement" were "two circumstances which have only little to do with the sort of opposition he has been facing": his changed attitude and his "natural growth as a pitcher."

In the meantime, though, the pennant chase continued, tightening up some as the Browns hit a losing stretch. The Red Sox pounded Gentry on August 19 and Joe Bowman beat the Tigers, 9-1. The next day the Senators took two from St. Louis, as Dutch Leonard and Early Wynn did the honors, and the Tigers beat the Yankees twice at Yankee Stadium. Overmire won the first game, 4-3, with Newhouser coming on to get the last two outs in the ninth, and Trout beat Atley Donald, 9-8, in the nightcap for an inelegant but nevertheless welcome 20th win.

On Monday, August 21, the Yankees' Walt Dubiel beat Gentry, 5-1, and the next day the Yanks beat Newhouser, 9-7, knocking Hal out with a six-run fifth inning. "Snuffy Stirnweiss and Oscar Grimes," trumpeted Dan Daniel, "made Newhouser look like Joe Dokes just off the bus from the Eastern Leagues."

The road trip was over and the Tigers headed home, six games behind the Browns, a game and a half behind the Red Sox, and a half game ahead of the Yankees. Still, Steve O'Neill thought he could catch the Browns. "We've got eight games left with those fellows," he said; "that gives us a chance . . . We're conceding nothing to them or to anybody else." He said he planned to throw

Newhouser and Trout at the Brownies in both starting and relief roles. When columnist John Lardner asked Newhouser about pitching in turn and out, the lefthander replied, "What's the difference, if we got a chance to win?" Four of those eight games with the Browns took place in Briggs Stadium, starting on August 25. In the first game Trout beat Denny Galehouse of the Browns, 1–0, for his 21st win, and the next day Overmire blanked Luke Sewell's team again. A huge crowd of 51,376 showed up for the Sunday doubleheader, and Hal Newhouser gave them what they wanted with a 5–3 win over Bobby Muncrief in the first game. Harold was shaky early and gave up nine hits and three runs in the first four innings; then he tightened up and, as H.G. Salsinger wrote, "In the last five Newhouser was all he had to be." In the second game, O'Neill was forced to start Walter "Boom Boom" Beck, and the Browns, behind Nelson Potter, pounded out a 17–2 win to salvage one of the four games.

After the close of games on August 27, the Browns held a three and one-half game lead over the Yankees, all but given up for dead a couple of weeks earlier, and a four-game lead over the Tigers and Boston. Over the next three days the Tigers split two games with Chicago, the Browns and Indians split a pair, and the Yankees and Red Sox divided four games. As the Tigers headed for St. Louis, the standings were unchanged from the start of the week.

On the last day of August, the Tigers arrived at Sportsman's Park, where, after a hot summer of almost constant baseball, "the infield . . . looks like something with a bad case of mange," according to one visiting baseball writer. In the first game of the series, Trout won in relief, 4–3, over Willis Hudlin, a veteran righthander making his first big league appearance since 1940, as the Browns gave away three unearned runs.

The Yankees took two from Washington, so the Browns' lead was now down to two over New York, three over

Detroit, and three and a half over the Red Sox. There
was a month to go.

Newhouser got the call on the first of September,
against Luke Sewell's best pitcher, Nelson Potter. York
and Wakefield hit home runs, Newhouser scattered six
hits and struck out eight, and the Tigers won, 6-3. It
was Hal's 22nd win.

The next day, Detroit took the third in a row from the
Brownies, as Johnny Gorsica notched a victory in relief,
beating Galehouse, 6-3. Wakefield's double with the
bases loaded was the big hit. The Browns' lead was now
one game over the Yankees and Tigers.

On September 3, Jack Kramer was Sewell's saviour,
as he ended the Browns' skid and beat Dizzy Trout, 4-1.
The Tigers had now completed the eight games with the
Browns that Steve O'Neill had been counting on, and
they had won six of them. They were two games behind
St. Louis. The Yankees won two more, from Washington,
so they trailed by just a half game. Most observers were
predicting that either Detroit or New York would win.
The Browns, Salsinger said, "lack the needed pitching
and hitting." He added that "the hopes of the Tigers rest
on two men – Trout and Newhouser."

On Labor Day, the Tigers and White Sox split a twinbill, Overmire winning but Gorsica losing. The Browns
and Indians split, as did the Red Sox and Senators. The
Yankees, behind Walt Dubiel and Mel Queen, shut out
the A's twice and moved into a half-game lead over the
Browns, two and one-half over Detroit, and three over
Boston. With St. Louis apparently fading, Joe McCarthy's Yankees looked like a pretty good bet for their
fourth consecutive pennant.

Steve O'Neill's Detroit Tigers refused to admit any
such thing. On September 6, Harold Newhouser won his
23rd with a 6-0 blanking of the White Sox at Comiskey
Park. Scattering six hits, the ace lefthander was in command all the way; Doc Cramer led the Tigers' attack with

three hits, and Newhouser told reporters of his appreciation for the veteran's work in center field: "It's a pitcher's greatest break to have Cramer behind him." The win pulled the Tigers to within two games of New York, and a 3-2 win by Gentry over the Chisox the next day reduced the margin to one and one-half games.

When Trout blanked Cleveland on the 7th, the Tigers were just one game behind the Yankees and Browns, now tied for first place. Boston was only three back, but the loss of star second baseman Bobby Doerr to the service had reduced the hopes of the Red Sox.

On September 8 the Yankees won and the Browns lost; the next day the Red Sox beat New York, the Browns lost, and Rufe Gentry won in relief over Cleveland. The Tigers trailed the Yanks by a half game, with the Brownies another half game back.

The doubleheaders of the 10th saw the Yankees and Red Sox split at Boston, the Browns and White Sox split at Chicago, and the Tigers and Indians divide at Briggs Stadium. Newhouser won the opener with another shutout, beating the Cleveland ace, Mel Harder, 5-0, on a four-hitter. Only three Indians got as far as second base, and two of them made it there when shortstop Joe Hoover twice threw ground balls into the dugout. "Newhouser," Salsinger noted, "pitched over these errors with power and considerable grace."

Unfortunately, Trout lost to Steve Gromek in the nightcap, so no ground was gained. Detroit still trailed the Yankees by half a game. The next four days were open dates for all four contenders (actually, the Yankees had a Wednesday game at Philadelphia rained out), caused by the vagaries of wartime scheduling.

With two weeks to go, the exquisite pressure of a tight pennant race was bearing down on the American League. It was exciting for the fans—particularly those of the Yankees, Tigers, Browns, and Red Sox—and for the players on the contending teams. The hours passed slowly from the end of one game to the start of the next, and then the game was on again, with each base hit, strikeout, or stolen base magnified because of its greater significance. The Tigers, paced by their pitching aces Newhouser and Trout, with occasional assistance from Overmire or Gentry or one of the others, were confident that they could come out on top. Wakefield was ripping the ball at a torrid .350 pace, Cramer and York boosted the attack, Richards held the pitching together, and second baseman Eddie Mayo, with key hits and great fielding, was simply playing the best ball of his life. And in the dugout genial Steve O'Neill kept everyone's head in the game. The Browns had superior overall pitching, with Kramer, Potter, Galehouse, and Jakucki, but nothing to match Detroit's two aces; Stephens, McQuinn, Don Gutteridge, and Chet Laabs led the St. Louis offense. Joe McCarthy's Yankees, paced by George Stirnweiss and Johnny Lindell, boasted pitchers like Ernie Bonham, Hank Borowy, and Joe Page. Joe Cronin had his Red Sox still in the hunt, although the loss of Hughson and Doerr to the service hurt substantially.

On Friday the 15th, the chase resumed, although Wakefield received word from his draft board that he had passed his army physical and was subject to call at any time. The Tigers played two more at Cleveland, with the same pitching matchups as on the previous Sunday. The results were about the same: Gromek beat Trout, 4–3, in the opener, while Newhouser won his 25th in the second game, beating Harder, 9–1. James Zerilli wrote in the *Free Press* that "Harold Newhouser took another long stride toward establishing himself as the pitcher of 1944" with his victory. Cramer had five hits and Hal himself made a remarkable play in the sixth inning, grabbing Roy Cullenbine's slow roller about five feet from first base and diving head first to the bag, nipping Cullenbine by inches.

When the Browns' Denny Galehouse beat Chicago,

Detroit and St. Louis were tied for second, half a game back. The next day Bobo Newsom of the A's beat New York, and Jack Kramer pitched a one-hit victory for the Browns over the White Sox, so Luke Sewell's men moved back into first place by a half game over Detroit and New York.

Sunday, September 17, saw another reshuffling, as the A's beat the Yankees twice, the Browns split with Chicago, and the Tigers, behind Overmire and Gentry, won two from Cleveland. When the smoke cleared, the Detroit Tigers were in first place, a half game ahead of the Browns, and two and one-half ahead of the Yankees. The Red Sox were four back, hanging close but running out of time.

The next day was another open date. The weary contenders rested, while James Zerilli published a column in the *Free Press* on "the pastime's greatest transformation in pitching fortune," that of Harold Newhouser. He talked to some of Hal's teammates about the change: "better control," one said; "he's a sharp student of the game," said another. "Poise, confidence, and one sweet fast ball that cuts the corners," offered another. One player said, "He's surer of his curve. He'll wheel that sharp curve time after time with the count three and two." Richards said, "In the last five games Harold has thrown some of the wickedest pitches I've seen in nineteen years of baseball." Newhouser, the writer concluded, had "moxie" in abundance, citing as an example the play on Cullenbine a few days earlier.

On September 19, the Yankees came to Briggs Stadium, and 29,386 fans showed up for a Tuesday afternoon game. They got what they came for, as Newhouser "was the complete master of the Yankees," beating the Bombers, 4–1, for his 26th victory of the season. Pitching with good control, plenty of stuff, and a baffling slow curve, Harold shut the Yanks out until Johnny Lindell hit a solo home run with one out in the ninth.

Johnny Niggeling of Washington blanked the Browns, and Cleveland beat the fading Red Sox. The Tigers now led St. Louis by a game and a half and the Yankees by three and one-half.

The next day Trout beat New York to push the champs four and one-half back, but Kramer won for the Browns over Washington. On the 21st, Nelson Potter of the Browns beat the Senators, and Detroit lost to the Yankees, 5–4, in 10 innings. Newhouser lost this one in relief, although he should have won it in regulation play. Substitute shortstop Joe Orengo fumbled two successive double-play balls in the eighth, giving the Yanks an unearned run which cost the win. Newhouser's record dropped to 26–9, and New York writer Dan Daniel, claiming "Hal had nothing at all" in the three innings he worked, said the lefty was starting to show the effects of overwork. The Tigers still led St. Louis by a slim half game.

On September 22, the Tigers won both games of a wild doubleheader from the Red Sox, 7–4 and 8–6, as Gentry and Beck won, the first win of the year for the latter. Wakefield's grand slam brought the Tigers from behind in the first game, while Cramer's two-run, inside-the-park home run was the key hit in the nightcap. The Browns and Yankees both won single games, so the Tigers led by a full game over St. Louis and by three and one-half over the Yanks. The Red Sox were now out of the running.

The next day all three contenders won, with Trout beating Boston for his 26th victory.

On Sunday the 24th, 50,718 turned up at Briggs Stadium to see Newhouser face the Red Sox, and Harold did not disappoint the crowd. He held the Sox hitless through four innings as the Tigers took a 3–0 lead, gave up a run in the fifth after Skeeter Newsome had ended the hitless skein, and then got a key double in Detroit's four-run fifth that knocked out starter Yank Terry. Hal coasted from there to a 9–5 win for Number 27 of his remarkable season.

The Browns beat the A's that day, 3–2, on ninth-inning errors by Edgar Busch and Roberto Estalella, so they stayed one game behind the Tigers. The Yankees lost to Mel Harder of Cleveland and fell four and one-half back. At this stage the Tigers and Browns had seven games left to play, the Yankees eight, with a week to go.

On Monday the 25th, O'Neill was forced to go with Rufe Gentry against the A's, and Ruffus pitched what Newhouser said "was probably the best he has pitched all year." Unfortunately Mr. Mack's tall, skinny side-armer, Russ Christopher, was even better, and the result was a 2–1 Detroit loss. Nelson Potter of St. Louis held the Red Sox to two hits and won, 3–0, and his team and the Tigers were once again dead even. The Yankees took two in Chicago, so they were three back with six to go.

It was that stage of the race when players tried to find something to do back at the hotel to take their minds off baseball for a couple of hours, to put today's game behind them, and to keep from anticipating tomorrow's game too much. The minutes ticked away slowly until it was time to head out to the ball park again.

The deadlock in the race continued through Tuesday the 26th. Trout shut out the A's, 6–0, for his 27th win, Sig Jakucki of the Browns beat Mike Ryba and the Red Sox, 1–0, and the Yanks took another from Chicago.

On Wednesday the 27th, the Red Sox won in the rain at St. Louis, 4–1, and the Yankees beat the White Sox. At Detroit Hal Newhouser shut out the A's, 4–0 on five hits, three of them somewhat fluky. The man who had led the American League in bases on balls in 1943 did not go to a three-ball count on a single batter until he went to three-and-two on Frankie Hayes with two out in the ninth before retiring him on a ground ball to end the game. It was a stunning performance.

With four games left, the Tigers led the Browns by a game and the Yankees by three. Joe McCarthy took his Yanks to St. Louis to close out the season, while the final four games for the Tigers would be with Ossie Bluege's Washington Senators, one of the disappointments of the year.

On Thursday the 28th, rain in the Midwest washed out both the Washington-Detroit and New York-St. Louis games, forcing doubleheaders for the next day and a little more strain on tired pitching staffs. O'Neill announced that Gentry and Overmire would pitch Friday, with Trout and Newhouser to go on Saturday and Sunday.

On Friday, Gentry came through, winning the opener, 5-2, but Stubby Overmire's arm was hurting and he could not pitch. Trout was named instead, but, pitching on two days rest, he was hit hard and beaten, 9-2, by Mickey Haefner. Stan Spence hit a three-run homer in the third inning to pace the Senators.

Meanwhile, in St. Louis, the Browns swept their doubleheader and eliminated the Yankees from the race. Kramer stopped the New Yorkers, 4-1, in the opener, and Nelson Potter outpitched Hank Borowy, 1-0, to win the second and move into a tie with the Tigers.

There were two games left to go.

On Saturday, with no margin for error, O'Neill was forced to send out Newhouser with two days rest. His left-handed ace was equal to the task, though, and came through with a 7-3 victory. In the first eight innings, Hal held the Nats to four hits, with Spence's sixth-inning bases-empty home run the only damaging one. York singled home a run in the first for Detroit, and Cramer did the same in the second. In the sixth, York hit a home run, and a Wakefield hit, bunt single by Outlaw, walk to Richards, and a two-run double by Doc Cramer put the game out of reach. A tired Newhouser gave up two Washington runs in the ninth, but he had enough left to finish up his 29th win of the season, tying the 35-year-old club record for wins in a season set by George Mullin back in 1909.

Down in St. Louis, though, Denny Galehouse shut out the dispirited Yankees, 2-0, so Newhouser's heroics only preserved the tie going into the last game of the season. For Detroit, the pitcher on that Sunday, October 1, would be Paul "Dizzy" Trout, trying to coax one more game out of his tired right arm. Hal Newhouser would be in the bullpen, but O'Neill knew that, realistically, he could not call on his ace after nine innings the day before, except perhaps to face one crucial hitter.

Ossie Bluege nominated his big knuckleballer, Emil "Dutch" Leonard, to pitch for the Senators. The Nationals, of course, were long out of the picture, and Leonard would be pitching for pride and professionalism. He had something more to think about, though, when he received a phone call in his hotel room from a caller who told the pitcher he would make it worth his while to make sure the Senators lost. Leonard was troubled by the call, which he reported to his manager, but Bluege told him to forget about it and pitch his ball game.

Some 45,565 fans crowded into Briggs Stadium, and they saw Dutch Leonard pitch the game of his life. Trout got through the first three innings successfully, but he ran into trouble in the fourth. Joe Kuhel singled, and the red-hot Stan Spence homered to give the Nats a 2-0 lead. Fred Vaughn, Jake Powell, and Johnny Sullivan followed with singles, and a third run crossed. The Tigers could not score against Leonard until the ninth inning, and the result was a crushing 4-1 defeat. Newhouser could only sit on the sidelines and watch, as the Tigers' chances were snuffed out.

In St. Louis, meanwhile, the largest crowd in club history, 37,815, showed up for the Browns-Yankees game; it was just as if only then — on the last day of the season — did the people of St. Louis take the Brownies seriously enough to acknowledge the possibility that they might

win. The alcoholic Sig Jakucki took the mound for Luke
Sewell, and behind two home runs by war worker Chet
Laabs and another by Vernon Stephens, the Browns won
the game, 5-2 – and the American League pennant. It
was the only one they ever won.

A weary and disappointed Steve O'Neill faced the
press and said, "We made a good, game fight and I'm
proud of our gang. At the same time, we've all got to
hand it to the Browns for the way they stood up under
pressure, especially in the last two weeks." He was surprised, he said, that the Yankees could not win at least
one of the final four games in St. Louis. What O'Neill
did not say, but what was very much in his listeners'
minds, was that it was almost impossible to win a pennant with what was virtually a two-man pitching staff.

One last proud and defiant statement came from Hal
Newhouser during the World Series, in which the under-
dog Browns gave the lordly Cardinals all they could handle before losing in six. After watching the Browns win
the third game, Harold told a reporter: "I believe that
if we had got into the series, we would have whipped the
Cards four straight."

It had been a remarkable season for the 23-year-old
lefthander.

9
OFF-SEASON
IN THE SUN

The off-season after the 1944 campaign was an active one for Harold Newhouser. Personally, of course, he could look back upon his own coming of age as a major league pitcher and the greatest season for an American League hurler since Lefty Grove's 31 wins in 1931. As a Tiger, though, he looked ahead to a new season, one in which he could help put Detroit into the World Series that had been so narrowly missed in 1944.

Dan Daniel, writing for *Baseball Magazine* in November, picked Newhouser as 1944's Player of the Year. "Hurricane Hal stood staunch right to the finish," Daniel wrote, "and wound up with a record which showed 29 victories and 9 defeats. This indeed was a throwback to the glorious era of pitching in which the 30-game mark was the yardstick by which superlatives were measured . . ." Newhouser, he said, "developed into a new and brilliant pitcher. Speed, curves, control, poise and a studious angle made Hal the most effective pitcher in the major leagues."

Hal's numbers for 1944 were awe-inspiring. He pitched 26 complete games and six shutouts (one of 12 innings), and he won four games (against two defeats) in relief. His earned run average was a sparkling 2.22, second to his teammate Trout's 2.12, and he pitched 312 innings, again surpassed only by Trout, who threw 352. New-houser's strikeout total of 187 led the league, and he reduced his bases on balls from 111 to 102, despite pitching 117 more innings than in 1943. He beat the Yankees six times, Washington five, the Browns, Cleveland, and Philadelphia four times each, and the Red Sox and White Sox three each. His most remarkable numbers were posted in the last month of the season. In September, when the pressure of the pennant race was at its heaviest, when the strain on his overworked left arm was at its greatest, Hal Newhouser started eight games, completed eight games, and won eight games, three of them shutouts. His only loss in September was in relief, on an unearned run. Dizzy Trout's numbers for the year were also extraordinary, as he won 27 and lost 14. But down the September stretch, where Newhouser was 8-1, Trout faltered to a record of four wins and five losses, including the two crucial ones in the final series with Washington. This comparison is certainly no criticism of the arm-weary Trout, without whom the Tigers would not have been in contention; it simply emphasizes the brilliant work of Hal Newhouser, who came very close to putting his team into the World Series.

This work was recognized on November 28, when the American League office announced that Newhouser had won the baseball writers' poll as the Most Valuable Player in the American League for 1944. Paul Trout actually received a few more first-place votes than Newhouser (10-7, with Vern Stephens getting four, Wakefield two, and second baseman Snuffy Stirnweiss of the Yankees one), but Newhouser received 10 second-place votes and six for third place to outpoll Trout by 236-232. (The 24th writer, probably the same one who voted for Stirnweiss, gave Newhouser, the 29-game winner, honorable mention.) *The Sporting News*, applauding the MVP selections of Newhouser and shortstop Marty Marion of the Cardinals, said they "represented pre-war baseball skills of the highest order." Newhouser and Marion, the paper said, "shed on the game a brilliance which could not have been brighter" in any peacetime season.

Newhouser's response to the announcement of the MVP award was to give credit for his turnabout to his manager, Steve O'Neill, and his catcher, Paul Richards. "I can't say too much for the encouragement I got from Steve," the pitcher said, "and from that guy behind the bat."

In December, *The Sporting News* named Wish Egan of the Tigers the top scout in the majors. The article quoted Egan on Hal Newhouser, at a time when the young lefthander was still struggling: "A boy with an arm like that can't miss. He'll get control sooner or later, and he'll be the best lefthander in the country."

Meanwhile, as the plaudits and awards for 1944 were doled out, momentous things were happening, in the world at large and in the world of baseball. Eisenhower's armies were racing across France, heading for Germany, only to come a cropper in late December with the German offensive through the Ardennes that was to be known as the Battle of the Bulge. Roosevelt was elected to the White House for an unprecedented fourth time, defeating Governor Thomas E. Dewey of New York. Bing Crosby and the Andrews Sisters sang "Don't Fence Me In," and Andy Russell had a big hit with "I Dream of You."

In early November, Hank Greenberg visited Briggs Stadium during a leave from the army; while there he told reporters that he intended to return to the game after the war. This was the latest in a series of contradictory quotes that Greenberg had given about his postwar intentions, but it indicated that he was feeling good. Greenberg, who would be 34 at the start of 1945, said: "I always figured I could play until I was 40." Later in the month, the Tigers learned that pitchers Al Benton and Les Mueller had been released from the service; they would be welcome additions to O'Neill's thin pitching corps.

On November 25, Judge Landis died. The crusty old commissioner, whose hard-headed rectitude had been one of the means of baseball's salvation in the 1920s, was succeeded for a year by an advisory council composed of the two league presidents, Frick and Harridge, and Landis' secretary, Leslie M. O'Connor. In the interim, a search was initiated for a new commissioner.

In early December the Tigers sent a two-man delegation, Zeller and Egan, to the winter meetings, as rumors buzzed that they were going to try to land slugging outfielder Jeff Heath from the Indians. As it turned out, they did make a trade, but it was of spare infielder Joe Orengo, sent to the White Sox for Jim "Skeeter" Webb, a good-fielding but light-hitting shortstop who just happened to be married to Steve O'Neill's daughter.

The Tiger brass received a scare after Thanksgiving, when the Associated Press reported on November 30 that Newhouser was likely to lose the second finger of his right hand, cut while sharpening a carving knife. The United Press got in touch with Beryl, who pooh-poohed the report. She said it was the middle finger, that indeed Hal had cut it, but that there was no infection and no danger. "I don't know how such a report got around," she said. Hal was holding down an off-season job in a factory supply plant, and the wire services sent photographers around to take pictures of him with a big bandage on his right hand.

On December 23, War Mobilization Director James F. Byrnes announced that he had recently written to General Hershey of Selective Service, asking that professional athletes previously found physically unfit be re-examined. He also asked that men in the 26-to-38 age bracket be looked at more closely. The first baseball-playing 4-F to be re-examined and then inducted was outfielder Ron Northey of the Phillies, taken into the army on January 29, 1945.

In late January, Senator Albert B. Chandler of Kentucky declared in a speech that baseball should continue and that the 200 or so 4-Fs playing baseball should do that rather than working in war plants. "That's about all they've ever done," Chandler said, adding, "They have no particular mechanical aptitude – not nearly as much as a woman – for war work." Baseball, of course, was happy to hear a friendly voice coming out of Washington, and it took note of Senator Chandler, as Senator Chandler no doubt intended.

Out in Ohio, old Denton True Young, "Cy" Young of the 511 big league victories, allowed as how Bob Feller and others coming back to baseball after the war might have a tough time of it. They would not automatically be stars again, Young thought, not even Feller. "His muscles will relax," Cy said, "and he will face new batters when he pitches again." Some of the players who had attained prominence during the wartime seasons, Cy felt, would displace the veterans returning from service. As it turned out, in quite a few instances that was just what happened. As to Feller, of course, old Cy was dead wrong.

With that thought for the future, the 16 major league clubs prepared for their third northern spring training. Both the world championship and American League pennants would fly over Sportsman's Park in St. Louis, but hopes were high in Detroit as the Tigers prepared for 1945.

10
HAL'S FLAG

In March 1945 the Detroit Tigers assembled for the
third time in Evansville, Indiana, for the start of spring
training. The players from the 1944 club had a continuing feeling of frustration at finishing that scant game
back of St. Louis; they still felt they had been a better
team than the Brownies. But, with a new season coming up, they had a new chance to win it all.

In early 1945 it was clear that Nazi Germany was on
its last legs; the Luftwaffe was gone, and there were increasing numbers of old men and young boys appearing
in the dwindling ranks of the Wehrmacht. Still, there
were disquieting rumors that Hitler would order the in-
stitution of guerilla warfare to defend a "National Re-
doubt" in the mountains of Bavaria, keeping the fighting
going for an indefinite period. And Japan was unvan-
quished. Although the United States Navy, Marines, and
Army had stripped away most of Japan's Pacific island
empire, the daunting task of an invasion of the home
islands still faced America's military and political leaders. Understandably, the government did not want a
relaxation of effort on the home front while these formidable realities remained.

Among those who entered the service between the
end of the 1944 season and the start of 1945 were Stan

Musial, Danny Litwhiler, Jim Tabor, Roy Partee, Al Zarilla, Ray Mueller, Clyde Shoun, Dominic Dallessandro, Thurman Tucker, Ralph Hodgin, Stan Spence, Ron Northey, Tony Lupien, and Ken Keltner, along with three Tigers who would be missed, Wakefield, Higgins, and John Gorsica. It was estimated that nearly one-fourth of those on 1944 Opening Day rosters were in the service by the start of 1945; in addition, roughly 80 percent of those who had finished the last pre-war year, 1941, on a big league roster were in the service when the 1945 season got under way. That was a substantial turnover. But what was taken for granted at the time, yet ignored in future years when wartime baseball was examined, was the fact that the replacements for those missing were themselves professionals. They knew how to play baseball.

The Office of Defense Transportation ordered a cutback in spring training travel (and thus in the number of possible exhibition games). There had to be increased reliance upon intra-squad games. Shortages in quality baseball equipment continued. There was, however, some good news. A few players were already returning from the service, and a steady trickle of such returnees would keep up throughout the season. Back already were two Tigers previously mentioned, Benton and Les Mueller, along with such others as Van Lingle Mungo of the Giants, Mickey Livingston and Peanuts Lowrey of the Cubs, Tom Earley of the Braves, and a young Cardinal farmhand named Albert "Red" Schoendienst, soon to be a Cardinal regular. Further help was afforded by a March 21 ruling from Paul V. McNutt of the War Manpower Commission that a professional baseball player was free to leave his war plant job or any other essential job until October. There would be no more part-time situations like that of Chet Laabs in 1944.

At Evansville, Newhouser found himself one of the reigning celebrities in camp. His fame had been boosted in early March by a Red Smith article in the *Saturday Evening Post*, entitled "Doghouse to Let: Apply Newhouser & Trout." The story, detailing the ascendance of Hal and Dizzy after their seasons in disfavor, gave the national reading public a more personal look at the young lefthander. Earlier, in October, a *Baseball Magazine* profile had informed its readers that Newhouser was "a great football and hockey fan. He hunts and fishes and collects stamps. He likes Gary Cooper and Irene Dunne on the screen and reads Western stories." What became clear, of course, was what the writers covering the Detroit club already knew: Hal Newhouser was a nice, rather shy young man, devoted to his wife and family, but slightly colorless off the field. He had been of interest to the writers before 1944 because of his incendiary temper; with that under control, he was of interest now because he had become a great pitcher. He was usually good for a quote, but his quotes were not earthshaking. A charismatic personality he was not.

At camp, the writers talked to Hal whenever they could, because he was what their readers were interested in and he always politely took the time to answer their questions. He told a writer from *The New York Times* that he would not win 29 games again; "I won't get enough work to win like that." He explained that, "With our improved pitching staff I'll be lucky to pitch enough games to win twenty. I'll never win twenty-nine again, probably not even twenty-five—because I won't have to." With an Associated Press reporter, Newhouser reflected on the 1944 season: "I'm glad to have that year behind me. I don't think all that work hurt me: it probably did me much more good than harm. But one season like that is enough." He told Sam Greene of the *Detroit News* that "I'll be satisfied to win fifteen games this year," although Greene noted that the lefty was "working with the industry of a pitcher determined to win thirty."

On April 6, the Tigers left Evansville after three weeks,

to complete training at Terre Haute, Indiana. O'Neill professed himself contented: "We had good weather and good workouts. I doubt that any other club is in better physical condition."

On April 11, the U.S. Ninth Army, under General William Simpson, crossed the Elbe; the next day all America (and the world) was shocked to learn of the death of Franklin D. Roosevelt in Warm Springs, Georgia. For many Americans there was hardly any recollection of anyone else as president; Hal Newhouser, for example, had not yet reached 12 when FDR was sworn in. The astonishment at Roosevelt's sudden death (despite the photographic evidence showing the ravages of the war years on the president) was compounded by the relative lack of public familiarity with his successor, Harry S Truman of Missouri. To Truman would fall the task of bringing the war to a successful conclusion, in Europe and in the Pacific.

In the midst of these momentous events, baseball prepared to open what was hoped would be its last wartime season and its first without Judge Landis. J. G. Taylor Spink in *The Sporting News* picked the Browns to repeat as American League champions, followed by the Yankees, Tigers, and Indians. And Hal Newhouser got ready to pitch the opener. On April 14, it rained in Terre Haute and the Tigers had the day off. But Newhouser took Paul Richards to the ball park and worked out for an hour under the stands. "I wanted to loosen up a little," he said. "I want to throw some more Sunday and then I'll be right for the opener, if I get the call."

Starting the season, Steve O'Neill was confident of his pitching; Newhouser, Trout, Overmire, Benton, Gentry, Les Mueller, and Walter Wilson, up from Buffalo, should be able to handle the mound duty. He wondered, though, what he was going to do for runs. His big gun was Rudy York at first base; Eddie Mayo was steady at second. Shortstop was in the hands of Jimmy Webb, his son-in-law, who was not much of a hitter, and at third, in place of the departed Higgins, he planned to play either Joe Hoover or Don Ross, neither of whom was much with the stick. He still had Cramer in center field, but the rest of the outfield was populated by people like Jimmy Outlaw, rookie Bob Maier, the elderly Hostetler, and young John McHale. The absent Dick Wakefield was sorely missed. The catchers, Richards and Swift, provided little offensive assistance. If York did not have a big year, the Detroit Tigers would have to scratch for runs.

They journeyed to St. Louis for the April 17 opening game, for which a disappointing crowd of only 4,167 turned out. (St. Louis, despite the Browns' pennant, was still a Cardinal town.) Newhouser pitched for the Tigers but lost, 7–1, to Sig Jakucki; George McQuinn and Milt Byrnes provided most of the firepower for manager Luke Sewell. Sam Greene of the *News* wrote: "Newhouser towers above Jakucki in the record books but on this one occasion the Browns' blond right-hander from the other side of the tracks was much superior."

Four days later, in 42-degree weather at Briggs Stadium, Newhouser beat the Cleveland Indians, 3–2, in 11 innings. Hal singled home the Tigers' first run, and then he grounded a hit to right against a drawn-in infield to win the game over Red Embree in the 11th. Before the game the Tigers were rejoined by Lambert "Dutch" Meyer, following his discharge from the army. Meyer, an infielder, had hit a modest .231 in parts of three pre-war seasons.

April 24 saw the Russian army engaged in bitter and destructive street fighting in Berlin, the surrender to the French government of Marshal Henri Petain, the head of the wartime Vichy regime, and the election as new baseball commissioner of Senator Albert Benjamin Chandler of Kentucky. Chandler, nicknamed "Happy," was a gladhanding politico totally unlike his austere predecessor, but he had an inner strength to him that

Tiger scout Wish Egan with the star American Legion pitcher.
(Photo credit: *The Sporting News.*)

Hal's parents see their son off at the railroad station for spring training in Texas, 1939. (Photo credit: *The Sporting News.*)

Ted Williams said the young Newhouser would "give you that rotten stare." Spring, 1940.
(Photo credit: *National Baseball Library*.)

The big bats of the 1945 Tigers. Left to right: Rudy York, Roy Cullenbine, Hank Greenberg, Doc Cramer, Eddie Mayo. (Photo credit: *Bettmann Archive*.)

Jack Kramer, Newhouser, and Bob Feller, after combining to shut out the National League All-Stars, July 9, 1946. (Photo credit: *Bettmann Archive*.)

Steve O'Neill, Paul Richards, and George Kell congratulate
Newhouser after his win over Feller in "the pitching duel of the
century," September 22, 1946. (Photo credit: *Wide World Photos.*)

Newhouser in a classic pose. (Photo credit: *National Baseball Library*.)

Prince Hal and a couple of admirers. (Photo credit: *Wide World Photos*.)

Hank Greenberg signs Newhouser to a 1954 Cleveland contract.
(Photo credit: *The Sporting News.*)

The Newhouser family. (Photo credit: *Bettmann Archive.*)

would eventually surprise the owners who put him in office. Happy Chandler would preside over – and take a substantial part in – the establishment of a players' pension system, the rebuffing of the Mexican League raids, and the destruction of baseball's longtime color barrier.

Newhouser's next start, scheduled for April 26 in Chicago, was called off because of rain and cold weather. Hal said, "That suits me. I don't like to work in cold weather. After that 11-inning game at Briggs Stadium last Saturday, my elbow was sore for three or four days."

Hal pitched on April 29, at Cleveland, but lost to Steve Gromek of the Tribe, 4–0, in the opener of a doubleheader. The same day Jack Zeller swung a trade with Cleveland, sending two infielders, Don Ross and the recently-returned Dutch Meyer, to the Indians for the much-traveled Roy Cullenbine, a strong switch hitter. Cullenbine was promptly installed in left field, where the Tigers had already tried Maier, Hostetler, and Hubby Walker. Maier was moved to third base. Cullenbine's acquisition made Detroit a legitimate pennant contender.

H.G. Salsinger, looking back on Newhouser's first three starts, wrote that the lefty was "having a hard time getting started this year, due not to weak pitching on his part but to lack of batting and fielding support." In the three games, Salsinger said, the Tigers scored a total of just four runs and Newhouser drove in two of them himself.

Harold's fourth start, though, was one which required little support. For a May 6 doubleheader with the Browns, 39,482 showed up in Briggs Stadium, and they were not disappointed. In the first game, Newhouser pitched a one-hitter and beat Sig Jakucki, 3–0; a clean single by Stephens in the fourth was the only safety for the visitors. Benton won the nightcap, 1–0, on a ninth-inning home run by Cullenbine for a Detroit sweep. The first game was played in an hour and 28 minutes, the second in a brisk 1:29.

Meanwhile, each day in early May 1945 seemed to bring new and startling news from Europe. First came the report, never confirmed, of Adolf Hitler's death in his bunker in the ruins of Berlin and the designation of Grand Admiral Karl Doenitz, commander of Nazi Germany's once-mighty U-Boat fleet, as the new head of state. Berlin fell to the Russians on May 2, Kesselring surrendered his armies in Italy on May 4, and on May 7 General Alfred Jodl, representing Doenitz and what remained of the German government, signed an unconditional capitulation to Eisenhower and the Allies at Reims. President Truman proclaimed May 8 as V-E Day, and Americans, whose hatred of Naziism had been reinforced by the horrifying discovery of Hitler's extermination camps, celebrated the liberation of Europe from the black night of National Socialism. The V-E Day festivities were necessarily restrained, however, in light of the task still ahead in the Pacific, where the conquest of Japan's home islands projected as a bloody and ghastly struggle.

There were indications that the manpower pressures on baseball would abate somewhat with the defeat of Germany; indeed, some players in the service would likely be mustered out. But the travel constraints would continue and perhaps even increase, as the nation switched its military emphasis from Europe to the Orient. J. Monroe Johnson, director of the Office of Defense Transportation, said that sports teams would be lucky to play out their regular schedules in the summer and fall of 1945, unless Japan were to fold up quickly, relieving the burden on transportation. Johnson said there was no possibility of playing baseball's All-Star Game that summer, and he thought the World Series could not be held unless the respective league pennants were won by two clubs in the same city, as in 1944.

The Tigers were hurting in early May: Richards had a sprained ankle and was out from April 29 to May 11, while Steve O'Neill missed 10 games because of gout. Richards handled the team while O'Neill was laid up; the veteran manager fretted about the slow start of Rudy York with the bat and, as always, he worried about the Yankees. "Their pitching figures to stand up," he said, and he felt that Lindell, Stirnweiss, and Nick Etten would give Joe McCarthy enough batting power. O'Neill felt good about the hitting of Eddie Mayo and Roger Cramer, and he appreciated the acquisition of Roy Cullenbine, whose bat was contributing to the Tiger offense.

Newhouser's next start was on May 11, when he lost to the Yankees and Hank Borowy at Detroit, 7–3. Out-fielder Tuck Stainback of the Yankees hit his first home run in four years, but Newhouser's main trouble came from his own infield, where Skeeter Webb committed three errors and Mayo one, and Bob Maier cost a run by cutting off a throw he should have let go through. Hal's record was 2–3, but no one was worried yet; the Tigers were up at the top of the league, with the Yanks and White Sox.

The next outing for Newhouser was not until May 19, after five days of rain had washed out baseball through-out the Midwest. The Senators captured the first game of the doubleheader, but Newhouser was at his best in the nightcap, blanking the Nats, 3–0, on six hits. Cullen-bine's leadoff home run against Mickey Haefner in the fourth inning was all that the Tigers' lefty needed to even his record for the season, but he himself singled home two more runs to ice the game.

Earlier that day Dizzy Trout pulled a muscle in his left side; on the 24th a line drive by the A's Bobby Estalella broke Benton's ankle. In the same game catcher Bob Swift wrenched his shoulder. A worried O'Neill moved Walter Wilson and Joe Orrell into his starting rotation. Luckily, he still had Prince Hal Newhouser. Harold stopped the A's in Philadelphia on May 23 with a 7–1 classic. He yielded seven hits (one a ninth-inning homer to Estalella to lose his shutout), walked one, and struck out 11. This game was no relaxing laugher for Newhouser; the score was only 1-0 until the Tigers struck for six runs in the eighth.

Four days later Newhouser won his fifth game of the season with a methodical 3-1 victory over the Senators at Griffith Stadium. The most noteworthy event of that contest was that, on May 27, slugger Rudy York hit his first home run of the season. Steve O'Neill could only hope that his first baseman would now make up for lost time.

On Memorial Day at New York, before a huge crowd of 67,816, O'Neill brought Newhouser back on two days' rest in the second game of a doubleheader, after Stubby Overmire had won the opener. Newhouser labored mightily, but the short interval affected his control and eight walks helped the Yankees to a 3-2 victory. The next day, though, O'Neill got a big boost from bespectacled Les Mueller, who shut out the New Yorkers on two hits. The Tigers ended May a half game behind New York.

As June opened, Newhouser's record stood at only five wins and four losses, although the lefty had pitched well in most of his games. In June, Hal got himself into a superb groove, and the wins started piling up one after another. On the 3rd he beat the Red Sox at Boston, 4-3, and on the 7th he beat Cleveland and Jim Bagby, 3-2. On the 12th he went 11 innings to top the Browns and Jack Kramer, 2-1, on a crucial single by Bobby Maier. This win put the Tigers in first place. On June 16, Newhouser scattered six hits to beat the White Sox, 6-1, and on the 20th he blanked the Indians, 5-0, driving in the first three runs himself with a double and a single. Four days later Hal set down the Browns at St. Louis, 5-1, with only Mark Christman's ninth-inning home run marring his effort. And four days after that, on June 28, Newhouser stopped the Senators, 5-2; suddenly his record had ballooned to 12-4. Along the way, in that remarkable month of June, Harold pitched a little relief, too, saving a win for Trout against the White Sox and another for Mueller with one and a third innings against the A's. By the time the month was over, the Tigers had ridden Hal Newhouser's strong left arm to a three-game lead over the Yankees.

The Tigers were starting to hit now, with Jimmy Outlaw, Cullenbine, and Cramer contributing, and Eddie Mayo keeping up his good work. Perhaps the biggest news of all was the word they received on June 14 that Hank Greenberg was being mustered out of the army and would join the team in a couple of weeks. O'Neill announced that he would install Greenberg in his outfield, and Jack Zeller crowed: "If he hits anywhere near his old clip we're the club to beat for the flag." Greenberg showed up on July 1 and, although he was clearly rusty from his four years away from the game, it was obvious that he could still hit.

Perhaps it would be appropriate at this point, with Greenberg making his reappearance, to take another overall look at big league baseball, as it stood in the summer of 1945, the last of the war years. The European war was over and Japan was reeling, but it was certainly not yet "business as usual" on the diamond. There were more unfamiliar names and faces than ever, and some familiar ones had returned from the past. Jimmie Foxx and Pepper Martin were among the pre-war heroes who turned up on major league rosters. On July 3, Branch Rickey announced that the Dodgers had purchased outfielder Floyd "Babe" Herman from Hollywood in the Pacific Coast League. Herman, of course, had been a hard-hitting and erratic-fielding star of the Dodgers from 1926 to 1931 and had continued with the Reds, Cubs, Pirates, and Tigers through 1937. But he had been out of the majors since then, and he was now 42 years old. Rickey, however, felt that the Babe could still pinch-hit (he was correct in that), and the old favorite would certainly not hurt the gate at Ebbets Field. On the same day, at the other end of the military pipeline from Greenberg, outfielder Al Gionfriddo of Pittsburgh, awaiting induction into the army, was given a 30-day deferment by his draft board because his wife was expecting a baby.

At Detroit, Newhouser's victory streak came to an end, when Jimmy Wilson of the Red Sox blanked the Tigers, 4-0, in a twilight game. Wilson, who was a rookie in 1945, would pitch in the majors through 1956, winning 86 games along the way. Newhouser's main problem in this game was a big outfielder named George Metkovich, from Angel's Camp, California. Metkovich, a left-handed hitter nicknamed "Catfish" because he had once suffered a foot injury by stepping on one, picked up four hits and stole a base. Metkovich had kicked around in the minors for five years, a farmhand of the Tigers and the Braves, before the Red Sox bought him from San Francisco in 1943. He developed into a useful performer and played in the big leagues off and on with six different teams through 1954. George Metkovich, incidentally, considered Hal Newhouser "the best lefthander I ever faced."

On that same July 3, the Indians beat the Yankees, 5-1, handing Atley Donald his first loss to Cleveland since 1939. The New Yorkers lined up with Etten, Stirnweiss, Mike Milosevich, and Oscar Grimes in the infield, ex-Phillie Herschel Martin, Tuck Stainback, and Bud Metheny in the outfield, and Mike Garbark catching. Metheny — Arthur Beauregard Metheny actually, a graduate of William & Mary College — had spent five years in the Yankee farm system before being brought up from Newark in 1943. He hit .248 over three wartime seasons for the Yankees, had three at-bats in 1946, and then departed. He would probably not have made the big leagues in peacetime — not as a regular, anyway — but he was a competent player and he did not disgrace the famous pinstripes. The Indians in this game used Mickey Rocco, Dutch Meyer, Boudreau, Al Cihocki, Heath, Felix Mackiewicz, Paul O'Dea, and Frankie Hayes, along with pitcher Al Smith. It was, as with most other teams, a mixture of solid big leaguers with wartime fill-ins.

The Senators pounded the White Sox, 12-2, behind Roger Wolff and a home run by Harlond Clift. Established players like Case, Clift, Kuhel, and Rick Ferrell were in the Washington lineup, as were George Myatt, George Binks, and Gil Torres, who played some in the majors in peacetime. Second baseman Fred Vaughn and centerfielder Jose Zardon disappeared when the veterans returned. The White Sox used an outfielder named Johnny Dickshot. Dickshot, a 33-year-old of Lithuanian descent, his name originally Dicksus, had played parts of four seasons during the '30s in the National League, but mostly he had played in places like Rock Island, Cedar Rapids, Little Rock, and Jersey City. The Sox picked him up from the Coast League and he hit .253 for them in 1944 and .302 in 1945, winding up his big league career.

The Browns beat the Athletics, 2-1, at Sportsman's Park, using mostly the same team that had won the pennant in 1944. The most noteworthy addition, of course, was one-armed Pete Gray in the outfield. The dismal A's, who finished 34 1/2 games out of first place and 17 games behind the seventh-place Red Sox, featured an infield of Dick Siebert, Irv Hall, Edgar Busch, and George Kell. They had Charlie Metro, Hal Peck, and Bobby Estalella in the outfield and Buddy Rosar behind the plate. There are some familiar names there, and some, like Hall, Busch and Metro, who were strictly wartime players.

Over in the National League, the same story prevailed. The Cubs crushed Boston at Braves Field, 24-2, piling up 28 hits, even though Boston's Tommy Holmes kept his hitting streak alive at 29 games. The veteran Claude Passeau coasted for the Cubs, as Cavarretta and second baseman Don Johnson had five hits each and Andy Pafko had four. Pafko was a youngster who had come to the major leagues during the war, but he was anything

but a "wartime player." Pafko compiled a .285 lifetime
average over 17 seasons in the National League and appeared in four World Series. The Braves used men like
Joe Mack, Dick Culler, Carden Gillenwater, Stew Hof-
ferth, Bill "Square Jaw" Ramsey, and Frank Drews, along
with Holmes, Joe Medwick, and Chuck Workman. Second baseman Whitey Wietelmann pitched the last inning of the lost cause, and the Cubs added six runs to
their total at his expense. His effort, though, was not
much inferior to that of Nate Andrews, Ira Hutchinson,
Al Javery, and Joe Heving, the real pitchers used by
manager Bob Coleman.

The Giants beat the Cardinals, 3–2, behind the pitching of Harry Feldman. Manager Mel Ott sprinkled himself, catcher Clyde Kluttz, and shortstop Buddy Kerr
among the Danny Gardellas and Sunny Jim Mallorys in
his lineup. The Cards, striving for their fourth consecutive pennant, lined up with Ray Sanders, Emil Verban,
Marion, and Kurowski around the infield, Schoendienst,
Buster Adams, and Augie Bergamo in the outfield, Ken
O'Dea behind the plate, and, on this particular day, righthanders Ken Burkhardt and Ted Wilks on the mound.

At Philadelphia, the Pirates beat the Phillies, 10–3,
behind the hurling of Nick Strincevich, a righthander
who had moderate success in the National League both
before and after the war. Frank Colman, a Canadian who
had started in the minors as a left-handed pitcher before
switching to the outfield, hit a home run and two doubles
for the Bucs, who had Bob Elliott, Babe Dahlgren, Frank
Gustine, and Al Lopez playing for them. The Phillies,
a very bad team playing for a newly-installed manager,
Ben Chapman, had an infield of Vance Dinges, Bitsy
Mott, Wally Flager, and John Antonelli, with Rene Mon-
teagudo, Vince DiMaggio, and Glenn Crawford in the
outfield. St. Louis Browns' retread Hal Spindel caught,
and Chapman used two pinch hitters, a very young Andy Seminick and a very old Jimmie Foxx. His ineffec-

tive pitchers for this game were Dick Barrett, Charlie Schanz, Marshall Scott, and Charlie Sproull. By definition, most of the '45 Phillies were "wartime players." Finally, the Reds beat the Dodgers, 5–1, at Brooklyn. Fastballer Frank Dasso won it for Cincinnati, one of the four victories of his brief big league career. The Reds' batting order of Dain Clay, Eric Tipton, Al Libke, Frank McCormick, Steve Mesner, Kermit Wahl, Woody Williams, and Al Unser contained several legitimate major league players as well as some who were questionable. For the Dodgers, basketball star Howie "Stretch" Schultz played first, Ed Stanky second, Eddie Basinski shortstop, and Luis Olmo third base. Augie Galan, Goody Rosen, and Dixie Walker were in the outfield, and American League veteran Johnny Peacock was behind the plate for pitchers Clyde King and Cy Buker. Olmo and Rosen are of interest here. Rosen was a little left-handed outfielder from Toronto, one of the few Jewish players in the big leagues. He had played all or part of three seasons for the Dodgers in the late '30s and then dropped down to the minors. After four and a half years with Syracuse in the International League, he was called up by the Dodgers in 1944 and hit .261. In 1945, he came on strong and hit .325 with 12 home runs, and he continued on with a .281 season for the Giants in 1946, after the war. "Wartime player?" One cannot really say that, even though it is clear that the war gave Goody Rosen the chance to return to the majors. Olmo, a young Puerto Rican, put in four and a fraction seasons in the minors before being brought to Brooklyn in 1943. He played very well for the Dodgers during the war, made the mistake of jumping to the outlaw Mexican League in 1946, returned in 1949 when the Mexican League suspensions were lifted, and played for the Dodgers and Braves through 1951. Again, Luis Olmo was a player who came up during the war, but he was more than simply a "wartime player."

It is easy to denigrate the men who were in the big leagues primarily because of the manpower shortage—players like Edgar Busch, Butch Nieman, Dick Barrett, Augie Bergamo and so many others—but baseball owes a debt to them. Playing the game because they loved it, for the most part, they earned modest salaries, benefitted from no pension plan, and enjoyed less than luxurious playing and living conditions. But they played at a professional level, kept the game alive, and preserved its continuity at a time when many expert observers expected baseball to fold up its tents and fade away for the duration. The Newhousers, Musials, and Borowys got most of the headlines, but the game would have been in a bad way without the Bitsy Motts and Steve Mesners.

Obviously, in mid-1945 the owners were having to scratch and scrape more for players than had been the case two years earlier. There were more young players and more players whose best days were clearly behind them. Still, there were a good number of established ballplayers in action, there were veterans returning from the service, and there was a lot of good, certainly interesting, and frequently exciting baseball being played.

After the Fourth of July holiday, Hal Newhouser's next action came on July 7, when he won his 13th game with a 3-2, 10-inning victory over the Yankees. Doc Cramer tripled off loser Bill Zuber in the 10th inning and scored the winning run on York's single.

When Newhouser took the mound on July 12 in Boston, his team had moved to a four and a half game lead over the Yankees and the surprising Washington Senators, who had moved up on the strong hitting of Harlond Clift, Joe Kuhel, and George "Bingo" Binks. Newhouser was unable this time to increase the Detroit lead; despite another strong performance, he lost again to the Red Sox, 2-1, as Wilson once more silenced the Tiger bats.

On July 18, Harold pitched the opener of a twilight-night doubleheader at Washington and won it, 6-4, for his 14th victory. Al Benton won the second game for Detroit, but two days later, in another doubleheader, the Senators won two to even things up.

The next day, July 21, the Tigers went to Philadelphia and played one of the more bizarre games in their history. It was a game which went on, and on, and on, for 24 innings, tying the record for the longest game in American League history, and nobody ever won it. At the end of the 24th, Umpire Bill Summers called the game on account of darkness, and it went into the books as a 1-1 tie. Everyone's batting average dropped substantially as each team got excellent pitching. Russ Christopher pitched the first 13 innings for the A's, with reliever Joe Berry going the next 11. For the Tigers, Les Mueller pitched an incredible 19 innings, giving up one solitary run, before Trout came in and finished it for him. It was a long afternoon, but the tie necessitated a doubleheader the next day.

Newhouser pitched the opener and handled the A's with little difficulty in a 9-1 victory. He scattered four hits and drove in three runs himself. In the second game, Philadelphia's Don Black beat Benton, 2-1, so the day was another long standoff. The Tigers still led by two and a half games over the Senators and by four over the White Sox, with the Browns, Red Sox, and Yankees another half game back.

On the 27th, back home in Detroit, Newhouser beat the White Sox in a most unusual shutout. He did not have his best stuff, and the Chicagoans collected nine hits and three walks. They had runners on in every inning, but not one scored. Catcher Bob Swift threw out four of them trying to steal, and Newhouser was able to get the crucial out every time. Finally, Mayo led off the ninth with a home run to win it, 1-0.

On the last day of the month, Newhouser won his 17th game, but he had to go 12 innings to do it, beating the Browns, 5-4. He had some handicaps to overcome. Third baseman Bob Maier, Salsinger wrote in the *News*, "is as inept today as he was at the start of the season at fielding ground balls hit to his left. It was Harold Newhouser's misfortune that two were hit to Maier's left yesterday and that Maier bungled both chances badly. His two errors made possible all four St. Louis runs." Hal himself scored the winning run in the 12th after singling to start the inning.

As July ended, Steve O'Neill was optimistic: "Sooner or later nearly every team falls into a slump. We've had ours," alluding to the recent mediocre eastern trip, "and now that we're home to spend nearly all of August I look for the boys to increase their lead." Rumors that Virgil Trucks might soon be discharged from the service excited the Detroit skipper too.

On August 4, Newhouser was cruising along toward another shutout after six innings at Comiskey Park when things suddenly unraveled. He walked Johnny Dickshot to open the seventh, and Floyd Baker grounded a single into short right field. Intending to sacrifice, Guy Curtright laid down a bunt toward third, but when Maier was late getting to the ball it went for a single. A two-run double to right by Cass Michaels and a squeeze bunt by Mike Tresh meant three quick Chicago runs before Newhouser clamped down and blanked the Sox the rest of the way. The Tigers could get nothing more against Orval Grove, however, and the result was a 3–2 White Sox win.

The next day the B-29 Enola Gay dropped the first atomic bomb on the city of Hiroshima, and world events started to move very quickly. Within the following three days the Russian army invaded Japanese-held Manchuria, the United States dropped a second atomic bomb, this one on Nagasaki, and the forces within the Japanese government favoring capitulation gained strength. The war in the Pacific was clearly in its final phase.

The Tigers bolstered their pitching staff for the pennant run by picking two veteran righthanders off the waiver wire – George Caster from the Browns and Jim Tobin from the Boston Braves. Both Caster and Tobin would contribute to the Detroit cause on a number of occasions. The disappointing Joe Orrell was sent back to the minors.

On August 8, Newhouser started against Boston and was wild to begin the game. Three walks, two singles, and a wild pitch gave the Red Sox three runs in the first, but after that the Sox were able to do nothing with the Detroit lefthander. The Tigers scratched out one run against Jim Wilson, but they still trailed, 3-1, when Zeb Eaton pinch-hit for Newhouser with one on and two out in the ninth inning. Eaton's home run tied the game and sent it into overtime. In the next inning Greenberg hit a line drive off Wilson's head that fractured his skull. In the 12th inning, Tiger reliever Walter Wilson gave up four runs to lose the game.

Newhouser's next outing was against the Yankees on August 12, in the second game of a doubleheader. Tobin had won the opener for Steve O'Neill. Newhouser, behind the heavy hitting of Roy Cullenbine, who had a homer and a double, won easily, 8-2, for his 18th victory. The sweep of the New Yorkers raised the Tigers' lead to three games over Washington. Between the games of the doubleheader Tigers' radio announcer Ty Tyson presented Newhouser with a gold watch from *The Sporting News*, emblematic of his selection by the baseball newspaper as the league's top pitcher in 1944. On hand for the ceremony were the commander and baseball coach of Roose-Vanker American Legion Post No. 286, beaming at the recognition of their top graduate.

On August 14, the *Detroit News* featured a banner headline reading, "JAPS QUIT," marking V-J Day and the end of the war. (The headline the next day was "GAS RATIONING ENDS!" In the Motor City the termination of gas rationing received an exclamation point that the close of the war did not merit.) With the surrender of the last of the Axis powers, the fighting stopped, and peace was supposed to reign. All that was left now, theoretically, was the dismantling of the mighty American war machine while things returned to normal. In actuality, of course, it did not quite work out that way.

One thing which the end of the war did accomplish was to remove the dark cloud hanging over baseball, the ever-present threat that the game might be forced to suspend operations because of no ballplayers, no transportation, or no customers. The pennant races would continue, and there would be a World Series in 1945. The Cardinals, gunning for their fourth straight flag, were encountering surprising resistance from Charlie Grimm's Chicago Cubs in the National League, while the Tigers led in the American, threatened by the Senators.

O'Neill was optimistic as August moved along. Eddie Mayo, who had missed 13 games after an injury early in the month, was back in the lineup, as was Doc Cramer in center field; Greenberg and Cullenbine were hitting well, Richards was holding the pitching staff together, and Newhouser was showing no signs of a letup in performance.

A club which few had thought of as a possible contender, Ossie Bluege's Washington Senators, had emerged as the Tigers' principal rival. In mid-August Bluege brought his team into Detroit and took three games out of four. Only Newhouser prevented a sweep; he beat the Senators, 9–2, for his 19th win, allowing only six hits. It was his 10th straight victory over Washington, and it meant that the Tigers still led the Nats by a game and a half.

On August 20, Hal won his 20th game with a 4–0 shutout of the Athletics. Cramer and Cullenbine hit home runs as the Tigers' lefty became the major leagues' first 20-game winner of 1945.

Four days later Newhouser pitched before a nighttime

crowd of 46,477 at Cleveland's Municipal Stadium, a throng which turned out for the return to baseball of the Indians' Bob Feller. "Newhouser was far from being at top form" for that game, Feller later wrote, and "I felt a strong sense of personal rivalry as I faced him that night." Feller's was a triumphal return as he struck out 12 and allowed only four hits, and a two-run Pat Seerey home run staked him to a lead which he carried through to a 4–2 victory. It was a disappointment to Newhouser, obviously, but a relatively minor occurrence in the context of the pennant race. Nevertheless, the symbolism of the encounter struck many observers – the returning hero against the wartime wonder, Ulysses coming home to Ithaca – and the symbolic loss would come back to haunt Newhouser in later years, when people were busy denigrating his record.

On August 28, Prince Hal throttled the Browns at St. Louis by a 10–1 count, coasting on a four-hitter behind home runs by Cullenbine, Greenberg, and Maier. His seasonal record now stood at 21–8.

Four days later Newhouser was matched with Feller again, this time before 25,742 at Briggs Stadium. For two innings, the Detroit lefty looked unbeatable, but in the third he suddenly seemed to lose his stuff. The Indians scored three runs, although Maier's error on a double-play ball with the bases loaded hurt badly. It turned out that Newhouser had pulled a muscle in his back in the third inning, and by the seventh, when he left the game, he could hardly raise his arm. Feller also failed to survive the seventh, and the Tigers eventually won, 5–4, with Tobin beating Ed Klieman. The second Feller-Newhouser encounter was a draw, but the Indians were going nowhere and the injury to his star pitcher was a major concern to O'Neill.

When play ended on Labor Day, September 3, the Tigers had a slim lead of two games over Washington. The Browns were three and a half behind Detroit, and the Yankees were another game back. With most of a month to go the Tigers could ill afford to lose their best and most consistent pitcher. They were leaving for the final eastern trip of the year, starting with a mammoth seven-game series in Yankee Stadium, and their pitching was thin at best. Tommy Bridges had returned, but the 38-year-old righthander looked like a shadow of his pre-war self. As the Tigers entrained for New York, Newhouser was left behind in Detroit for treatment at the Henry Ford Hospital. Steve O'Neill wrote his ace's name tentatively into his pitching rotation for Friday, September 7; Newhouser was scheduled to fly in from Detroit the day before. Whether he would be able to pitch effectively, no one knew.

On September 4, Dizzy Trout won the opener of the New York series, beating Allan Gettel, 10-0, as Cramer and Greenberg hit home runs. The next day the two teams split a doubleheader; the Tigers took the opener 10-7 behind home runs by Mayo, Cullenbine, and Greenberg, but the Yankees and Joe Page beat Al Benton in the nightcap, 5-1. Meanwhile the Browns and the Senators also split a doubleheader.

On the sixth, Washington took two from the Browns, while the Yankees and Detroit split another doubleheader. Roy Cullenbine homered in each game, but the Yankees pounded Tobin, 14-5, in the opener before Les Mueller came back for O'Neill with a 5-2 victory over Bill Zuber. The Tigers now led Washington by a game and a half. They waited anxiously to see how Newhouser would pitch the next day. They knew that he still complained of soreness in the area of his left shoulder blade, but O'Neill had already used 11 pitchers in the first five games of the series. The Tigers were desperate for Prince Hal to bail them out. As Dan Daniel wrote in the *New York World-Telegram*, "O'Neill must have a winning Newhouser the rest of the way."

Before the game Newhouser visited the trainer's room,

and Dr. Raymond Forsyth, an osteopath, gave him a shot of novocaine to dull the pain in his shoulder. O'Neill told his pitcher simply to "see how far he could go." Then Newhouser went to the mound for what he later called "the most peculiar game I ever pitched."

In the first inning, facing the dangerous Charlie Keller, back from the service and hitting as well as ever, Newhouser needed a strike. He threw a good curveball past the left-handed "King Kong," but, as he later related, "a terrific pain shot up my back and I knew I couldn't throw any more like it." Newhouser called catcher Richards out to the mound and told him what happened. "Might as well forget about a curveball signal," Newhouser said; "I just can't throw one."

He went the rest of the way throwing just fastballs and change-ups while the Yankees looked for that wicked curve again. Harold never threw another one, but the Yankees never figured out that he could not throw it again until the game was out of hand. Newhouser limited the New Yorkers to four hits, all singles, as he won, 5–0. Rudy York hit a home run, Eddie Mayo was four-for-four, and Prince Hal had his 22nd win. "Believe me," he said, "you don't beat the Yankees very often on just one curveball."

Roger Wolff of the Senators beat St. Louis, 3–2, to keep his team one and a half games back, but a relieved Steve O'Neill said of his ace, "I don't think he was ever better," and the Detroit players felt a renewed jolt of confidence. The next day Dizzy Trout finished off the Yankee series (and the Yankee pennant hopes) with an 11–4 win over Joe Page. The Tigers could still not shake Washington, however, as the Nats, behind Pete Appleton, beat the Browns again while the new president, Harry Truman of Missouri, watched.

On September 9, the Senators took a doubleheader from the White Sox. The Tigers played two at Boston, but they won only the opener, 6–3. The second game was called on account of darkness after 11 innings, still tied at 3-3. The Tigers led by one. On the 10th the Senators and White Sox split another doubleheader, as did the Tigers and Red Sox. Dave Ferriss of Boston won the opener, 9-2, but Stubby Overmire took the nightcap for Detroit, 2-1, to maintain the one-game lead over Washington.

The next day it was Hal Newhouser's turn to pitch, but the lefthander was bothered by a lump under his left shoulder blade. O'Neill called upon Trout instead, and Dizzy rewarded the skipper with a two-hit, 5-0 victory over the Red Sox. In Washington, when Guy Curtright pushed a ninth-inning run home on a squeeze bunt, the White Sox beat the Senators, 2-1. The Tigers led by two.

On the following day the Tigers had another doubleheader scheduled in Philadelphia. Newhouser warmed up for five minutes but then advised O'Neill that his shoulder was still too sore to pitch. Benton beat Bobo Newsom of the A's, 7-4, in the first game, with relief help from George Caster. In the second game, unfortunately, the Tigers and Trout lost, 3-2, in 16 innings on a hit by Roberto Estalella. With the state of his pitching staff, Steve O'Neill needed no extra-inning games. Wolff of the Senators beat Cleveland, 5-1, to cut a half game from Detroit's lead.

On September 13, with Newhouser still unable to pitch, Jim Tobin led the A's, 2-1, going into the ninth, only to give up two runs (the second on a bases-loaded walk) to lose the game. When Walt Masterson of the Senators beat Feller, 4-0, on a two-hitter, Ossie Bluege's club had climbed to within a half game of the lead. A big headline in the *Detroit News* that day read: "HOW TO GET WORLD SERIES TICKETS," but the race was still very much up for grabs.

The next day, a rainy day in Philadelphia, with the game scoreless in the top of the fifth, O'Neill sent Bobby

Maier from third to try to steal home. Dick Fowler, on the mound for the A's, pitched out and should have had Maier, but catcher Buddy Rosar missed the tag. After Les Mueller retired the home team in the fifth, the rains came for good and the Tigers escaped with a 1-0 win. The Senators, though, came back with three runs in the ninth to beat Cleveland, 6-5; they still trailed the Tigers by a mere half game as the Detroit club journeyed on to Washington for a five-game series.

The big matchup began with a doubleheader on September 15. Newhouser started the first game; he gave up a hit and a walk in the first inning and struck out one hitter. Unfortunately, there was more rain, and the game was held up for an hour and six minutes. When play resumed Stubby Overmire was on the mound for Detroit. O'Neill explained later: "There was nothing wrong with Hal after that opening inning but the time taken out was so long that it wouldn't have been good for him to warm up again. He'll be all right tomorrow."

Overmire came through, with relief help from Caster, and beat the Nats, 7-4; Cullenbine's three hits led the way. In the nightcap Trout won his 18th, beating Mickey Haefner, 7-3, behind the bats of York, Hoover, and Outlaw. The jubilant Tigers were now two and a half games ahead. They got word, too, that Virgil Trucks was getting out of the navy and was on the way to help them.

On the 16th there was another twinbill. Again, Newhouser started the first game. "They needled Newhouser before the game," wrote Joe Williams of the *New York World-Telegram*, "injections to ease the anguish of a torn back muscle." The novocaine helped – some. Although his control was far from sharp, Hal pitched the entire game. Unfortunately, so did Roger Wolff, and the Senator knuckleballer was effective as he beat the Tigers and their ace, 3-2. Hal's record fell to 22-9. In the second game, Benton beat another of the many Washington

knuckleball pitchers, Johnny Niggeling, to boost the
Detroit club's lead back to two and a half games. A fine
relief job by Trout helped to nail down the win.

The final game of the series was rained out on September 17, but it was rescheduled for the open date on
the next day. The Nats took an early 5-0 lead, but the
Tigers came back with five to tie. In the seventh inning,
though, the Senators scored four runs against Caster
and Newhouser; Prince Hal came in just long enough
to give up a bases-loaded triple to George Case that made
a 6-5 Washington lead 9-5. Zeb Eaton allowed three
more runs in the eighth as the Senators coasted to a
12-5 win.

As the Tigers left Washington for Cleveland, they
could feel good with a three-out-of-five victory in the
Senators series. They had a one and a half game lead,
with eight games to play. And they knew that the
Senators had only five games left; Clark Griffith, the
Washington owner, never dreaming that his club would
be in contention, had arranged before the season that
his team's campaign would end a week ahead of everyone
else in the league, so that he could rent his ball park
to the pro football Redskins. Now his Senators would
have to sit and watch their pennant race go on without
them for that last week. With all this going for them,
the Tigers still had one big worry – Hal Newhouser. Since
his shutout of the Yankees 11 days earlier, Newhouser
had been able to pitch only 10 2/3 innings, over three
games, and none too effectively. They had to worry about
the condition of his left arm and shoulder.

In Cleveland, Feller beat Les Mueller, 2-0, on September 19, cutting the Detroit lead to one game over
the idle Senators. It stayed that way the next day, when
Allie Reynolds of the Indians beat Benton, 6-1, and the
Nats lost a big chance to move up by losing to Joe Page
of the Yankees, 6-3. On the 21st the Tigers had an off
day, and New York's Bill Zuber beat the Senators' Master-

son, 5–3, on homers by Nick Etten and Snuffy Stirnweiss. The Tigers now led by a game and a half; they
had six games left while Washington had only three.
Then, on September 22, Prince Hal Newhouser announced that he was back. Not with words, but, more
effectively, with actions. He was back in town as the
Tigers returned to Briggs Stadium after their long road
trip, and he was back in form. In a game which mathe-
matically eliminated the defending champions from the
race, Newhouser stifled the Browns on four hits and
won, 9–0. Newhouser, Salsinger wrote, "dominated the
game . . . was in complete charge all the way and . . . got
stronger as he went along." Along with his pitching, Hal
drove in three runs with a double and triple. It was Hal
Newhouser's game and, once again, Hal Newhouser's
pennant race.

At Shibe Park in Philadelphia, Roger Wolff kept the
Senators one and a half games behind with a 2–0 gem
over the A's and sidearming Russ Christopher. But the
schedule was running out for Washington.

On September 23, Nelson Potter of the Browns beat
Trout, 5–0. In Philadelphia, the Senators' Dutch Leonard
had a 3–0 lead after seven innings but the A's came back
on an umpire's bad call to tie the game and send it into
overtime. In the 12th inning Washington outfielder
George Binks forgot his sunglasses and lost a fly ball
in the sun to set up a 4–3 win for Connie Mack's club.
The Senators won the nightcap, 4–3, their last game of
the season. But the first-game defeat meant that they
were still one game behind with none left to play, rather
than tied with Detroit. The Tigers had four games still
to play and could win the title with two victories. Ossie Bluege and Clark Griffith, Roger Wolff and Dutch
Leonard, George Case and George Binks – all they could
do was wait to see what happened.

The Tigers' game with Cleveland on September 24 was
rained out, and there was no game scheduled for the 25th.

O'Neill opened the doubleheader on September 26 with his ace, and Newhouser was brilliant once again. Paired against Allie Reynolds of the Indians before a crowd of 41,880, Prince Hal simply blew the opposition away. He scattered seven hits, gave up no runs, and struck out 10 as the Tigers won easily, 11–0. Greenberg and Cullenbine each had a home run and three runs batted in, Richards drove in a pair, and Newhouser hit two doubles. The victory clinched at least a tie for the pennant and gave Hal a record of 24–9.

In the second game, however, with a chance to win the flag before the big home crowd, the Tigers were unable to handle Steve Gromek, the local boy from Hamtramck, and the Indians' righthander beat Benton, 3–2. The Tigers still led by a game, but the Senators were not yet dead.

The Tigers had two games to play at St. Louis, and two losses to the Browns would necessitate a playoff on Monday, October 1, at Briggs Stadium. O'Neill considered the possibility of leaving Newhouser home in Detroit, because if they lost both games he would want Newhouser ready and rested to pitch the playoff game against Washington. He ultimately decided to take his star lefthander along to St. Louis – he wanted Hal to share in the celebration if they won the pennant at Sportsman's Park – but he announced that his pitching for the series would be the newly-arrived Trucks on Saturday and Overmire on Sunday. Potter and Muncrief were the probable Brownie pitchers.

On Saturday the 29th, rain falling in St. Louis for the ninth consecutive day postponed the game, forcing one final doubleheader on the season's last day. At that point one last dreadful possibility, almost too dismal to contemplate, loomed up before poor Ossie Bluege, the Senators' manager: if rain should force the cancellation of the final Browns-Tigers games, or even one of them, Detroit would win the pennant. Under league rules at the time, any games not played by the end of the scheduled season were lost forever, even though they might have a bearing on the championship. For Bluege's team to have a chance, the Browns and the Tigers must play both games on September 30, and the Tigers had to lose them both.

Sunday, September 30, was another dark and rainy day in St. Louis. It was an intermittent rain, and, as game time approached and passed, the groundskeepers at frowzy old Sportsman's Park worked hard to get the diamond in condition to play baseball. The field was muddy but playable—barely. It was drizzling, and the game began an hour late. Virgil Trucks started the opener of the doubleheader against Potter.

Trucks, making his return to baseball in the most dramatic circumstances possible, gave up a run in the first on a double by Gutteridge and a single by veteran Lou Finney, but he settled down after that. In the fifth inning a walk and singles by Skeeter Webb and Mayo tied the score. In the sixth Cullenbine walked and took second after York fouled out to catcher Frank Mancuso at the screen. After an intentional walk to Outlaw, Richards singled home the go-ahead run for the Tigers. The Browns loaded the bases with one out in the sixth, and O'Neill lifted Trucks. For relief he brought in Hal Newhouser, leading many to wonder what he would do for pitching if he had to face a playoff on Monday. It was obvious that the Detroit skipper wanted to win the flag then and there.

Newhouser worked his way out of trouble and the Browns failed to score in the sixth. In the seventh inning, though, Gene Moore doubled and Stephens drove him home with a hit to tie the score once again. In the top of the eighth, Detroit mounted another threat, but Greenberg was caught off third to kill the inning. In the bottom half, Finney singled again. He was forced by Pete Gray, the Browns' one-armed outfielder, but George

McQuinn's double off the right-field screen brought the speedy Gray around, and the Browns led 3–2, as the day grew darker.

Newhouser was due to lead off the ninth, but O'Neill chose to pinch-hit for him with little Hubby Walker. Hub, a 39-year-old who had not been in the big leagues since playing a couple of seasons with Cincinnati in the mid-1930s, was hitting only .091 for the Tigers (2-for-22) while Newhouser was a .257 hitter, and Walker was 0-for-14 for the year as a pinch hitter. Still, O'Neill made the switch, and Hubby promptly rewarded him with a base hit. Red Borom went in to run for him. When Webb bunted, McQuinn played the ball late to second and both runners were safe. Mayo laid down another bunt; this time the throw went to first and the two runners moved up. The Browns walked Doc Cramer intentionally to set up a double play, even though Greenberg was on deck.

Big Henry watched Potter's first pitch go by, but his swing on the next delivery sent the ball sailing into the left-field bleachers for a grand slam home run; Borom, Webb, and Cramer scored ahead of him. The Tigers suddenly led, 6–3, and that dark and gloomy afternoon seemed bright and sunny to Steve O'Neill and his men. The manager sent Al Benton to the mound for the bottom of the ninth, and Benton retired the Browns with no further damage. The Detroit Tigers were the American League champions for 1945, and Hal Newhouser, though struggling, picked up his 25th win in the clincher.

The players whooped and shouted for a few minutes as the photographers got the necessary pictures, but then they had to get ready to go out and play the second game. After a half inning, however, the rains came down hard again and the umpires called the game off. In the gathering darkness it was unlikely in any event that the required five innings could have been played. Regardless of the rain and regardless of the darkness, Hank Greenberg's slam had won the pennant for the Tigers on the field; they were spared the embarrassment of being called "Umbrella Champs."

As the Tigers rode the six o'clock train back to Detroit and the roaring welcome which awaited them in the Motor City, they could look back on a most satisfying season. Their home attendance of 1,280,341 led the majors and was just 9,000 shy of the league record set by the Yankees in 1920. They had vanquished a gallant challenger in the Washington club – a team which hit only one home run all season in its home ball park, massive Griffith Stadium, but which had the deepest pitching staff around in 1945. Mayo, Cullenbine, Greenberg, and Cramer all had fine seasons, and Paul Richards set high standards for a catcher. Towering above them all was their linchpin, the ace on whom they depended time after time to win the big one, the man they called Prince Hal, Harold Newhouser. He pushed and pulled and carried the Tigers to a pennant.

11
CHAMPIONS
OF THE WORLD

The 1945 World Series between the Tigers and the National League champion Chicago Cubs has become famous through the years as the one about which Chicago baseball writer Warren Brown said beforehand that neither team could win. As it turned out, there was quite a lot of sloppy play in the series (as there frequently is), and there were a number of very good performances. Part of the problem with the 1945 Series, one suspects, is that the Cubs' consistently mediocre performance in the years since makes it fashionable to poke fun at their last success. Nevertheless, both clubs featured top-notch players for whom no apologies were needed, such as Stan Hack, Bill Nicholson, Phil Cavarretta, Andy Pafko, Hank Borowy, and Claude Passeau of the Cubs and Tigers Cramer, Cullenbine, Greenberg, York, Newhouser, Benton, Trout, and Trucks.

The start of the Series was scheduled for Wednesday, October 3, at Briggs Stadium. The first three games were to be played in Detroit, as federal travel restrictions limited baseball to just one change of scene. Steve O'Neill said that Newhouser would open for the Tigers after the two and two-thirds innings he had pitched in the pennant-clincher; "the work he did against the Browns Sunday will just set him up right," the Tiger manager said.

For the Cubs it would be Hank Borowy, the blond righthander who had come to Chicago from the Yankees in a mysterious midsummer waiver deal; Borowy had pitched the Cubs to the pennant. Hank told reporters, not too diplomatically, "Naturally, I like the assignment of pitching against the Tigers in the opener. I always like to face clubs I can beat, and I think you'll find I've beaten this club pretty often."

Big words, thought Detroit rooters, but Borowy made them stand up. Before the game Newhouser was given another shot of novocaine in his shoulder. Then he went out to face the Cubs, amid all the hoopla of a World Series opener, with the new commissioner, Senator Chandler, on hand for the first time.

The first inning was a frustrating nightmare for Newhouser. With one out, Don Johnson beat out an infield squibber. He stole second while Newhouser was working on Lowrey, who flied out to Cramer. Cavarretta hit a slow bouncer to Mayo and just beat the throw to first, with Johnson taking third. After a Richards passed ball allowed the first run to score, O'Neill ordered an intentional walk for Andy Pafko. Nicholson then hit a high fly to the screen in right that Cullenbine probably should have caught. When he missed it, the hit went for a triple and two more runs scored. Mickey Livingston's single to score Nicholson completed the four-run damage. In the boxscore it looked like Newhouser had been pounded, but it was really two infield hits, an intentional walk, a passed ball, and a fly that might have been caught that did him in.

In the bottom of the first, the Tigers collected two hits and two walks against Borowy, but Cramer's double-play ball in the middle of it all meant that no runs scored. In the second inning, Newhouser struck out the three men he faced — Roy Hughes, Borowy, and Hack — and it appeared that the lefty was settling down.

In the third inning, however, trouble erupted again and

this time Newhouser was hit hard. Johnson led off with a line drive which Cramer misplayed into a double. Lowrey sacrificed, and Cavarretta's single through the pitcher's box made the score, 5-0. Pafko hit a long double to left-center field, and Cavarretta scored. Hal retired Nicholson on an infield popup, but Livingston's single scored another run. O'Neill brought in Benton, and Newhouser headed for the showers, to the shock and amazement of the crowd of 54,637.

The Tigers never did get to Borowy, and the final score was 9-0. In the locker room after the game, Newhouser told the press, "I thought I had good stuff and my control was all right. If I had gotten past the first inning I would have been all right." Then he thought it over and said, "After looking over those hitters, I'll be a lot better pitcher against the Cubs next time."

Manager Charlie Grimm of Chicago said, "He had good stuff out there, but we waded right into him. He's still a great pitcher in my book." The Cubs would see a lot more of Hal Newhouser, but it was a jolt to the Tiger faithful to watch their ace being treated so harshly. The principal topic of conversation in the Motor City that evening was the surprising ineffectiveness of Newhouser, whom Detroit fans now relied upon to win every time out. That he could simply have had a bad day – to which even the best are entitled from time to time – did not seem to occur to many people. Besides, with the game Borowy pitched, even a shutout would have netted Newhouser only a tie.

The next day, before a crowd of 53,636, the Tigers evened the Series. Virgil Trucks pitched a steady seven-hitter, holding Chicago to one run, on a fourth-inning double by Cavarretta followed by Nicholson's single. The Tigers came back in the fifth on a run-producing single by Roger Cramer and Greenberg's three-run home run. The third game saw the Cubs' Claude Passeau put together the best pitching performance in World Series history to that time, a one-hit, one-walk masterpiece for a 3–0 win. Rudy York singled over the shortstop's head in the second inning, and that was it for Detroit. Stubby Overmire pitched well, but not well enough.

After Game Three, the two clubs moved on to Chicago, and O'Neill trotted out Paul "Dizzy" Trout for the first game in Wrigley Field. Trout and Ray Prim of the Cubs were working on even terms until the top of the fourth, when a one-out walk to Mayo was followed by singles from the bats of Cramer and Greenberg and a Cullenbine double, producing two runs. Prim was replaced by the veteran Paul Derringer, and an intentional walk and a single by Richards got two more runs home. This was more than enough for Trout to win it, 4–1, to tie the Series at two games each.

The fifth game was a rematch of the first game starters, Newhouser and Borowy. The Detroit lefthander had appeared jittery in the opener, but for Game Five he was all business and too much for the Cubs. The final score was 8–4 Tigers, which was somewhat misleading. Newhouser pitched an excellent game but was plagued by his teammates' poor fielding. Clifford Bloodgood of *Baseball Magazine* wrote that the game was "a comedy of errors . . . loosely played . . . The official box score can never come close to revealing the true story." Standing out in bold relief, Bloodgood said, was Newhouser: "He hurled a far better game than is shown in the records and could sue his colleagues for non-support."

In the third inning, after the Tigers had scored a run on a walk, a Mayo single, and a fly ball by Cramer, the Cubs came back when, with two out, Borowy doubled to left for the first hit against Newhouser. Stan Hack then poked a hit into center, and when Cramer fumbled it, Borowy, who had been held up at third, was sent home. Newhouser then picked Hack off first base.

After two more scoreless innings, in which Prince Hal retired all six Chicago hitters, Borowy came apart.

Cramer led off the sixth with a single and moved up a base when Pafko bobbled the ball. Greenberg drove Cramer in with a double down the left-field line, and Cullenbine followed with an infield hit. When York lined another run-scoring single to center, Borowy was finished. Against reliever Hy Vandenberg, Outlaw sacrificed and Richards was purposely passed to load the bases. When Newhouser walked, too, Cullenbine scored and it became 4–1. York scored an additional run on Webb's infield grounder.

After Newhouser pitched another one-two-three inning, the Tigers picked up a run in the seventh against Paul Derringer. In the bottom of the inning Johnson fanned, but Lowrey looped a hit to center. After Cavarretta walked, Pafko grounded to the pitcher, who threw to second to force Cavarretta, Lowrey moving over to third. Nicholson grounded a ball to third baseman Outlaw, who committed what writer Dan Daniel called "the boner of the series." Instead of throwing to first for the easy third out on the slow-moving Nicholson, Outlaw for some reason elected to go to second. The startled Eddie Mayo was late covering the bag, Pafko was safe, and Lowrey scored. Another run came around when Livingston hit a ground-rule double to right, but Newhouser then calmly fanned pinch hitter Dewey Williams to end the inning.

The Cubs got another hit in the eighth when Mayo lost Frank Secory's wind-blown popup in the sun, but they scored no runs in that inning. In the ninth Detroit picked up two more runs on doubles by Greenberg and Cullenbine, but the Tiger fielders were not yet through with Hal Newhouser. Cavarretta led off the inning with an easy fly ball to right center, which dropped between Cramer and Cullenbine for a two-base hit.

Cramer later said, "I could have caught the ball but Cullenbine kept shouting 'All right — All right.' When I heard this I stopped and then, to my surprise, the ball plopped to the ground. I asked Cullenbine why he didn't make the catch and he told me: 'When I called all right, all right, I meant, all right, you catch it.'"

After Pafko struck out, Nicholson nubbed a ball into center for a base hit, scoring Cavarretta. Livingston flied to right – a ball Cullenbine *did* catch – and then Bill Schuster fouled out to Richards to end the game.

Newhouser was charged with four runs, all earned, and seven hits. He walked two and struck out nine. Daniel said that "with good fielding and throwing," the Tigers . should have had a shutout rather than an 8–4 victory. Joe Williams of the *New York World-Telegram* said of Newhouser: "It was easy for him to handle the Cubs. Handling his own Tigers was something else. What he did was beat two teams in one game."

The teams were just warming up for the sixth game, which was another bizarre exhibition of baseball. "One of the dizziest World Series games ever played," *The Sporting News* called it. The Cubs won it, 8–7, in 12 innings to tie the Series again and force a seventh and final game. The game featured errors, baserunning blunders, Rudy York converting a bunt into a base hit by falling down as he tried to field it, and the play which has created an enduring image for the 1945 Series – elderly Chuck Hostetler rounding third with a crucial run in the seventh inning, falling down between third and home, and being tagged out as he lay sprawled in the dirt. Hank Greenberg hit a two-out homer in the eighth inning to tie the game at 7–7. Borowy and Trout, both pitching in relief, restored some order as they each held the opposition scoreless through the ninth, 10th, and 11th innings. In the bottom of the 12th, with two outs and a Cub runner on first, Hack hit a line drive to left that bounced in front of Greenberg and then up and over his shoulder as the winning run scored. Originally scored a hit and an error, it was later changed to a double for the Cub third baseman.

October 9 was an off-day before Game Seven, but it was so cold in Chicago that neither team worked out. Charlie Grimm, the Cubs' manager, looked at his ragged pitching staff and tried to come up with a starter for the final game. He considered Derringer, ancient Hy Vandenberg, and fastballer Paul Erickson, and none of these possibilities held much appeal for him. Finally, on the theory that it's always best to go with one's best, he decided on Borowy, even though Hank had pitched four innings in Game Six. For O'Neill, there was never any doubt; he would use Hal Newhouser, even on two days rest. That night Newhouser pulled the cord out of the telephone box in his room in the Stevens Hotel; he wanted no disturbance of his sleep.

There were 41,590 spectators in Wrigley Field the next day, and they had hardly settled into their seats before their Cubs were far behind. Skeeter Webb led off the game with a hard single to right. Mayo also singled to right, and Webb raced around to third. Cramer lined a single to left to score Webb, and it was apparent that the arm-weary Borowy had nothing. Charlie Grimm made a hasty appearance at the mound to take his pitcher out. Derringer relieved, and Greenberg laid down a sacrifice bunt. Cullenbine was given an intentional walk, and after York popped up, Jimmy Outlaw walked, to force a run home. It was the third bases-loaded walk the Cubs had given up in the Series. Paul Richards then struck the key blow, a big double to left which scored all three baserunners. The Tigers had a 5-0 lead for Hal Newhouser before he had thrown a pitch.

Unfortunately, Newhouser, coming back on short rest, did not appear to have his stuff. As he warmed up, his curve was not breaking and his fastball was not moving. Second baseman Mayo told himself that "I don't think Hal's going to get past the first two or three innings." Richards could see the problem, too, so he started calling for change-ups, on perhaps four of every five pitches. The Cubs, who had seen more fastballs than anything else in Newhouser's first two appearances, were looking for the same thing again, and Hal kept them off stride with the slow stuff. Chicago scored a run in the first inning, but Newhouser blanked them in the second and third. In the fourth inning, he gave up another run on a triple by Pafko that Cramer might have caught, but by now the movement had returned to his fastball. Just as the Cubs were adjusting to the soft pitches, Hal switched to his fastball for the rest of the game. He shut down the Cubs again until the eighth.

In the meantime the Tigers scored one run in the second inning (on another walk with the bases loaded), another in the seventh, and two in the eighth. A Chicago run in the bottom of the eighth made it 9–3, and that was the score as Newhouser went out to pitch the last frame. After Hughes singled through the box, Newhouser fanned pinch hitter Clyde McCullough for his 10th strikeout of the game. Hack flied to Cramer, and when Don Johnson grounded to Webb for the final out, the Tigers were the champions of baseball.

The story of the 1945 World Series was the incredibly bad Tiger outfield play, the gritty mound work of Hank Borowy, timely hitting by Greenberg, Cramer, and Richards, the one-hitter by Passeau, and, ultimately, the outstanding pitching of Trout, Trucks, and especially Newhouser for Detroit. Prince Hal's left arm was tired from the heavy load it had carried throughout the season, and his shoulder was still sore. Nevertheless, he came through when O'Neill and his teammates counted on him.

Dan Daniel wrote: "Hurricane Hal Newhouser . . . was acclaimed the hero of the 42nd classic . . . At no stage of the Series was Newhouser in his best form. Like all the other participants, he went into the competition over-tired physically and frazzled mentally. But when Hal had to win to give the Bengals a three-to-two edge, he won.

And when he had to triumph in the grand finale, he still had enough of his spectacular speed, baffling change of pace and cunning curve to make the Bruins look very bad." Hal's 22 strikeouts in the series set a new record, one which stood until broken by Sandy Koufax 18 years later, in a much more free-swinging era.

Newhouser was, once again, the key man for the Detroit ball club, the one man who was indispensable to them. After the season ended, he was voted the Most Valuable Player in the American League for the second year in a row, finishing far ahead of teammate Eddie Mayo, the runner-up. He was named Player of the Year by *The Sporting News*, and his numbers for the season were once again spectacular. He won 25 and lost nine, and his percentage of .735 led the league. His earned run average of 1.81 was far below everyone else's, and he led in innings pitched, 313, complete games, 29, shutouts, 8, strikeouts, 212 (83 ahead of the next closest competitor), fewest hits per nine innings, and most strikeouts per nine innings. As H. G. Salsinger wrote, "When the final story of the American League season of 1945 is written, the main character will be Harold Newhouser." Newhouser pitched one critical game after another for Steve O'Neill, and, as a result, the Tigers were champions of the world.

But there was still a nagging question as Newhouser and his teammates celebrated their triumph. Salsinger had tried to deal with it early in September when he told of getting a letter from overseas asking where Newhouser would rank if he had to pitch against pre-war hitters. "Pitching against pre-war lineups," the letterwriter stated, "you'd never have heard of Newhouser." Answered Salsinger: "It is true that Newhouser has pitched against inferior batters in the last two years, but it is equally true that Newhouser has been supported by an inferior cast. The Detroit club has been correspondingly weak in batting and fielding. You see, it all evens up."

Or does it? Even Salsinger was giving only an opinion. The test would come when all the players were back from the military service. Would Prince Hal Newhouser overwhelm the hitters in 1946 as he had done in 1945? That question could only be answered on the ball field.

12
THE BIG BOYS
COME BACK

Jack Zeller went out on top. The veteran general manager of the Detroit club announced his retirement after the World Series, effective at the end of the year. A longtime minor league executive named George Trautman was named to succeed Zeller, with the dual responsibility of keeping the Tigers winners and moving the franchise into the post-war world.

Obviously, conversion back to a peacetime basis was the key to everything Americans were doing in late 1945. The most popular songs in the country that November were sung by Kitty Kallen, with the Harry James band, and they expressed what millions of people felt: "It's Been a Long, Long Time" and "I'll Buy That Dream." The war was over, the Depression was just a bad memory, and now Americans were anxious to have the things they had been told they were fighting and sacrificing for – peace, prosperity, and the good life. Unfortunately, the end of the war brought problems with the Russians, shortages, labor strife, and inflation; the good life had not quite arrived. Conversion to a peacetime economy, the country learned, would not be without some painful adjustments.

The return to peacetime baseball was very much on Harold Newhouser's mind after the 1945 season. He spent the winter in Detroit, working for a company that distributed display cases for fruits and vegetables, and the first thing he had to do was to regain the 15 pounds he had lost during the pennant race and the World Series. Then he concentrated mentally on the challenge of pitching once again to the best hitters in the game, the men who were returning from the war – Williams, the DiMaggios, Doerr, Appling, Dickey, Chapman, Gordon, and the rest.

Newhouser knew that he had matured as a pitcher, knew that the sensational records of 1944 and 1945 were not achieved simply because the quality of baseball played was lower during those years. "I learned something about pitching," he said, "I learned something about myself." Still, he had reservations about the challenge of post-war baseball:

> Naturally I was leery of going back after I had pitched to DiMaggio and Williams and all for four years and was not a winning pitcher. And all of a sudden to come back, well, anybody with any common sense would say, "well, yeah, you've been winning but now the big boys are back. What are you going to do?" Well, I was a different pitcher, too. I was in a different frame of mind. They didn't know that. They just thought the old Hal Newhouser's here. They didn't know that the kid grew up a little bit. He's not a boy anymore; he's a man.

On January 10, 1946, Trautman traded Rudy York to the Red Sox for infielder Eddie Lake. "I'm counting on Lake to be my shortstop," he said, and he planned to move Greenberg back to first base: "I believe Hank will find it easier at first base and will not object to the switch." The Detroit club also announced the appointment of Lou D'Annunzio, the "bird dog" who tipped off

Wish Egan to the sandlot play of Hal Newhouser, among others, to the position of a full-time scout.

Four days later, Newhouser participated in a dinner honoring Egan at Detroit's Hotel Statler. Among the other players present, also discoveries of the old Irishman, were McCosky, Wakefield, Cullenbine, and White Sox catcher Mike Tresh. "He's not [just] a scout," Newhouser said of Egan, "he's a real friend."

Several weeks later, the Tigers headed for spring training in Lakeland, Florida. It was like old times; Evansville, Indiana, was long forgotten. Hal Newhouser took his family down from Detroit before camp opened, even though he had not yet signed a contract for 1946. With two consecutive MVP awards in his pocket, Prince Hal felt that he was entitled to a rather more substantial share of Walter Briggs' money.

Steve O'Neill was soon in mid-season form. The Tigers, O'Neill said, would be the "team to beat" in the upcoming pennant race, although he conceded that New York and Boston might give them trouble. He projected an infield of Greenberg, Mayo, Lake, and Mike Higgins (or Billy Hitchcock, if age had taken its toll on Higgins), an outfield of Wakefield, Pat Mullin, and McCosky, Birdie Tebbetts and Richards behind the plate, and a pitching staff led by Newhouser, Trout, Trucks, and Benton. On paper, Detroit looked formidable, but there was a long gap between the start of spring training and the days of early October.

Newhouser became an official holdout on the 20th of February, when training opened. Still, O'Neill knew his man: "Hal will sign all right," he said. "He wouldn't be down here if he didn't intend to sign. I hope he signs soon so that he'll have plenty of time to get ready."

On the 21st, Newhouser donned his uniform and posed for photographers, and the next day he ended his brief holdout by signing for a reported $45,000, which made him at the time the highest-paid pitcher in the history of baseball. "There was never any vast difference between what Newhouser asked and the club offered," Salsinger reported. "After several conferences the club agreed to his request," which may or may not have happened, but it appears that Newhouser was able to work out a pretty good contract for those reserve-clause, pre-free-agency days. It was time to go to work.

Spring training in 1946 turned out to be a rather unsettling time. In Daytona Beach, Branch Rickey's two black players, John Wright and Jackie Robinson, were working out with the minor league Montreal Royals, but everyone in baseball was aware of them. There were a number of lengthy holdouts — the new Detroit infielder Eddie Lake did not sign his contract until mid-March — and the wealthy Pasquel brothers raided American camps for their upstart and outlaw Mexican League. Among the major leaguers who succumbed to the lure of Jorge Pasquel's golden pesos were George Hausmann, Roy Zimmerman, and Sal Maglie of the Giants, Murray Franklin of the Tigers, Roberto Estalella of the A's, and — the two biggest names — Mickey Owen of the Dodgers and the Browns' Vern Stephens, though Stephens was unimpressed by what he found in Mexico and escaped back to the United States on April 5. There was big money in the post-war air, in the United States as well as in Mexico, and the players wanted to share in it. Snuffy Stirnweiss of the Yankees, the defending batting champion, held out for more pay, and Larry MacPhail, the new owner of the Yanks, decided to shop Stirnweiss around. Only one team, MacPhail said, showed any interest, and that was Detroit, which might need infield help with the defection of Franklin, the holdout of Lake, and the advanced ages of Higgins and Mayo. MacPhail said, "The Tigers asked for him [Stirnweiss] and wanted to know if they had anybody in whom I might be interested. I told them, 'Yes . . . Hal Newhouser,' and the conversation lagged appreciably thereafter."

Since Steve O'Neill permitted his ace to work himself into shape on his own schedule, Newhouser mapped out a program that called for conditioning by easy stages. He tried to reach his pitching peak just before the season opened, and he could not understand how so many of the other Detroit pitchers could be working as hard as they were so early. He told Salsinger he thought they were making a mistake. Of course, many of the pitchers in that first crowded post-war camp were pitching for survival in the big leagues and did not have the luxury of rounding into shape gradually.

On March 23, Newhouser became the first Tiger hurler to pitch a complete game, shutting out the Syracuse Chiefs of the International League on two hits. "Newhouser," a reporter wrote, "just breezed along against Syracuse."

As spring training progressed, the Tiger brass felt some concern about the rest of the team. Lake's long holdout was a bother, Eddie Mayo had problems with his back, Greenberg (the highest paid player on the club at $75,000) was very slow in getting into playing condition, and Hoot Evers, a highly-touted outfield prospect, fractured his thumb and ankle in a freak accident and was feared lost for at least two months.

About their great lefthander, however, Trautman and O'Neill had no worries. "I've never been in better condition," Newhouser said, shortly before the opener. He was at 174 pounds, a good weight for him, up from the 160 he weighed when he pitched the final game of the 1945 World Series. He told Salsinger this would be the most critical season of his career. He said he had "insatiable curiosity" as to how he would fare against all the returning veterans.

Finally, the time came. J.G. Taylor Spink made his annual predictions in *The Sporting News* (he picked the Yankees, Red Sox, and Tigers one-two-three in the American League), the teams worked their way north, the red, white, and blue bunting went up on eight ball parks, and Opening Day was at hand. On April 16, the *Detroit News* wrote:

> This was a day to forget about nylon lines, black marketeers, high rents, low beer supply, sugar rationing, shortage of shorts, shirts, suits, and the delay on the delivery of that 1946 automobile. It was a day even to forget about the Iranian question and the atom bomb. Baseball, the genuine pre-war brand, was ready to take over the American sporting scene . . .

At Briggs Stadium, the Tigers sent out their ace to take on St. Louis. Newhouser allowed the Browns a first-inning run on two cheap hits and then shut them down the rest of the way. The Tigers tied it in the second and went ahead on Greenberg's fourth-inning home run off Nelson Potter. That was enough for Newhouser, who struck out eight on the way to a 2–1 win. Salsinger wrote, "He had stuff, control, and he pitched to spots." In the jubilant clubhouse after the game, someone said, "Say, Bob Feller struck out 10 at Chicago. How many did you get, Hal? Eight? You two ought to be close all season." Newhouser demurred: "I won't get within 75 strikeouts of that Feller. I don't care much, either, just so I keep winning." He pointed out that Feller once fanned 261 in a year and that his own high was the 212 of the prior season. He said he had no idea of trying to match Feller in strikeouts.

Four days later, before a crowd of 42,775 at Cleveland, Newhouser spoiled the Indians' home opener with a two-hit shutout, winning 7–0 as Dick Wakefield drove in five runs with a single, double, and triple. There was a cold breeze blowing off Lake Erie, which made conditions a little uncomfortable. Several Cleveland sportswriters criticized O'Neill for not holding Newhouser back to pitch against Feller the next day, but O'Neill shrugged off the carping by pointing out that it was Newhouser's turn to pitch. He had the last laugh anyway, when Feller lost on the following day by a 3-2 score.

On the 25th, Hal won his third game of the young season, beating the Browns at St. Louis, 6-5. He gave up all five runs in one inning, the fifth, but there were a bunch of scratch hits and fielding misadventures which were not called errors. Catcher Birdie Tebbetts said, "Everything happened in that one inning, but with perfect fielding support the Browns wouldn't have scored a run, or scored only one at the most." Newhouser held the Browns scoreless over the last four innings, and the Tigers rallied to win with two in the eighth inning, the winning run coming across when first baseman Babe Dahlgren lost a Tebbetts popup in the sun.

On April 30 at Fenway Park, Newhouser lost his first game, 4-0, to the Red Sox behind Joe Dobson's three-hitter. After the game, Harold's pitching elbow swelled up, and X-rays disclosed the presence of several bone chips, although the examining physician was unable to say whether they had been there a few days, a week, or even a year. The doctor recommended rest or, if the elbow pained Newhouser too much the next time he tried it, an immediate operation. The next time out, after skipping one start, was May 9, in Griffith Stadium, Washington, with Prince Hal matched against the Senators' Roger Wolff. In the third inning, with men on first and second and no outs, Newhouser deflected a Gil Torres line drive with his bare hand to Eddie Mayo, who caught the ball, stepped on second to double the lead runner, and then threw to first to triple the runner off that bag. A spectacular play, it took the heart out of the Senators. In the fifth, Detroit scored a run on an error by Jerry Priddy, and that was all Newhouser needed. He yielded only two hits in winning, 1-0, and answering, for the time being, the questions about his elbow.

While the Tigers were winning with Newhouser, they were less successful with the other pitchers on the staff, and they were having trouble attaining consistency at the plate. In the meantime, the Red Sox ran off a 15-game winning streak from April 25 to May 10 and took command of the American League race. With the heavy hitting of Ted Williams, Bobby Doerr, Rudy York, Dom DiMaggio, and Johnny Pesky, and the excellent pitching of Tex Hughson, Dave Ferriss, and Mickey Harris, Joe Cronin's team took off and never looked back.

On the 13th, Newhouser won his fifth, 6–5, over the White Sox, with late-inning help from Hutchinson. On May 16, with Jimmy Bloodworth returning from the service, the club sold Hitchcock to Washington. Two days later, Trautman traded veteran outfielder Barney Mc-Cosky, slumping at .198, to Philadelphia for young third baseman George Kell; the next day Higgins, hitting only .217, was shipped off to the Red Sox. The Kell deal was a spectacular success for the Tigers, even though Mc-Cosky resumed his accustomed .300 hitting when his chronic back problems allowed him to play. Kell, four years younger, was just coming into his prime when he arrived in Detroit. He had six-plus seasons of excellent play with the Tigers, including a batting championship in 1949, on his way to enshrinement in Cooperstown in 1983.

The sale of Higgins to the front-running Red Sox, though, backfired on the Tigers. Pinky hit .275 for the Sox and gave Joe Cronin the punch at third base which Boston was not getting from Rip Russell. Higgins was the final piece in the Red Sox pennant puzzle.

Higgins was unable to help the Sox much on May 19, however, as they succumbed to Newhouser by a 3–1 count at Briggs Stadium. Harold yielded only four hits to the hard-hitting Red Sox, striking out nine, while Greenberg, Outlaw, and Wakefield all hit home runs. On the 24th, Newhouser stifled the White Sox at Chicago, 3–1, for his seventh victory in eight games. It was the last game for manager Jimmy Dykes of the White Sox, who was replaced by veteran pitcher Ted Lyons. Another managerial change the same day hit the American League like a thunderclap: Joe McCarthy quit as skipper of the Yankees, to be succeeded by Bill Dickey. McCarthy had won eight pennants in his 15 years with the Yankees, and it just seemed as if he had been there forever. In the National League the St. Louis Cardinals were stunned as three of their mainstays, pitchers Max Lanier and Fred Martin and infielder Lou Klein, jumped to Mexico. The Pasquels were not finished vexing the moguls of organized ball.

One day Dan Daniel wrote in the *New York World-Telegram*, "O'Neill offers up a fervent prayer every morning that those slivers of bone in Newhouser's elbow do not kick up again and force Hal out of action." For the stumbling Tigers, such a development would have been disastrous. With their weak hitting, the Tigers were dragging along in third and fourth place; only the steady pitching of Hal Newhouser was keeping them that high. Thus it came as an unpleasant shock to the Tiger brass when, at a meeting requested by Newhouser, he told them that he had received a huge offer from Pasquel to jump to the Mexican League. The offer was for $300,000 to be deposited in the pitcher's bank account up front, with an additional $200,000 for pitching three years in Mexico. "They [owner Walter Briggs, his son Spike, Trautman, and O'Neill] almost fainted when I told them what had happened," Newhouser said later. "I told them I didn't especially want to jump, but that the money meant a lot."

Finally, the elder Briggs said tersely, "Don't do it, Hal. Stay with us. You won't regret it." Newhouser did stay, and he apparently did not regret it. He frequently said that he was treated generously by Walter Briggs over the years.

On the 29th of May, Newhouser won his eighth game by beating Cleveland, 4-1. Rookie Hoot Evers, finally in the lineup, hit a key triple against Allie Reynolds in the three-run third inning to give Hal the runs he needed. Four days later, Newhouser won again, this time a 10-2 victory over Washington. He struck out 13, with each Nat in the lineup going down on strikes at least once. Twice he fanned four in a row. It was a good thing that O'Neill had Newhouser's pitching to savor, because the next night a collision on a pop fly resulted in a broken jaw for Evers and a leg injury for Mayo. In the same game, Stubby Overmire sprained his pitching hand sliding into second base. The Tigers were 11 1/2 games behind the Red Sox, tied with Washington for third, and going nowhere.

Early in June baseball was rocked with another crisis, as the Pittsburgh Pirates players announced their affiliation with a putative players' union, the American Baseball Guild, organized by a young Boston labor lawyer named Robert Murphy. The players could see that the huge crowds pouring through the turnstiles in this first post-war season were making lots of money for the owners, and they felt that they were entitled to a larger piece of it. When the Pittsburgh ownership refused Murphy's demand for collective bargaining over alleged grievances, Murphy called upon the Pirates to strike on the night of June 7. An hour before game time, the players voted 20-16 in favor of striking, but this was short of the three-quarters vote needed. The strike was averted, and, in a subsequent vote on August 20, the Pirates rejected Murphy's Guild. For the first time in many years, however, the players had some bargaining clout, with the Mexican League raids and the possibility of a union. The lords of baseball and a special players' committee worked out a more generous agreement on a pension fund, minimum salary, and limitation of salary cuts. Baseball was spared labor strife at this time—for more than two decades.

On June 8, Hal Newhouser took the mound against the Red Sox at Fenway Park, but he had nothing that day. Four hits and two walks led to five runs for the Sox in the first inning, an early shower for Prince Hal, and a 15-4 Boston triumph. Three days later, though, Newhouser whipped the Yankees at New York, beating Floyd Bevens, 8-3. His record was now 10-2.

On June 15, the Tigers officially raised their world championship flag at Briggs Stadium, with Commissioner Chandler and league president Will Harridge participating in the ceremony. Chandler also presented world champion rings to members of the Detroit club; only 15 of the 30 recipients of those rings were still on the roster. As another reminder of the 1945 outcome, Hal Newhouser went to the mound and beat Dutch Leonard and the 1945 runner-up Senators, 3-1.

In the next outing Newhouser won the 100th game of his career, and 12th of the season, beating the Yankees, 6-2. He scattered four hits, struck out 10, and took a shutout into the ninth, when Keller doubled and DiMaggio homered for two runs. Newhouser then fanned Billy Johnson and Johnny Lindell to end the game. The next day manager Dickey said, "I never before saw him with the kind of stuff he showed us yesterday. His curve ball and change of pace were deadly."

Two days later, Newhouser lost one to New York, coming in to pitch relief in the 10th inning and surrendering a two-run home run to Tommy Henrich in the 11th. But three days after that, on June 26, Prince Hal breezed by the Red Sox, 16-2, to raise his record to 13-3. In addition to racking up 11 strikeouts, Newhouser hit a three-run home run, the first of his career, and a run-scoring double.

He closed out a brilliant month of June four days later with a 1-0 win over the Browns at Sportsman's Park. Jack Kramer was in fine form for the Brownies but could not match Newhouser's four-hitter and the lone run which scored on a Greenberg sacrifice fly.

On July 3, Prince Hal unveiled another classic, against the White Sox, winning 2–1 in 10 innings. A second inning homer by Whitey Platt accounted for the only Chicago run, and the Sox picked up just two more hits and one walk. In the meantime, Newhouser was striking out 10. In the last of the 10th, Richards doubled and rode home on Newhouser's two-base hit to win the game. Four days later, in the last game before the All-Star break, Newhouser brought his record to 16–3 with a five-hit shutout over the Browns, winning 3–0. Hal even stole a base in this game.

Why was Newhouser pitching so sensationally and winning so consistently against the good post-war competition? Looking back, he said, "I think I caught them all by surprise, because my pitching techniques had changed. Instead of ball one, ball two, it was strike one, strike two. Then ball one. So the whole pattern changed." The balls that in pre-war days had been three or four inches outside were now on the corners of the plate. "Now it was strike two and no balls and then throw the ball two or three inches outside. They couldn't gamble by taking it. So therefore I think before they realized, half the season is over with and I already have 15 wins before the All Star Game." [Actually 16] The other thing, of course, was that Newhouser's stuff was not a mirage. He still threw the blazing fastball, great curveball at three different speeds, and stunning change-up, just as he had to wartime hitters in 1944 and 1945. And the returned veterans and new stars were no more successful at hitting him than the Oris Hocketts, Ray Macks, and Bud Methenys had been during the war.

The All-Star Game, back after a year's absence, was played on July 9 in Boston's Fenway Park. Claude Passeau for the Cubs started against Feller, and the

American Leaguers, managed by Steve O'Neill, took a two-run lead on Charlie Keller's first-inning home run. After three innings, Newhouser came in to pitch, and he hurled three innings of shutout ball, giving up one hit to Peanuts Lowrey, and striking out four. Hal even picked up a base hit against Brooklyn's Kirby Higbe and scored his club's fifth run. By the time Newhouser left, the Americans led, 6–0. Kramer pitched three scoreless innings to end it, while his teammates piled up six more runs, including Ted Williams' second home run of the game, a three-run shot in the eighth against the famous "blooper ball" of Pittsburgh's Rip Sewell. It was the most lopsided All-Star Game ever.

After the mid-season break, Prince Hal went back to work against the American League. A 5–1, three-hitter against the Yankees, two straight complete-game wins over the Senators, and a 4–2 win over the A's meant that Newhouser had notched his 20th victory of 1946 by July 26, the first in the majors to do so.

Following the victory over Philadelphia, however, Newhouser developed a soreness in his pitching elbow, diagnosed this time as a nerve injury. He missed one turn, and when he came back on August 4, he was hit hard by the Red Sox, particularly Bobby Doerr, who banged a home run in the fourth inning and a grand slam in the fifth to bring an end to Newhouser's day. The 9–4 loss brought Hal's record to 20–4.

On July 31, Feller won his 20th game to match Newhouser, and shortly thereafter *The Sporting News* ran a page full of articles on the two pitchers, headlined "Extremely Rare – a 30-Victory Pair!" Shirley Povich of the *Washington Post* wrote the main article, saying, "The Newhouser vs. Feller debate is raging among all the ballplayers of the league and the only concession that is made is that Feller has a better strikeout pitch than the Detroit southpaw." Newhouser, Povich wrote, "has a better assortment of pitches than Feller, no two of them as good as Feller's fast ball or curve. But he does have better control and can pitch to a spot with less effort. He conserves himself better than Feller in a game, saving his good pitch [for] when there is trouble." The argument among partisans of the two pitchers continued on for several years, until Newhouser's arm miseries made it academic; there was general consensus for those several years that they were the two best pitchers around.

The problem with his elbow in early August and the resulting delay in picking up his 21st win eliminated the possibility of Newhouser winning 30 in 1946. Five days after the loss to Boston, he relieved Hutchinson in the ninth inning with a 5-4 lead over the White Sox, two runners on base, and none out. He kept the runners where they were, retired three in a row (including strikeouts of Frankie Hayes and Bob Kennedy), and saved the win. Two days later, though, he started against the White Sox and lost, 3-0, to Eddie Lopat, pitching seven decent but not brilliant innings.

Just when Steve O'Neill was starting to show some concern over his ace, Prince Hal came back on August 15 at Detroit and blanked the White Sox, 3-0, on four hits, for win number 21. His next outing was August 20, at Philadelphia, where Bob Savage of the A's pitched a three-hitter and won, 2-0. Newhouser scattered seven hits and struck out 10, but the loss made his record 21-6.

After a brief relief stint in Washington, Newhouser won his 22nd in New York with a brisk five-hitter over the Yankees, winning 7-2 with 10 strikeouts. He even hit his second home run of the year. "Newhouser," wrote a New York reporter, "was at the top of his game yesterday."

On the last day of August, and the first day of Zack Taylor's tenure as manager of the Browns, following the release of Luke Sewell, Newhouser beat St. Louis, 11-3, giving up five hits and fanning 10. His strikeout total

for the year, though far behind that of Feller, had now
reached 220, eight more than his previous seasonal high,
set against all those wartime batters in 1945.

A big September helped the Tigers beat out the Yankees for second place, as the Detroit bats, silent for most
of the season, came alive. A slugging spurt down the
stretch by Greenberg enabled him to win the home run
and RBI crowns over Ted Williams. The pitching staff,
led by Newhouser and with solid contributions all season
from Trout, Trucks, Hutchinson, and Benton, did its
part, too, although the team still finished far behind the
Red Sox.

Newhouser started the month with a solid 4–1 victory over the Indians for win 24. He then lost two in
a row, 3–2 to the White Sox and 5–4 to the Yankees,
before shutting down the Athletics and their ace, Phil
Marchildon, 2–1, in 10 innings. Prince Hal had 11 strikeouts in this game, which raised his season record to 25–8.

On September 22, showman Bill Veeck, the new owner
of the Cleveland Indians, ballyhooed the day's game with
Detroit as "the pitching duel of the century" and attracted a crowd of 38,103 to Municipal Stadium to see
two clubs which were well out of the pennant race. The
lure, of course, was the pitching matchup of Feller against
Newhouser, a game about which Feller later wrote, "I
was eager to come to pitches with the man who was my
chief rival, although a friendly one."

It was quite a game, but there was no doubt who was
the better pitcher on that day. The Tigers won, 3–0, as
Newhouser yielded just two hits, a solid single by Jim
Hegan in the third and a ball off Newhouser's glove by
Heinz Becker in the seventh. Hal walked none, and neither
runner moved beyond first base. The Tigers' ace even
racked up more strikeouts than Feller, nine to seven, and
earned a standing ovation from the Cleveland crowd
when he came to bat in the ninth inning.

A week later, 47,896 people showed up at Briggs Stadium in a cold rain for the final game of the season, another pairing of the same two teams and same two pitchers. Feller by this time had accumulated 343 strikeouts during the season, and he was striving to set the all-time record. In the books it was held by Rube Waddell at 343, but research by Ernest Lanigan at the Hall of Fame in Cooperstown indicated that Waddell's actual total was 347. For three innings, Feller said, "it appeared that Newhouser was the man intent on breaking a strikeout record. I had never seen him faster or with better control. He struck out six men in three innings. I couldn't throw the ball past anybody." In the fourth, five consecutive Cleveland singles netted three runs, but it was not until the fifth inning that Feller picked up his first strikeout, with Newhouser the victim. That may have set the record; for good measure Feller struck out Greenberg twice, Wakefield, and Jimmy Bloodworth to finish at 348. Cleveland won the game, 4–1, and Harold Newhouser's season record finished at 26–9.

Despite the sour note on which it ended, it was a magnificent season for Newhouser, recognized as such by Walter O. Briggs, who gave his great lefthander a $10,000 bonus. Feller tied him with 26 victories, but Feller lost 15 games to Newhouser's nine. The Tiger ace led the league in earned run average with a sparkling 1.94, surrendered the fewest hits per nine innings, held opposition hitters to a league-low batting average of .201, and struck out 275, far above his previous high. Even though Feller broke the strikeout record, Newhouser led the league in most strikeouts per nine innings, 8.47 to Feller's 8.43. Feller led in games, innings pitched, and complete games, but these statistics were distorted somewhat by the Indians' practice of leaving Feller in a game no matter what, or pitching him on short rest, for his run at the strikeout record. Newhouser was a solid second to Ted Williams in the voting for the league's Most Valuable Player, and he answered, as well as could be done, the questions of those who pooh-poohed his record against wartime opposition. Ed Lopat, the crafty lefthander of the Chicago White Sox, said that by this time Newhouser "dominated the pitching. He had a beautiful easy smooth delivery with a good fast ball, a good curve, and a good change plus good control. He had learned how to pitch . . . He was a fierce competitor and . . . a tough loser." Feller himself said, "If anyone had any doubts about Newhouser being a great pitcher, they should have been dispelled." The 1946 season, Newhouser said, gave him his "greatest feeling." No matter what people say about the war years, the Tiger lefthander has said, "I can look back with great satisfaction on 1946. I just shut the door right in their face."

13
AN OFF-YEAR

In preparing for 1947, the Detroit ball club made another major front office change: George Trautman was named head of the National Association, the governing body of the minor leagues, and Billy Evans, a veteran administrator and former big league umpire, took over as general manager of the Tigers. Evans started his new job with a bang; on January 18 he sold Hank Greenberg to the Pittsburgh Pirates.

Greenberg had led the American League in home runs, with 44, and runs batted in, with 127, in 1946, and he was still a great favorite with Detroit fans. But his batting average had slipped to .277, he was 35 years old, and he had fallen prey to a series of aches, pains, and injuries during that first full post-war season. As he recalled later, "When I got back I was really playing from memory." In addition, with his salary of $75,000, big Hank took home the Tigers' heftiest paycheck. Greenberg had been making noises about possible retirement, and Evans and owner Walter Briggs decided the time had come for him to move on.

The deal produced a great amount of criticism for the Detroit brass, from the paying customers as well as from some baseball people. Among those who voiced their dissatisfaction with the transaction was Hal Newhouser.

Newhouser as a teenager had watched Hank Greenberg
as the Tigers' young slugging star; as a rookie pitcher
he had played with Hank before the war, and in 1945
and 1946 he had relied upon him when Greenberg returned from the service. Newhouser had come to know
Greenberg's quiet dignity and solid character, and he
cherished big Hank as a friend. The deal underlined once
again the fact that in baseball loyalty was seldom a two-
way street.

A couple of weeks later Newhouser told the press that
he was not ready to sign the contract the club had sent
him. While not necessarily unhappy with the salary
figure, he said, he wanted to sit down with Evans to
discuss other phases of the contract, "such as television
rights and so forth." He also said he was not interested
in debates about whether he or Feller was the highest-
paid pitcher in the game: "you'd be surprised how close
my salary compared with Bob's for last year. I had a
bonus clause based on attendance in my contract, too.
And I'm not worried about trying to match Feller's pay-
check this year."

Signed or not, Newhouser was, as *The Sporting News*
put it, "lighthearted when he left for the South." He had
put back on the weight lost during the 1946 season, he
had made some money as a manufacturer's representative during the off-season, and he felt good about the
club's chances for 1947. He said his pitching arm felt
all right; the removal of a wisdom tooth a couple of weeks
earlier should relieve any shoulder soreness. On February
21 Newhouser in Lakeland and Evans in Detroit settled
Hal's contract with a long distance phone call, for a
salary of more than $60,000. Steve O'Neill had already
nominated Newhouser to pitch the season's opener against
the St. Louis Browns. "You couldn't pick anyone else,"
the skipper said.

Billy Evans went down to Lakeland to watch his team

in action and commented, "I knew this club had good pitching, but I never imagined it was that good." The Cincinnati Reds watched Newhouser work against them for five innings and then told reporters he was better than any lefthander in the National League. And veteran pitcher Bobo Newsom disagreed with those who said Feller was the best in the American League. "He's just a thrower," Bobo said; "the real pitcher is Hal Newhouser of Detroit . . . He not only has the stuff but he knows how to pitch." It was spring training and everything was rosy.

Just before the season opened, though, H.G. Salsinger wrote that the Tigers were coming north with a poorly-conditioned team. "The players," he said, "preferred loafing to training. The Tigers did less running this year than we ever saw a Detroit squad do. How the boys hated to run!" Later, Salsinger would specify Newhouser as one of those to whom he referred.

The Tigers' lefty ace opened the season with a 7–0 shutout of the Browns at Sportsman's Park. With two rain delays, Newhouser had to warm up three different times, and his control was a bit shaky, but he held the Browns to four hits for his 13th straight win over St. Louis.

Six days later, on a bitterly cold and windy day in Detroit, Newhouser started his second game, against the Chicago White Sox. He got in trouble with his control in the first inning, put a couple of men on base, and then hit Ralph Hodgin, a little left-handed batter, in the head. Newhouser still remembers the situation vividly:

> Hodgin came up and had two strikes and no balls on him . . . He hit the ball to all fields and bent over a little bit. And I said to myself he's looking for a breaking ball. And I'm gonna throw him a tight fastball up here. [Motion-

ing] And I did. I got the fastball from the
catcher. I came in here tight, and he stayed in
there a little bit too long . . . waiting for the
breaking ball, I think.

Ted Lyons, the big, strong ex-pitching star who now
managed the White Sox, charged out of the visitors'
dugout, furious at the beaning of his outfielder, until
Newhouser calmed him down, pointing out that in the
situation he had needed an out, a strikeout, not another
baserunner, and that he had certainly not hit Hodgin
intentionally.

Hodgin was carried from the field and taken to a
nearby hospital, a shaken Hal Newhouser walked in a
run with the bases loaded, giving up three runs in the
first inning on just one hit, and the White Sox went on
to win the game, 6–4, as Newhouser left after five
innings.

Newhouser was not a headhunter. He was not afraid
to come inside to a hitter, to lay claim to his share of
the strike zone. "I crowded them, I'll put it that way,"
he says now. But he did not throw at batters to hit them.
He tells the story of a game against the Yankees when,
to put a halt to a burgeoning New York rally, he knocked
down Charlie Keller, the powerful, beetle-browed slugger. He did it with a pitch about six inches over Keller's
head, but, as Newhouser recalls, "it looked like he was
gonna come out [to the mound]. I said, well, I'll just have
to fight him. I did it. I'm gonna have to live up to it.
And I can't say I'm sorry." But Keller just glared and
dug in for the next pitch. This pitch, which Newhouser
was trying to throw for a strike, went right at Keller's
head. "By God, I knocked him flat. But I didn't mean
it. And twice in a row . . . And he just looked at me . . .
long enough to tell me to stop it, that's the end of it."
A couple of years later, when Keller joined the Tigers,
Newhouser greeted him. "I said, 'hi, Charlie,' and he said,

'Aah, two times in a row!'" He said he had seen the first one coming, but "well, the second time you almost got me."

Although Ralph Hodgin recovered, he was never quite the same player again and was soon out of the major leagues. As for Newhouser, he seemed somewhat unnerved by the mishap, and his control was poor in his next few outings. He lost, 6–0, to the Indians and Feller at Cleveland and 7–1 to the Red Sox at Briggs Stadium. Then he pitched a 2–2 tie in a game against the Yankees that was rained out after six innings, and lost, 2–1, to the White Sox at Chicago.

His record stood at 1–4 with a third of the month of May gone, and there were suddenly all sorts of theories about why the great Hal Newhouser was not winning. There was the sale of Greenberg, of course, and the retirement of Paul Richards (although in 1946 Newhouser had been caught more by Birdie Tebbetts than by Richards). There was the plain fact that the club was not scoring a lot of runs in the games Newhouser pitched and the claim that he had not gotten into top shape in Florida. Billy Evans was quoted as saying that "Newhouser will have to pitch himself into shape." Those who remembered the heart problem that had kept the lefthander out of the service came up with other theories, such as rheumatic fever or some other dread disease. Newhouser scoffed at all of this: "That's ridiculous, of course. I've never felt better in my life. I'm at 184 pounds, my best weight. It's just a matter of pitching luck. Things are bound to break better soon."

Indeed, on May 13 Prince Hal shut out the Washington Senators, 8–0, on four singles, and the talk quieted down somewhat. Four days later, in Philadelphia, Newhouser and Joe Coleman of the A's hooked up in a classic pitchers' battle; Hoot Evers hit a two-run homer in the ninth to break a 0–0 tie. In the bottom of the ninth, the A's loaded the bases with none out, but Newhouser

turned them back with just one run, which scored as
Gene Handley bounced into a double play. The Tigers
won, 2–1.

On May 20 Detroit traded Tebbetts to Boston in ex-
change for catcher Hal Wagner. There were persistent
rumors, always stoutly denied, that the Tigers traded
away the veteran catcher because he and Newhouser did
not see eye-to-eye on things. Perhaps it was simply that
any catcher replacing Richards would have seemed less
in tune with Newhouser than the tall Texan, and Tebbetts found it difficult to erase from his mind the wild
and angry young man he had caught before the war.

The next day Newhouser lost to the New York Yankees,
5–0, as the Yanks' rookie pitching sensation Frank "Spec"
Shea blanked the Tigers. Again, it was first-inning trouble which hurt Newhouser: he loaded the bases in front
of Joe DiMaggio, and the Yankee Clipper unloaded them
with a three-run double. On May 25, though, Newhouser
beat the White Sox, 10–1, striking out 11, and on the
30th he beat the Browns and Bobby Muncrief, 2–1, the
winning run scoring on a throwing error by Johnny Berardino. Newhouser's record was now even at 5–5, and
it seemed that he was back to normal.

But 1947 was not to be another great year for Harold
Newhouser. There was always to be one more thing going wrong, and it seemed as if the vision of Ralph Hodgin
lying on the ground haunted him all season long.
Newhouser himself, looking back on 1947, said, "I just
think I had a little bit of a mental collapse. I started
off a little bit poorly, and I got to fighting it because
I wanted to have another good year."

Despite the problems their ace was having, the Tigers
played well at the start of the 1947 season. On May 10
they took over first place and held onto it for a little over
a month, before a 10-game losing streak knocked them
out of contention.

On June 3, Newhouser lost to the Yankees, 3–0, as Spec

Shea once again blanked the Bengals. DiMaggio's four hits paced the New Yorkers, now under the guidance of veteran manager Bucky Harris. In his next start, though, Prince Hal shut down the hard-hitting Red Sox, 5–0, holding them to four hits and driving in the first two runs himself against Dave Ferriss.

On June 15, Newhouser lost to Washington, 1–0. The Tigers could do nothing with Senators' pitcher Walt Masterson, and a scratch run Eddie Yost scored in the sixth was enough to beat Newhouser. Five days later, in New York, he lost again to Frank Shea, this time by a 5–3 score. Finally, on the 25th, Prince Hal ended the club's 10-game skid by beating the Red Sox and Tex Hughson at Fenway by a 4–2 score. Four days later he beat the Browns, 7–5, to even his record at 8–8.

Watson Spoelstra, writing in *The Sporting News* of "this . . . exceedingly disappointing season for Newhouser," pointed out how often the Tigers' run production fell off when Hal was pitching. Four times they had been shut out with Newhouser on the mound. Still, Spoelstra felt the lefthander could reach 20 wins: "Hal is sound of wind and limb. While a little unsteady at the start, he has pitched himself into shape. He can't keep drawing blanks on the days he works."

At about the same time, columnist Red Smith asked a Detroit writer how Newhouser's disposition was. "He's all right," was the answer. "Better than you'd expect, considering the breaks he's been getting. He's had a right to walk off the mound more than once this year, the way this club has been kicking the ball games behind him."

As July opened, Newhouser moved his record into the winning column for the first time. He beat the Indians on July 2 by a 6–5 score. The Tigers scored four in the first inning, and Newhouser, though without his best stuff, was effective in the clutch. After throwing two innings of relief on July 6 in St. Louis, Harold departed for Chicago, where manager Joe Cronin named him to start for the American League in the annual All-Star Game, to be played in Wrigley Field.

Newhouser hooked up with the pitching sensation of the year, side-arming righthander Ewell Blackwell of the Reds, the National League starter. And while Blackwell lived up to his advance billing, Newhouser was just as effective over his three-inning stint. Prince Hal retired the first eight men he faced, including Walker Cooper and Harry Walker on strikes, before pinch hitter Bert Haas of the Phillies lined a single into left. Newhouser then retired the side, bequeathing a 0-0 score to his successors in what was ultimately to be a 2-1 American League victory.

Newhouser, of course, could not know it, but the All-Star Game start was to be the high point of his 1947 season. As the second half of the year got underway, he was frustrated in a 2-2, eight-inning tie against the Red Sox, called because of darkness, and hit hard in a bad start against Washington. Newhouser gave up five runs and seven hits in just two innings, but his teammates rallied to win, 9-8.

On July 20, the biggest crowd in Briggs Stadium history, 58,369, showed up to watch the Tigers sweep a doubleheader from the Yankees. Hal Newhouser won the opener, 4-1, with a three-hitter in which he walked none. It was his 10th win of the season. On the following eastern swing, however, Newhouser lost to the Senators, 3-0 (to Walter Masterson again), and to the Yankees and Vic Raschi, 5-1, before beating the Red Sox at Fenway Park, 10-3.

Back home on August 8, Newhouser took a 2-0 lead into the ninth against the White Sox before uncharacteristically tiring. Successive singles by Taft Wright, Luke Appling, Cass Michaels, and Red Ruffing tied the score, and a two-run, 10th-inning homer by Rudy York won it for the Sox. Four days later Newhouser's record fell to 11–12 as he lost to the Indians and Steve Gromek, 3–1, at Cleveland. The next day Prince Hal picked up a particularly frustrating loss in relief against the Browns. Hal White, working with a two-run lead, walked the leadoff hitter in the ninth, so O'Neill brought his ace in from the bullpen. Willard Brown, one of two black players the Browns had signed to try to bolster their sagging attendance, hit a liner between the outfielders which turned into a game-tying, inside-the-park home run. Then Henry Thompson, the other black Brownie, walked, stole second, went to third on an infield out, and scored the winning run on Hal Wagner's passed ball.

The next time out, at Comiskey Park, Newhouser beat the White Sox, 4–3, although he was not particularly effective. Al Benton pitched the last three innings and blanked the Chicagoans. On August 21, Newhouser lost to Early Wynn and the Senators, 3–2, again pitching fairly well but not well enough to win.

By this time the Yankees had the pennant race all but wrapped up. The Red Sox were second, 13 games back, with the A's, Tigers, and Indians clustered close behind. There were rumors that Steve O'Neill was on his way out as Tiger manager, but Dizzy Trout said, "No other manager could keep this club up in the first division like Steve has done."

After a 5–4 win over the Athletics, Newhouser started against the Red Sox on August 28 at Briggs Stadium. He gave up a run in the first inning and then sat through a rain delay. When he came out again for the third inning, he did not have a thing. The Red Sox pounded seven hits and scored five runs, and finally Steve O'Neill motioned from the dugout for Newhouser to leave in favor of reliever Hal White. Newhouser turned his back on the manager and, since catcher Bob Swift was holding the ball, got a new baseball from the home-plate umpire.

O'Neill stormed out to the mound, grabbed the ball from Newhouser's hand, and angrily threw it on the ground, as he directed his pitcher to leave. After the game, won by Boston, 13–3, O'Neill announced that Newhouser had been fined $250 for "an indifferent performance"; it was the first fine of a player levied since O'Neill had taken over the club in 1943. "I just don't think Newhouser was putting out the way he should have been," the irate manager said. "His pitching was definitely inferior and I wanted him out of there."

Newhouser told the AP reporter, "I was bearing down all the time. I thought I could get 'em out and didn't want to leave." He added that, "It's the first time I ever was fined by a manager, and I don't see how he could have thought I wasn't trying." The next day the genial O'Neill had calmed down, but he reiterated, "The fine is going to stick. As far as I'm concerned the whole thing is a forgotten incident. I'm for Newhouser 100 per cent. He is a great pitcher. He has always worked hard and has lost a lot of tough ball games this season." Then he scratched his head and added, "I don't know what got into Hal." It was an embarrassing and unfortunate incident, one which put the final touch to Hal Newhouser's 1947 season. It also produced in the press a flurry of stories recalling the angry and headstrong Newhouser of pre-war days.

There was still a month to go, however, and three days later Newhouser gave anything but an "indifferent" performance as he shut down the Browns at St. Louis by an 11–2 score. He fanned seven and scattered eight hits and coasted behind an attack that featured Roy Cullenbine's home run.

Back in Detroit, and hearing catcalls and boos from the hometown fans for the first time in years, Newhouser faced the Brownies again on September 7. Again the Tigers were shut out, this time by Jack Kramer, and Newhouser lost by a 3–0 score.

His remaining four starts were all out of town – a 7–2 win over the Yankees, a 4–1 loss to Early Wynn at Washington, a 4–1 victory over Ed Lopat and the White Sox (before 942 people in Comiskey Park), and a closing 4–2 win over Bob Lemon and the Indians. In this game, a rookie named Al Rosen, just up from Oklahoma City, pinch-hit against Newhouser. As Rosen recalls it, "His first pitch was a fast ball (you must remember I was not used to seeing fast balls of this nature), his second pitch was another fast ball that I took for strike two, and on the third pitch he threw me that great overhand curve of his. I swung straight down, and the top of the bat hit home plate!"

The fact that Newhouser won four of his final six starts helped the Detroit club to finish second, two games ahead of Boston (but 12 behind the Yankees), and it gave him a season record of 17 wins and 17 losses. His earned run average of 2.87 was among the league leaders. For most pitchers that would have been regarded as a fine year, but Prince Hal Newhouser had erected such high standards the prior three years that it was considered a failure for him. People all over the league were debating what was wrong with Newhouser. Watson Spoelstra said he'd had bad support in many games, "but nearly everyone is disturbed by Newhouser's apparent loss of his blazing speed and his baffling assortment of stuff." Columnist Oscar Ruhl quoted "a veteran American League star" to the effect that Newhouser had "lost his poise and not his stuff." He said that it looked as if Hal had "discarded his slow curve and his various changes of pace to the almost exclusive use of the fast ball." What was amusing was that if the Tigers had gotten one or two more runs in three or four games for Newhouser none of that would have been written; the press would have written about another good year for the Detroit southpaw.

H. G. Salsinger sat down over the winter and predicted that Harold Newhouser would win more than 20 games in 1948, because "he learned a number of things that will be of inestimable value to him in the future." Salsinger continued:

> When the breaks went against Newhouser in the early weeks of the season, he tried to buck them in the wrong way and all he did was produce more bad breaks. His pitching for three seasons had been distinguished by finesse and poise. He pitched smart baseball, using his stuff with fine discretion. When the breaks went the wrong way last year, he seemed to become panicky. He lost his poise, discarded his finesse. He lost games that, with adherence to his former plan, he would have won. He bucked luck in the wrong way. He no longer paced himself and he lacked what he needed in the clutches.

With all his problems, Newhouser led the league with 24 complete games. Steve O'Neill said, "Newhouser still is a great pitcher in my book. He had a little trouble with his control last summer. That's all that ailed him. I look for him to come back with a big winning season." Once again there would be pressure on Harold Newhouser to prove himself.

14
BACK ON TOP AGAIN

For the 1948 season, Hal Newhouser knew he was in for a pay cut. He had received considerably more than $60,000 the year before, based on his great 1946 record, and 17-and-17 did not warrant that kind of money. He did not sign what was sent to him by Billy Evans on January 12, but there was no undue haggling, and on February 27 he signed his contract, for a reported $50,000.

Newhouser concentrated on baseball during the off-season because he was determined to show that the mediocre performance of 1947 was an aberration. He worked out to stay in good shape, and he sweated over a book that he was writing, a book that would describe for his readers the mechanics and philosophy of pitching a baseball as he had developed it in his own mind over his career. He was writing the book, with a working title of *How to Pitch Baseball*, without the aid of a ghostwriter.

Once he got to Lakeland, he worked hard and looked forward to the start of the exhibition season. When his teammates complained that six days between the opening of a camp and the first game was not enough, Newhouser told a reporter, "I was in pretty good shape when I got down here. I get into playing condition quickly." He told Dan Daniel, of the *New York World-Telegram*,

"If anything impedes me this season, or any other year, it will not be failure to keep in shape. I ran forty laps around this field this morning. I have made two hundred laps within ten days. My legs are in shape right now."

He said, "I will pitch three innings my first time out, six the second, longer the third or fourth. I expect to go the distance four times before we open the season." Newhouser went on to explain, "I figure that normally I will average a hundred pitches in nine innings. So when I train to go the route, I throw a hundred times. Somebody on the bench keeps track of how many are curves, how many fast balls, or change of pace, and how many of each find the mark. Once I have pitched a hundred balls, I quit. I figure I have gone nine innings. Then I examine the chart. If my percentage of hooks for strikes or outs was poor, I spend the next couple of days working on my curve. If my fast ball failed, I concentrate on that. I have reduced this whole business to a matter of arithmetic."

With his scientific conditioning behind him, Prince Hal was anxious for the regular season to begin. The baseball writers picked the Yankees and the Boston Braves to win the league pennants. In *The Sporting News*, J.G. Taylor Spink chose the Red Sox as his American League flagwinner, to be followed by New York, Cleveland, Detroit, Philadelphia, Washington, the Browns, and the White Sox. H.G. Salsinger wrote that the Tigers had to be regarded as contenders, since their pitching looked "stronger than expected, due to [the] improved condition of Dizzy Trout and Virgil Trucks and indications Hal Newhouser will regain 1946 form." Salsinger was not impressed by the club's catching, infield, and outfield.

Manager O'Neill named Hal Newhouser as his opening day pitcher on April 19 and was not disappointed. Before 14,801 at Comiskey Park, Newhouser was locked in a 2-2 tie with the White Sox after eight innings. The Tigers scored three runs in the ninth off Joe Haynes of the Sox, with a Newhouser hit one of the keys to the rally. Hal then snuffed out the home team in the bottom of the ninth for a 5-2 victory.

On the 25th Newhouser was rocked for two home runs by Kenny Keltner in a 7-4 loss to Cleveland, and two days later he lost to the Browns when he gave up a run on Al Zarilla's single in his third inning of relief. Three days after that he lost to the White Sox, 5-4, on four runs in the eighth inning. Suddenly his record was 1-3, and columnist Oscar Ruhl was writing: "Note to Hal Newhouser, a hard loser who dropped three straight decisions after copping the opener: 'Watch that temper.'"

On May 6, Newhouser started against the Red Sox, gave up hits to the first five Red Sox hitters, and departed, although the Tigers won the game, 8-3. Two days later, Hal started again but was routed by the Yankees in the seventh inning in a 9-1 loss. The Detroit club suffered a grievous loss in this game when George Kell's wrist was broken by a Vic Raschi fastball.

On May 12 at Washington the Tigers staked Newhouser to a 7-3 lead and were dismayed to see him unable to hold it; he was knocked out in the fifth inning, though Detroit rallied to win, 14-9. It was now mid-May, Hal Newhouser had won just one game and lost four, and he had been ineffective in five straight starts. All the theories for his lack of success were trotted out once again, with a new one added. (Interestingly, Feller and Blackwell also started slowly and were subjected to the same kind of analysis.)

John P. Carmichael, the Chicago writer, suggested that Feller and Newhouser had had too many "great years." "It isn't that either Hal or Bob is in danger of going to pieces overnight," he wrote; "just that the 'big years' finally may have become just the wee bit burdensome, with maybe a hidden kink here and there beginning to take its toll." Watson Spoelstra wondered "how can a pitcher lose the winning touch so completely?" He said that Newhouser, "a devoted family man, has always taken care of himself, in and out of season." His fastball, everyone agreed, was just as fast as ever. Spoelstra thought that Hal had discarded his slow curve, that he was unable to control his best curve, and that hitters were sitting on his fastball. He pointed out, too, that Newhouser had never been the same since the departure of Richards. Bill Corum of the *New York Journal-American* suggested that perhaps Newhouser was telegraphing his pitches, then added the possibility "that Hal really was just one of the many wartime phenoms of recent seasons – the mice who have looked so good when the cats were away," overlooking of course the cats whom Newhouser beat 43 times in 1946 and 1947.

Newhouser soon proceeded to demonstrate that perhaps the experts had overlooked another possibility: that he was simply off to a slow start. On May 19, he beat the Red Sox, 4-1, despite five errors by his teammates. He held the Sox to just four singles and tied a major league record by initiating four double plays himself. On the 24th he beat Early Wynn and the Senators, 5-2, and on May 30 he beat St. Louis, 6-4, in 11 innings, going all the way. Suddenly his record was 4-4, and the chorus of analysts faded away.

Starting June, Newhouser went 11 innings to beat the Yankees and Ed Lopat at New York, 6-2. Moving on to Philadelphia, he scattered seven hits to beat the A's, 2-1. He won his sixth in a row at Washington's Griffith Stadium, beating the Nats by a 4-1 count, as Wakefield's four hits led the attack on Ray Scarborough.

On June 15, the Tigers turned on the newly-installed lights at Briggs Stadium for the first time, proudly announcing that 1,458 lighting units would provide 2,750,000 watts of electricity. A huge crowd of 54,480 showed up for the occasion, and naturally local favorite

Harold Newhouser was selected to pitch for the home team. It was all a great success; the lights worked, Dick Wakefield and Pat Mullin hit home runs, and Newhouser, pitching on two days' rest, held the Athletics to two hits in a 4-1 triumph.

With his seven wins in a row, Hal said, "I'm finding those corners again. I never felt that I had lost my stuff even in the darkest days, but I'll admit I worried plenty. I couldn't figure things out . . . Now I can see that it is mainly a matter of regaining my control." Steve O'Neill said, "I would not trade him for any pitcher in the game." And Salsinger said Hal looked like "the very best pitcher in baseball."

On the 20th the winning streak came to an end when Vernon Stephens of the Red Sox knocked Newhouser out with a three-run homer in the ninth inning, but five days later Hal ended the club's five-game losing string with a 4-2 decision over the Yankees.

A bad outing against the Indians on June 29 – a 6-2 loss and a third-inning departure – was matched by a relief victory over the Tribe two days later, a win highlighted by Newhouser's triple with two men on base in Detroit's five-run eighth inning. Hal's record was now 10-6.

On July 3, Newhouser went the route to beat Chicago, 6-2, and two days later Hal came in to save Hutchinson's win over Feller and the Indians in the ninth inning. On July 7, pitching every other day for the third time in a row, Newhouser shut out the Browns for win number 12. On July 10, the Associated Press carried an item saying that Newhouser had a sore arm that would sideline him at least 10 days. Yet the next day he beat the White Sox and then headed for St. Louis and the All-Star Game with a record of 13-6.

In the All-Star Game itself, Newhouser told manager Bucky Harris that he had a touch of bursitis in his shoulder and that he probably should not pitch. Harris got him into the game by using him as a pinch runner for Ted Williams in the sixth inning.

When Newhouser returned to the Tigers, O'Neill gave him and his achy shoulder a couple of extra days of rest before pitching him in the first game of a doubleheader at Yankee Stadium on July 18. Before 62,990 spectators, Hal beat the Yankees, 5–3, despite a couple of costly infield errors. In his next outing, however, despite being given a six-run lead in the first inning, Newhouser could not hold the Senators. He departed in the seventh inning with no decision in an eventual 9–8 Washington win. This was followed by a poor relief job in Philadelphia and a quick ouster by the Red Sox in Boston. It was clear that the arm and shoulder problems were affecting his pitching. His record at the end of July stood at 14–7.

Trainer Jack Homel told O'Neill that Newhouser's arm should have at least a 10-day rest, so the manager shuffled his pitching rotation to accommodate his ace. In early August, Hal's book, now entitled *Pitching to Win*, reached the market, which was gratifying to the blond lefthander, but his enforced inactivity was not. Finally, on August 8, O'Neill sent him to the mound at Briggs Stadium, against the Senators and their ace, Early Wynn. Newhouser responded once again, beating the Nats, 5–3. He gave up 11 hits, but the three Washington runs were all unearned, scoring on an error by shortstop Johnny Lipon in the fourth inning.

The win over the Senators made O'Neill feel good, and it boosted Newhouser's chances to win 20 games. "I gotta make it 20 and no foolin'," the lefty said; "I figure I can do it, too." Unfortunately, his work during the rest of August demonstrated that his arm problems were not over. On the 13th he lost to the Browns, 4–1, leaving in the fifth inning, and on the 22nd the Browns knocked him out again in the fifth, as the Tigers lost, 10–1. On

August 26, poor relief work by Art Houtteman helped Newhouser to a 4–3 loss to the A's, and on August 30, he lost to the Yankees, 3–0. In this last game, though, he went the route and pitched very effectively after the Yankees scored all three in the first inning. Spec Shea pitched a one-hitter for New York, that lone hit a single by Hal Newhouser in the third inning. The Newhouser record at the end of August was 15–11. The chance for a 20-win season was looking a lot slimmer, but the pitching performance in New York rekindled some hope.

And, indeed, in his next start Hal Newhouser beat the White Sox, 4–3, pitching the whole nine innings. It was his 16th victory. Five days later he started against Feller before a big crowd at Cleveland, come to celebrate Ken Keltner Night and to watch their Indians contend for first place. After eight innings the two aces were tied at 2–2, and O'Neill pinch-hit for Newhouser in the ninth. Neither starter was involved in the decision when the Indians won it, 3–2, in the 13th inning.

On September 14, Newhouser had to go 11 innings for a 2–1 win over Washington at Briggs Stadium, and four days later he pitched a complete game, 4–3 win over the Yankees, with the winning run scoring on his own squeeze bunt. On September 22 Newhouser beat the A's, 5–1, for his 19th win of the season and the 150th of his career.

On Sunday the 26th, 57,888 people poured into Briggs Stadium to see Newhouser oppose Feller once again. This crowd raised the Tigers' home attendance for the season to 1,735,117, a new club record and a great tribute to the Detroit fans who watched a fifth-place team that was never in contention. The Indians won that day, 4–1, to take a one-game lead over Boston and New York.

Three days later, though, Newhouser shut out the Browns once again, beating Ned Garver by a 4–0 score. It was his 20th win of a troubled and troubling season;

unbeknownst to Hal Newhouser, neither the season nor the trouble was over for him. The next day, at the season's last home game, he and Dizzy Trout, who was on the bench in civilian clothes, got into an argument which nearly became violent. Newhouser, according to Trout, was needling him about the cold which was keeping him out of uniform. Trout took exception to this line of conversation and there was some kind of scuffle. It was all quickly patched up, but it was an unwelcome item in the newspapers. In addition, it gave credibility to an article in *Baseball Digest* by a writer named Kyle Crichton, who wrote, "At twenty-seven Newhouser is probably as immature as any man who ever dominated his profession. He is still a big blond kid and will possibly end that way." The article, which rehashed all the old stories about the pitcher's bad temper and his problems with teammates, was titled "The Newhouser Nuisance."

The Tigers, though, still had to go to Cleveland to finish up the season. Pennant fever was raging in the Ohio metropolis, fueled by Bill Veeck's promotions and the heroics of a team led by Lou Boudreau, Joe Gordon, Keltner, Lemon, Feller, Larry Doby, and a rookie pitcher named Gene Bearden. After the first two games of the series, the Indians needed to win the final game on Sunday, October 3, to wrap up their first pennant since 1920. If they won, the Yankees and Red Sox, tied for second a game back, could do nothing about it. Manager Boudreau sent Bob Feller to the mound for the pennant-clincher, and Fred Hutchinson was scheduled to go for Detroit. Hutch had been lined up to pitch the day before, but he was ill with the flu; O'Neill had been forced to use rookie Lou Kretlow. Now for the final game, Hutchinson was still sick and had been left back at the hotel. Steve O'Neill gave the ball to Newhouser.

That day, before 74,191 fans, with all the pressure, after all the innings that had gone before, all the arm trouble, all the questioning of his ability, Hal Newhouser was simply at his peak. He had not prepared himself mentally or physically to pitch that day; he thought his season was over. It made no difference. Through eight innings, he scattered three singles and held the Indians scoreless while his teammates knocked Feller out of the box and took a 6-0 lead. As the scores came in from the East, and it was clear that the Red Sox were beating the Yankees, Boudreau and Gordon discussed the pitching choice for a playoff the next day, because they were convinced they were not going to touch Newhouser. The Tigers scored another run in the ninth, and then the Indians scratched out a run on two hits, and the game ended with a 7-1 Detroit win. The Indians were thwarted in their effort to win the pennant before their own fans; they were now tied with Boston.

Boudreau met with the press after the game and said, "We were trying to beat the greatest lefthander in baseball on one of his greatest days." He looked around and then continued, "Newhouser beat us almost single-handed. We could have batted against him for two days and still lost the game. He's one of the greatest pitchers of them all." Asked about Cleveland's chances in the playoff at Fenway Park, with the World Series against the Braves for the winner, Boudreau said, "There is no Hal Newhouser in Boston, and we're going there just a day early for the World Series."

Boudreau was right. His two home runs and Bearden's pitching led the Indians to a victory in the first American League championship playoff ever, and they went on to win the Series against the Braves. Back in Detroit, Newhouser could look back on a season in which he won 21 games (tops in the American League) while losing 12, pitching for a very mediocre Tiger team. Spoelstra, writing in the October 20 *Sporting News*, said, "Most baseball men figure this was Hal's best year, even better than the war years and the 1946 season in which he reached or surpassed the 25-victory mark three times in a row."

In any event, Hal Newhouser had proven once more that he was not a wartime flash and he had proven that the off-year in 1947 was just that, an off year. And his contemporaries considered him one of the two or three greatest pitchers of his time.

15
THE SLIDE BEGINS

After the close of the 1948 season, there was a spate of rumors of the Tigers' intention to trade Hal Newhouser for the good talent they would need to return to the first division. A Detroit paper printed a story that there were only four untouchables on the roster – Kell, Evers, and young pitchers Ted Gray and Billy Pierce – and that everyone else was expendable (except, it was added, new players like Johnny Groth, Lou Kretlow, and Joe Ginsberg). When Billy Evans was asked about this story and the obvious omission from the list of the club's ace lefthander and biggest winner, he exclaimed, "Trade Newhouser? That's ridiculous and preposterous. Not a chance."

At the World Series, though, there were several reports of Newhouser trades, one in an even-up swap for Ted Williams, another for several Red Sox players. Evans responded flatly, "We aren't disposing of Newhouser. He will be nowhere but Briggs Stadium. You can put that down and remember it."

The trade rumors eventually subsided, to be followed by speculation on the Detroit managerial situation. This was brought to a climax in early November, shortly after Harry Truman's electrifying presidential victory over Tom Dewey, when the club announced that it was releasing Steve O'Neill as manager. The genial Irishman's six-year tenure at the helm of the Tiger ball club was one of the more successful in the history of the franchise, but the 1948 fall into the second division brought about O'Neill's ouster. Two of his players, Pat Mullin and New-houser, sent him wires of regret after the news came out. Newhouser's read, "Dear Steve: You are still the best. My kindest regards. Hal Newhouser." O'Neill later told a reporter, "You'll never know what a lift those two messages gave me." A few days later, the Detroit club named Robert "Red" Rolfe, the old Yankee third baseman, as its new manager. Rolfe had been working for the Tiger farm system as its chief of scouting.

In mid-January 1949, reversing his usual pattern, Newhouser was the first member of the Detroit club to sign his contract. After his fine 1948 season, he had no difficulty in reaching a settlement at about the $60,000 figure. Newhouser was eager for a new year to start. When he got down to Lakeland, he told a reporter for the United Press that he'd like to set a goal for himself of one win per week. "If a guy could do that, figuring of course that he still would get beat occasionally," New-houser said, "he could win 30 games. And that's what I would like to do—just once." (A look at the calendar, however, shows that such a pace would produce no more than 25 wins; still, it was a laudable goal.)

On March 10, near-tragedy struck the Tigers' camp when promising young pitcher Art Houtteman was in-volved in a serious collision with a fruit truck. Houtte-man suffered a basal skull fracture, and his future career was in great jeopardy. The Detroit club was counting heavily on Houtteman, whose poor record in 1948 re-flected an incredible string of hard-luck losses, and now that ill fortune continued. The young righthander re-covered from the accident and went on to win 15 games in 1949, but no one could predict that at the time. As the team came out of spring training, there were no very high hopes for it. Fifth place seemed to be the consensus prediction for the Tigers.

On Opening Day, Red Rolfe did what Steve O'Neill had done so often: he gave Hal Newhouser the ball and turned him loose. Despite cold weather, 53,435 people came out to Briggs Stadium and they were rewarded with a Newhouser three-hitter as he beat Allan Gettel and the White Sox, 5-1. Highly-heralded rookie outfielder Johnny Groth hit two home runs for the Tigers and Aaron Robinson (picked up from Chicago in a swap for the supposedly "untouchable" Billy Pierce) added another. "Hal didn't have his stuff early in the game because of the cold weather," Rolfe said, but the Sox did not seem to notice; there were only two innings in which Newhouser faced more than three hitters.

Four days later, on a day when Newhouser did not seem to have his good stuff, he beat the defending world champion Indians at Cleveland, 5-4, going 10 innings. Spoelstra wrote that "Newhouser was magnificent when he had to be." In his next start, too, Hal pitched well, even though he lost, 4-3, to the Browns in 12 innings.

On the first of May, before another big crowd at Briggs Stadium, Dick Wakefield slugged a three-run homer against Cleveland's Bob Lemon in the first inning, and Newhouser made it stand up for a 3-2 victory, in a quick game of an hour and 45 minutes.

As Newhouser was once again claiming his place as one of the game's premier pitchers, he received a nice tribute from Lyall Smith, a young Detroit newspaperman. "Quite a man is Prince Hal," Smith wrote. "But his hat size is the same as it was when he broke into baseball in 1939." Earlier, Joe Williams, a writer for the *New York World-Telegram*, in a column in which he called the pitcher "the greatest lefthanded pitcher in baseball today," said that "Newhouser is a matured, pleasant, intelligent young man." So many stars become filled with their own importance, but Harold Newhouser remained friendly, approachable, and a bit shy.

On May 6, Newhouser had no decision in a game against Philadelphia which featured a spectacular debut by another left-handed pitcher. Hal gave up three runs before leaving in the eighth inning of a game the A's won in 13 by a 5-4 score. Early in the game Connie Mack inserted a small southpaw who had just arrived from the Buffalo club before the game. The young man's name was Bobby Shantz, and he proceeded to unroll nine innings of hitless relief pitching to pick up his first major league victory.

A loss to the Yankees and Allie Reynolds followed, before Newhouser beat the Browns, 9-3, for his fourth win. He then lost three games in a row, to the A's, Yankees, and White Sox, although two of these were by the score of 2-1, both five-hitters and route-going performances by Newhouser.

On June 3, Harold beat the A's, 4-3, defeating another talented young Philadelphia lefthander, Alex Kellner. Newhouser served up home runs to Sam Chapman and Eddie Joost, but otherwise he was impeccable. The next day he pitched a scoreless inning in relief to save a 10-9 win over the Red Sox; this was in line with a decision by Rolfe to use his starters—Newhouser, Trucks, and the others—in relief in between starts. Spoelstra wrote, "It wasn't that Hal was shirking his work. He had worked every fifth game almost without exception and the records showed he had pitched the most innings."

The Yankees came into Detroit and Newhouser pitched against them on June 7. The New Yorkers had a new manager for 1949, the veteran Casey Stengel, and they were once again leading the league. Nevertheless, Prince Hal stopped them by a 5-2 score with another complete game. The Tigers were in second place, four and a half games behind.

On June 12, Newhouser shut out the Senators on four hits, but he lost at Philadelphia four days later, despite pitching the whole way. With a little soreness in his arm, Newhouser missed a start, but he picked up a win in relief over the Red Sox on June 22. Entering the game in the fifth inning, behind Kretlow and Trout, Hal pitched five innings of scoreless ball as the Tigers came from behind to win. Three days later, he pitched a complete game at Yankee Stadium to post a 9–3 win, and four days after that he beat the Indians at Cleveland, 4–0, on six hits (four of them by outfielder Dale Mitchell). His record, as June came to a close, was 10–6.

On July 4, Newhouser had another no-decision in the nightcap of a doubleheader with Cleveland. The score was tied, 3–3, when he left in the eighth inning; the Indians scored four off Hutchinson to win it in the ninth. Manager Boudreau of the Indians then set off a noisy controversy when he named three lefthanders, Kellner and Lou Brissie from the A's as well as Boston's Mel Parnell, to his pitching staff for the All-Star Game but not Newhouser. There was a lot of heat over this snub — one Detroit official said, "I'll never know how they can pass up the best lefthander in baseball" — and it was not confined to the Motor City. Dan Daniel wrote that Boudreau should have picked Newhouser, "not only for his high potentialities of today, but . . . his eminence among the pitching fraternity of the major leagues." One who did not regret Newhouser's omission was Billy Southworth, the National League manager, who had assumed that his team would have to face the Detroit star for the first three innings.

After the All-Star Game, though, the second half of the 1949 season was not a happy time for Hal. He lost his first start, to the White Sox, and then had four straight starts in which he had no decision. Although the Tigers won three of these games, Newhouser pitched well in only one of them. He finally won his 11th game of the season on August 2, beating the Yankees, 10-2, but did not win his 12th until August 19, when he stopped the Browns, 4-2.

In the meantime, Newhouser started having the trouble with his left arm which eventually ended his career prematurely. One evening he was driving home from the ball park; he had the window down and his arm on the window ledge. "I went to take my arm off the ledge," he said, "and I couldn't pick it up." He thought that perhaps the arm had gone to sleep; "I finally picked it up and put it in my lap." Later it felt better, so he dismissed the incident as an aberration and went on pitching. Asked to account for his ineffectiveness, Newhouser responded with the caution and vagueness of a man whose contract ran only to the end of the current season. "I'm sure I don't know," he told a reporter. "I haven't had a sore arm and I feel stronger than any time before. But I just don't seem to have the pitching luck I've enjoyed in the past."

In late August, Hal picked up a complete-game victory against New York and a win over Washington, which Hutchinson saved for him, and his record at the end of the month was 14-9. He then put together a very fine month of September, starting with a route-going 5-4 win over the White Sox and his former staffmate, young Billy Pierce.

On September 8, Newhouser won his 16th game with a magnificent one-hit shutout of Cleveland. Detroit writer Sam Greene reported: "It is doubtful that Newhouser ever surpassed the brilliance of his sixteenth victory." He retired the first 17 Indians before walking pitcher Frank Papish with two out in the sixth. Boudreau, leading off the seventh, lined a 3-1 fastball to right for the only hit; a double play followed, so that Newhouser faced only 28 batters. Catcher Aaron Robinson said that the lefty had never been faster: "This was the only time I ever caught Hal that he didn't throw a single slider. His curve was breaking beautifully and he was lightning fast."

In his next outing, against the pennant-contending Red Sox at Fenway Park, Newhouser lost, 1–0, as Ellis Kinder won his 20th game for Boston. Ted Williams hit a home run in the sixth inning for the only run of the contest. Prince Hal won his next two starts with complete-game wins at Washington and Cleveland, the latter against Feller, before losing his last game on September 30, also to Feller and the Indians.

The Tigers finished fourth in 1949, one notch up from their second-division placement of the year before, and Hal Newhouser, with an arm that was slowly dying on him, won 18 and lost 11. His earned run average was a bit higher than usual at 3.36, but he piled up the substantial total of 292 innings, his heaviest workload in four years. Besides, his strong finish gave the club high hopes for the future.

For 1950, Billy Evans cut Newhouser's salary to $53,000, and this resulted in a brief holdout by the pitcher. He also wanted to register his concern over the pitching schedule followed by Red Rolfe in 1949. As baseball writer Sam Greene put it, Rolfe "frequently picked his starting pitchers without regard to rotation. This caused some grumbling on the staff." There is no indication that Newhouser complained about it, but he was not happy with Rolfe's system. With Steve O'Neill, he could always count on just when he would pitch, and this knowledge gave him a certain psychic comfort which helped his performance. As Greene put it, "it is probable that the changed program was partly responsible for his ineffectiveness at some stages of the race." When the contracts were sent out, Newhouser took off for Florida for a two-week vacation with Beryl. "There will be time to talk contract when I return February 6," he was quoted as saying. He came back to Detroit, however, picked up his two daughters and some clean clothes, and returned to

Lakeland without so much as a phone call to the club offices. Finally, when Evans came down to camp, Newhouser sat down with him for 35 minutes, got a few gripes off his chest, dickered a little on his salary, and then signed the contract. He was anxious to get to work.

Unfortunately, spring training was a disaster for Harold Newhouser. He reported on March 5, and he was scheduled to start an exhibition game against the Yankees on the 14th. While he was warming up, he told Rolfe that his arm did not feel too good but that he would like to give it a try anyway. Scheduled to pitch three innings, he worked only two, in which he gave up three hits, three walks, and a run, and then took himself out of the game. He never pitched another inning in Florida.

Scheduled to work batting practice on March 28, Newhouser threw 12 pitches and then went to the clubhouse, saying, "My arm hurts." He said, later, "That was pain. I mean real pain." But Jack Homel, the club trainer, said that he could not find anything wrong. Rolfe commented to the working press that he did not know how Newhouser could have hurt his arm. On April 1, the club had Newhouser X-rayed and examined by a physician named Edgar Watson, and Watson said he could see no signs of calcium deposits, arthritic conditions, or abnormalities in the pitching arm. Given the results of the X-rays, Newhouser said, "Mentally and physically I feel a lot better. I'm not worried a bit now. I was greatly worried before the X-rays showed nothing wrong." Then he added, "All I know is that whenever I threw for a few minutes, I got a dull pain in my shoulder. When I stopped throwing, the pain stopped." Anyway, he said, "the doctors told me everything will be all right. All I need is a few more days rest."

But the pain continued. As the Tigers headed north from Florida, Rolfe still could not figure out why his star lefthander could not pitch; had not those X-rays said there was nothing wrong? He was skeptical, and there was a clear inference that he suspected Newhouser was malingering. Rolfe finally used Newhouser for three innings in Louisville against the American Association Colonels and was not happy with what he saw. One correspondent pointed out that the two runs Louisville scored were meaningless; "what concerned Rolfe was the 'nothing ball' he [Newhouser] tossed up."

Homel the trainer said Newhouser's trouble was "muscular inflammation that will leave when the weather gets real hot." This was the only cheery note in a gloomy picture as the Tigers prepared for the season opener. Detroit and its fans had high expectations for their Tigers for 1950, but the bright picture required a healthy Hal Newhouser. It became more and more evident that that element was not present.

In fact, the season opened without Newhouser, and the team headed into its regular schedule without him. On April 30 he pitched batting practice in Chicago, "with results," wrote Spoelstra, "that made Rolfe happy." Still, Newhouser's shoulder ached. One day, as the pitcher recalls, "Rolfe . . . said to me, 'Hal, you're gonna have to pitch.' Pretty soon we're going to have to do something, either they put me on the voluntary retirement list, or they put me on the hurt list, or trade me, and nobody wants to take me because my arm's bothering me . . . I got to where I got my arm built up a little bit . . . so I went out and pitched and I was in misery. But I pitched."

Sam Greene of the *News* wrote that Newhouser's arm, "because it is attached to the highest-paid pitcher in the major leagues," had been for weeks a subject of "inquiry, speculation and innuendo." Newhouser, he said, had been pictured "as sulking over a paycut; as selfishly indifferent to the needs of his team; as pretending that his shoulder was sore to escape the demands of duty." All of this had been fueled in part by the statements being made by Rolfe and Homel. Greene went on: "this is an absurd assumption by persons who have never talked with Newhouser . . . an assumption in conflict with the pitcher's pride and principle . . . Nothing in his professional background suggests a disposition to dodge his share of the load."

Newhouser's first outing was on May 14, against the Browns at Detroit. Watson Spoelstra covered the game for the *Detroit News*:

> After watching Newhouser for three innings, nobody could tell whether he is bound for recovery or oblivion. The pitcher reported that he felt no soreness in his long-ailing shoulder. That was the only encouraging word . . . Newhouser's performance against the Browns was a pathetic sight to those in the crowd of 30,794, who remembered his solid efforts of the last decade.

In the game with the Browns, Newhouser pitched three innings, struck out two, walked four, hit one, and gave up four hits and five runs. A grand slam home run by Roy Sievers in the first inning was a crusher, and the Browns won the game behind Cliff Fannin, 7–3. Hal Newhouser certainly looked as bad as all the gloomy news coming out of Lakeland would have figured him to look.

Yet eight days later, on May 22, Newhouser made another start and looked like the Prince Hal of old. He pitched a complete game and beat the Senators, 5–1. Rolfe and the Tigers were tremendously encouraged, and Newhouser talked of his possibilities for winning 20: "I've got a chance to make it if I hit a hot streak." Four days later, he took on the Browns and Fannin again, at Sportsman's Park, and scattered six hits to beat them, 11–2. And four days after that, he went the route again in beating Cleveland for his third win, 5–2. On June 3, Newhouser went the distance in stopping the A's at

Shibe Park, 6-1. His four-game winning streak ended in New York with a 5-4 loss, but in Boston he beat the Red Sox, 6-2, in the first route-going win for a visiting lefthander at Fenway since Gene Bearden's win in the 1948 playoff.

On June 17, Newhouser beat the Red Sox again, at home, 4-1, before 54,086 happy Tiger fans. He then lost three in a row, to the Senators, Yankees, and Indians, in all of which he was hit hard. He picked up a win in relief with a strong inning and a third against the Indians but was then hit hard in a no-decision with the White Sox. He beat Cleveland on July 8 in a game which Dizzy Trout saved for him, and he seemed back on track on July 13 with a complete-game, 5-2 win over Washington. It was Newhouser's ninth win of the year, and it moved the Tigers into a three and a half game lead over the second-place Yankees.

Hal won his 10th in a sloppy game at Philadelphia, beating Carl Scheib, 8-6, with two innings of relief help from Paul Calvert. This game was followed by a 10-4 loss to the Yankees, a bad start with no decision against the A's, and a relief performance against Mr. Mack's team to save a win for Hutchinson.

Newhouser did not work again for six days, when he was brought in again in relief of Hutchinson. Newhouser was a little shaky in his two and a third innings, but with the tying run on third in the ninth he fanned the Senators' Mickey Vernon to end the game. Five days later he started against the White Sox but had to be satisfied with a 1-1 tie when rain washed the game out after seven innings. On August 14 he lost a heartbreaker to Cleveland when rookie Al Rosen hit a game-tying homer with two out in the ninth and the Indians scored the winner in the 10th on a late throw home by Neil Berry.

On the 20th, Newhouser was scheduled to start against his old road roommate, Stubby Overmire, now pitching for St. Louis. Hal invited Stubby to bring his

wife down from their home in Grand Rapids for Sunday
dinner after the game at the Newhousers' in Franklin
Village. The Browns knocked Hal out in the fourth inning and Overmire won the game, 6–2, but Newhouser
carried out his hosting assignment with perfect aplomb
afterwards. His record now stood at 10–8.

A complete-game win over the Yankees, a game-saving
relief job against the Red Sox, and a loss at Philadelphia
ended Newhouser's month of August. He was 11–9, and
the Detroit club now trailed New York by two games,
with the Red Sox a half game farther back.

In the first week of September, Newhouser posted two
complete game wins, beating Chicago and Cleveland, as
Wertz, Groth, and Charlie Keller had big hits for the
Tigers. As of September 7, the Tigers and Yankees were
in a virtual tie for first place, with Boston one and a half
games back. Rolfe announced that his starting pitchers
for the stretch run would be Houtteman, Newhouser,
Hutchinson, Trout, and rookie Ray Herbert. Hal Newhouser was back in a pennant race, for the first time since
1945.

On the 8th and 9th, Trout and Houtteman beat the
White Sox while the Yankees were idle, and the Tigers
took a game lead. The next day the Yankees beat Washington in the first game of a doubleheader (a game in
which Joe DiMaggio became the first player ever to hit
three home runs in a game at Griffith Stadium) and then,
with usual Yankee good fortune, saw the second game
rained out while trailing, 6–2, in the fourth inning. At
Chicago, the Tigers split, reducing their lead to one-half
game. The opener of their twinbill was a 1–0 classic by
Hal Newhouser in 12 innings. Randy Gumpert of the
Sox was almost as effective, but Evers tripled in the 12th
and scored on Groth's single. It was Newhouser's 14th
win.

Over the next three days the Yankees and Tigers traded
the lead back and forth, and then the New Yorkers moved

into first place with a 7-5 win over Newhouser and the Tigers. Detroit scored four against Vic Raschi in the first, but home runs by DiMaggio and Johnny Mize helped rout Newhouser after four. The two front-runners split the next two games before the Yankees moved on to St. Louis. On September 17 the Yanks split with the Browns while the Tigers lost to Boston, and New York's lead was a full game over the Tigers. The next day Newhouser carried a 2-1 lead into the ninth inning, only to lose, 3-2, on two infield hits, an intentional walk, and a Walter Dropo single off reliever Hal White, followed by Doerr's sacrifice fly. This was a very tough loss, and it dropped the Tigers behind the Red Sox.

On the 19th, the Tigers won and the Yankees lost, and the next day the Tigers won again over the A's. The Yankees won, but Boston lost two to Cleveland. The following day Hutchinson beat the A's, 8-2, and the Tigers and Yanks were again tied for first place. Boston was two games back. On September 22, Newhouser hooked up with Bob Feller in a game that was 3-3 in the ninth, until the Indians' Joe Gordon ended it very suddenly with a home run. The next day the Yankees' Lopat shut out the Red Sox, and Art Houtteman lost to Cleveland.

On the 24th the Tigers fell two and a half back. The Yankees beat Boston, and Detroit lost, 2-1, to Cleveland in 10 innings, the winning run scoring on a mental error by the Tigers' catcher Aaron Robinson, who stepped on the plate but neglected to tag the winning run coming in, thinking that a force play was in effect. After this game, the Tigers' chances were slim indeed, and they never got any closer than two and a half games to the end of the season. Newhouser pitched two more games, both effectively, winning one and losing one, to finish with a record of 15-13. The Tigers had been in first place for 119 days of the 1950 season, compared to 51 for New York, but the Yankees were there at the end, and they were the ones who would meet the surprising Philadelphia Phillies in the World Series. Red Rolfe was named Manager of the Year, but this was scant consolation for second place.

No one knew what to think of Hal Newhouser after the 1950 season. Clearly his fastball and snapping curve were not what they had been in years past, but he had pitched surprisingly well considering the arm and shoulder miseries with which he had started the year. A few games he pitched were masterpieces reminiscent of his best years. He was a pitcher now, not just a thrower, and cunning and craft could make up for some of the lost physical ability. How much was the big question. The club chose to look hopefully toward 1951 and to figure Newhouser as a steady winner. The pitcher himself, though, in spite of brave and optimistic words uttered for public consumption, knew that there was something seriously wrong with his pitching arm. When the pain started, he said, it "was worse than a toothache." The exact cause of his trouble – whether it was bursitis, a pinched nerve, muscle damage, whatever – was never determined. Newhouser later said that at least 26 specialists looked at his shoulder at one time or another – "not one of them could give me the reason for the pain." The state of medical understanding of the physiology of a baseball pitcher's arm and shoulder was still rather primitive, and the doctors really did little if anything for Newhouser. Whether he could continue to pitch and win remained problematical.

16
A FADING TIGER

Art Houtteman, Detroit's best pitcher in 1950, was drafted into the army in October, so the Tigers were almost forced to look to Hal Newhouser as a big winner again. Rolfe, in February, told Watson Spoelstra, "He pitched his best ball last August and September when we needed it most. With a little luck he could have won five more games to climb to twenty, and I have a feeling he'll reach that figure this year."

Newhouser signed his 1951 contract before training camp began, taking another cut to about $42,000. Before he signed it, he said, he seriously considered quitting baseball to take a job paying $30,000 a year with a Detroit industrial concern. "The job offered tremendous possibilities for me in a new occupation," Newhouser told Lyall Smith. "I argued with myself for days before deciding to play ball again." He reported to camp saying that he was aiming for 20 wins in 1951. Later on, though, asked how long he thought he could keep pitching, Prince Hal replied, "This season will decide it. I'll hang up the glove if I don't have a good year."

The Tigers, hoping to improve on their second-place finish of the year before, had a terrible spring. General manager Billy Evans said his team was the "worst club I saw in Florida." Houtteman was gone, Ted Gray was terrible, and George Kell fractured his ring finger in a collision with Monte Irvin of the Giants. Newhouser started a game against the Memphis Chicks and was literally knocked out of the box. The first four Memphis batters got hits, the fourth a line drive off the pitcher's instep which sent him to the clubhouse. Luckily there was no fracture, and aside from that misadventure, Newhouser had a good training camp.

Shortly before the season opened, on April 13, Wish Egan died in Detroit at the age of 68. Father Charles Coughlin, the famous "radio priest" of the '30s, a close friend of the old scout, said the Solemn High Mass. Hal Newhouser served as a pallbearer and said of Egan, "He did a lot for me. He practically lived at our house for a year before I decided to go with the Tigers. I was very fond of him."

Newhouser's seasonal debut was on April 17 against Cleveland, and he lost it, 2–1. Spoelstra wrote that "the way the 'big fellow' looked gave the entire Detroit club a lift." The temperature was 40 degrees, but Newhouser had sharp control, good speed, and an excellent curve. He lost when shortstop Johnny Lipon booted an easy grounder in the ninth inning.

Four days later he was knocked out early at Chicago, even though the Tigers won, and he lost again on April 29 to the White Sox, 4–0, though he pitched fairly well. On May 4, however, Newhouser won his first game, going all the way to defeat Boston, 8–4; after the game, Rolfe said, "Hal can be a 20-game winner. His stuff and control are good. All he needs is some runs."

Five days later, Newhouser shut out Washington, 4–0, and six days after that he coasted to another win over the Senators. On May 20, his 30th birthday, Prince Hal went the route once again to beat the Red Sox at Fenway Park, 8–4. Spoelstra wrote in *The Sporting News* that Newhouser was once again the ace of the Detroit staff. Before May was over, though, he lost a couple of games, one to the Browns and the other to Cleveland, to even his record at 4-4. As June opened, the disappointing Tigers were in fifth place, 10 games behind the red-hot Chicago White Sox. Hoot Evers, upon whom the Tigers rested many of their hopes, was hitting very badly, but Virgil Trucks, who had missed a large part of the 1950 season, was healthy and winning again.

On June 4, Newhouser started slowly against Washington, giving up five runs in the first three innings. After that, he shut down the Senators completely and the Tigers came back to win, 6-5, on Groth's two-out hit in the ninth inning. It was Hal Newhouser's fifth victory. Six days later he had a no-decision start against the A's. On June 15, Newhouser lost, 2-0, to the Yankees at New York; trouble struck him in this game when he was forced to leave after four innings with an arm that was so painful he could no longer pitch.

He was unable to pitch again until the first game of the Fourth of July doubleheader, when he threw a complete-game victory over Chicago, winning, 6-3, and temporarily knocking the White Sox out of first place. Four days later Newhouser came in to relieve Hal White in the fourth inning of a game against Cleveland. He pitched to one man, Dale Mitchell, who hit a home run; Newhouser left with his arm hurting again.

On July 9 all of Detroit was saddened at the death of Harry Heilmann, once one of the club's greatest hitters and the broadcast voice of the Tigers for the past 18 years. Five days later Hal Newhouser gave it another try; he started against Washington but was forced to leave after an inning and a third. The loss evened his record at 6-6 and, though neither he nor the Tigers knew it at the time, ended his 1951 season. The Associated Press reported that "the pitching future of Prince Hal Newhouser is in doubt," and it certainly seemed so. In mid-August Rolfe used him in batting practice, but the lefthander's arm and shoulder still hurt. "It doesn't look like Hal can be any use to us the rest of the season," Rolfe said.

On August 10, Charlie Gehringer replaced Evans as the Detroit club's general manager, and on August 19 Bob Cain of the Tigers had the dubious honor of pitching to the only midget to bat in the major leagues. Bill Veeck of the Browns sent Eddie Gaedel to bat against the Tigers, and photographers caught the classic picture of catcher Bob Swift on his knees behind the plate trying to establish a strike zone for Gaedel.

Gehringer tried to figure out what to do about Hal Newhouser and his aching pitching arm. He had a series of meetings with the pitcher, and on September 6, Gehringer told the press, "We would like to see him pitch a game or two before the season ends to allow us to make a judgment on him . . . [H]e constitutes quite a problem, for we can't fill our roster with sore-armed pitchers."

Later on Gehringer denied that Newhouser would be released. He admitted that waivers had been asked on the pitcher but added that the same had been done on many other players, simply to gauge interest in them. "We aren't going to give Newhouser away," Gehringer said. In late September the general manager said, "The report on Newhouser is good. He is throwing better and that is encouraging. We haven't given up on him."

On January 17, 1952, an era ended in Detroit baseball. Walter O. Briggs, the wealthy owner of the Tigers, died in Miami of a kidney infection. Briggs had been an unobtrusive participant in the operations of his ball club over the years, letting the baseball people run things but helping to set general policy directions. It was he who had turned down the Newhouser-for-Bagby trade after the 1943 season and had assured Newhouser in 1946 that his best future interest was in Detroit and not in Mexico. His son, Walter O. Briggs, Jr., known to one and all as "Spike," took over the ownership of the franchise.

In February Hal Newhouser stopped in for a chat with

Gehringer. He assured the general manager that his arm would come around and that he could help the team. Gehringer told him that he figured strongly in Tiger pitching plans if his arm was all right. By this time Hal had made up his mind to stay with baseball, after several months of doubt and indecision. "If I can't be a good pitcher," he told a reporter, "it may be better to turn to something else."

Dizzy Trout weighed in with his contribution. It seems he and Newhouser had gone deer hunting in the north woods following the 1951 season. After they had each shot a buck, they and their companions got involved in a snowball fight. "Hal got right into the thick of it," Trout said. "He forgot himself for a few minutes and let go with one hard throw after another." Thinking back, Dizzy said, "his arm looked pretty good to me and I'm betting that it will feel good in training camp."

When contract time came around, Newhouser made the club a novel offer. He knew that he would have to take the full 25 percent cut from $42,000 down to about $31,000; what he suggested to Gehringer and Spike Briggs was a five-year contract at $20,000 a year. If his arm went bad and he could not pitch, he would work as a roving pitching instructor in the club's farm system. As he pointed out, if he had a good year in 1952 and won 15 to 18 games, with the usual year-to-year contract, the club would have to restore the 25 percent pay cut and he would be assured of at least $100,000 in three years. The five-year contract represented security for the pitcher and little risk for the club, he said. Briggs and Gehringer kicked the concept around for several days before finally telling Newhouser that club policy dictated no contracts longer than one year.

The Detroit executives had other things on their minds besides Newhouser's creative contract proposal. The club was receiving much criticism from the Detroit Negro Labor Council for running "a lily white organization."

Gehringer lamely denied the charge, but the facts were plain. Not until 1953 would the Tigers even sign any black minor league players, and the first black player to appear in a game for the Detroit club itself was Ossie Virgil, in 1958.

A major problem Gehringer faced was that he was running low on quality ballplayers of any color. The 1951 Tigers had finished eight games under .500, and things did not look much brighter for 1952. In February the club traded Bob Cain, Gene Bearden, and Dick Kryhoski to St. Louis for four players, but logic said that not much improvement could come from trading with the hapless Browns.

As spring training approached one writer wrote that manager Rolfe "had decided to throw away the kid gloves in dealing with Prince Hal." Whatever this meant – was he going to make Newhouser pitch even with excruciating pain in his left shoulder? – was never tested, because Rolfe denied the thrust of the story. "Newhouser has pitched hard a good many years," he said, "but if his arm is right, there is no reason why he couldn't be very effective working once a week." Former general manager Billy Evans was of another mind; talking to reporter Dan Daniel, Evans said, "Hal Newhouser's chances are not too bright."

In spring training at Lakeland, Newhouser took things rather easy. He worked four times in Florida and did not shirk his conditioning, but he tended to baby his pitching arm. He never had learned the exact nature of the trouble that had shelved him in 1951, so he was concerned. "I went from doctor to doctor," he said, " . . . and they gave me all kinds of tests, but I never did find out for sure what was wrong. The best explanation I got was that a tendon in the shoulder had pulled away from the bone structure. If that should happen again, I suppose I'd be all through. That's the reason I'm going to take my time about cutting loose." Rolfe said, "We'll let Hal take his time . . . We have reason to hope he will be all right, but it's still too early to tell."

In mid-March, columnist Joe Williams, of the *New York World-Telegram*, dropped in on the Tigers' training camp and learned that Newhouser, once the Tigers' ace, was now just another "hopeful name on the roster." Naturally, Williams wrote,

> a sore-armed pitcher cannot be at his best—but now you find critics wondering if his best was ever really big league. They remind you, that when he was winning 29, 25 and 26 from '44 through '46, all the power hitters were off to the wars . . . Gone were Williams, DiMaggio, Keller, Vernon, Chapman, Dillinger, Pesky, Stephens, Priddy, Valo, Johnson, Zarilla, and the like. This is a thought, however unjust and uncomplimentary it may be to Newhouser's record and talents. Yet some fantastic things happened when grown men were away. Even Snuffy Stirnweiss led the league in hitting and Dizzy Trout the pitchers and the Browns, of all people, won a pennant.

So, it had started: the whispering, coming usually out of New York, that Newhouser was never "really big league." It will be noted, of course, that Williams somehow managed to extend the war through 1946, ignored the years after 1946 completely, and contrived to send Vern Stephens and Bob Johnson off to a war they did not fight in. And the Browns; always the Browns' pennant would be cited as proof positive of the utter incapacity of wartime players. Williams *did* overlook Pete Gray, who would, in years to come, usually be mentioned as typical of wartime players. The Browns, Pete Gray, Snuffy Stirnweiss (that "Snuffy" was a nice touch, a nickname that helped to convey a picture of the inade-

quacy of wartime players): they were all useful in denigrating Newhouser's accomplishments.

Hal Newhouser was at the time concerned more with
his ability to pitch in 1952 than with his reputation for
1944 and 1945. He figured that his work from 1946
through 1950, when he had averaged more than 19 wins
a season over a five-year post-war span, had taken care
of that. He baked his arm in the hot Florida sun, and
that made it feel better. He learned that Red Rolfe intended to use him in the regular rotation when the season
started, and he pitched two batting practice sessions on
the trip north without any ill effects.

As the opening of the season approached, the Tigers
were a consensus pick for seventh place, although infielder Don Kolloway said, "If Hal comes back, we'll have
enough good pitching to figure in the race."

On Good Friday, Hoot Evers was hit on the hand by
a pitch from Cincinnati's Herman Wehmeier, and his
thumb was broken. It was not a good omen. The Tigers
opened the season by losing their first eight games and
10 of their first 13. Newhouser made his first appearance
on April 17, losing to the Browns, 3–1. Actually, he looked
good for seven innings until his arm grew weary; he gave
up a home run to Les Moss in the eighth and another
to Bob Nieman in the ninth. He threw no curves but
relied on a fastball that he moved around. After the game,
he grinned and said, "There was not the slightest twinge
of pain." Despite the loss, Prince Hal's showing encouraged the Tiger leadership.

Nevertheless, by May 2 the club had fallen into last
place, a position from which it never rose. On the 4th,
Newhouser was given the ball again, at Shibe Park in
Philadelphia; he lasted into the fifth, was not effective,
but did not figure in the decision as the Tigers lost, 6–5.
On May 11, Prince Hal lost to the White Sox, 6–5, leaving in the fourth inning, and he did not see further action
until the 27th. He relieved Marlin Stuart in the first

inning at Cleveland, with none out and a run in, and pitched five fairly good innings before leaving for a pinch hitter. A six-run outburst by the Tigers against Bob Lemon in the sixth inning gave Newhouser an unexpected 6–4 victory, his first of the year.

On June 3, the Tigers made a blockbuster trade with the Red Sox, sending Kell, Evers, Dizzy Trout, and Lipon to Boston for Pesky, Dropo, Fred Hatfield, Bill Wight, and Don Lenhardt. It was a trade that helped the Sox much more than it did the Tigers. When Johnny Pesky reported to Detroit, he was given a locker next to Newhouser's. After a few days Johnny ventured to tell Hal that when he was playing for Boston he had always thought the combative Newhouser "a horse's ass." Newhouser looked at him and responded, "I felt the same about you." The two players laughed and became good friends.

Newhouser had three brief relief outings in mid-June; he faced a total of only eight batters, although he permitted no runs over that stretch. Finally, on June 22, he pitched the last seven innings of a 12-inning game against the A's, picking up his second win of the season. He gave up no runs and scored the winning run himself on a single by Wertz against old Bobo Newsom.

Five days later, Rolfe gave Hal a start at St. Louis. He went the route but lost, 2–1, both runs scoring on throwing errors (one of them his own bad throw). He gave up only three hits, and visions of the old Newhouser suddenly appeared in Detroit. Prince Hal was seven wins short of a lifetime total of 200, and he now had hopes of reaching that goal in 1952. "I believe I can do it, too," he said, after being restored to the starting rotation. "When I was going good, I could always count on 12 to 14 victories in the last half of the season. With regular starts, I know I can win again."

On July 2, Newhouser lost to the White Sox, 3–2, on a home run by Minnie Minoso. Again, he pitched well in defeat; one of the Chicago runs scored on Steve Souchock's error. The next day, with the club record standing at a dismal 23–49, Rolfe and third base coach Dick Bartell were fired. Fred Hutchinson was named the new Tiger manager.

Newhouser beat the Browns and Satchel Paige on July 6 by an 8–6 score. Hal pitched seven innings and gave up four earned runs, and he contributed a single, double, and run batted in to his cause. The game was marred for the Tigers when infielder Jerry Priddy broke his leg sliding into the plate.

After absorbing a pounding in New York on the 13th, Newhouser came back four days later to go the distance in a 1–0 loss at Washington. Jim Busby singled home the only run of the game in the ninth, and Newhouser's record fell to 3–6. In his next outing, Harold pitched eight strong innings against the Senators but had nothing to show for it as the game went 16 innings before the Tigers managed to lose. On July 28, though, Prince Hal went the route against the Yankees, holding them to seven hits and two runs as he won his fourth game of the season.

Newhouser lost to the Red Sox and Dizzy Trout on August 2, but a week later he won a five-hitter over the White Sox at Chicago, 6–1. A few days after that, Spike Briggs negotiated an eight-player deal with the Browns, with Vic Wertz (going) and Ned Garver (coming) the key individuals. The Tigers stayed mired in last place. On August 17, Newhouser pitched a complete game against the Browns but lost, 4–2, on a two-run home run by ex-teammate Wertz in the eighth inning. He beat the Senators on the 23rd, 6–3, yielding three runs in the first and then shutting them out the rest of the way. And five days later, Newhouser won again, this time by 4–1 over the Indians in another complete game.

He now had 198 wins, and he told a reporter he felt he could have two or three more good years. "I'm really enthusiastic about 1953," he said. "If my arm had been right all season, I'm sure I could have helped keep Detroit from sliding into the cellar." And in fact he *had* been pitching well. His strikeout totals were way down and the velocity on his fastball was nothing like it had been, but he was a smart veteran by now and he could get batters out with craft and guile. "I've learned how to pace myself," he said. "Now I throw, for instance, a change of pace, a little slider, a curve, and then come in with a fast ball."

On the 3rd of September, he started a game at Cleveland against Feller, but it was a far cry from the old days. Feller was stumbling through a dismal season, and only 13,897 fans showed up for a matchup that could have filled the park a few years earlier. It turned out to be, as a United Press reporter wrote, "some unscheduled batting practice," as Feller was routed early and Newhouser was driven out in the Indians' eight-run fifth inning. The Tigers won, 11–8, but Newhouser did not figure in the decision.

After another undistinguished start, Newhouser was brilliant in a relief effort against Washington on the 15th. He snuffed out a Senator rally in the eighth, pitched a one-two-three ninth, and picked up the win when Harvey Kuenn tripled and scored on Fred Hatfield's single. He lost to Cleveland and Early Wynn on the 19th, 4–1, but he had one start left.

On the evening of September 25, only 569 people showed up to see the last-place Tigers take on the seventh-place Browns. It was the smallest crowd in Briggs Stadium history. What those fans saw, though, was Hal Newhouser's 200th career victory. He won it, 3–2, holding the Browns to six hits, and he struck out eight, his high for the year. The three Detroit runs were driven in by rookies who were in grade school when Harold Newhouser pitched his first big league game—Russ Sullivan, Harvey Kuenn, and Bill Tuttle. When third baseman

Hatfield threw out Don Lenhardt to end the game, his teammates surrounded Newhouser and thumped him on the back. He was the 55th pitcher in baseball history to win 200 big league games.

Newhouser's record for the year was nine wins and nine losses, the best on the last-place Tigers' pitching staff. It was the first time in the 51-year history of the franchise that the club had ever finished in the cellar. But it was not even close: the Tigers won 50, lost 104, and ended up 45 games behind the pennant-winning Yankees. Indeed, they were 14 games behind the Browns. All they could do was look to the next year. Hal Newhouser was certainly doing so: "I hope to be back," he said after the final game; "my arm has been all right since Hutch gave me a chance to work regularly." He said he would start training for 1953 immediately, with a lot of swimming and badminton. "My arm feels better than at any time in the last three years."

The Tigers were not so sure. In November, Watson Spoelstra wrote that Newhouser posed a problem for the club in 1953. Granting his remarkable comeback after arm trouble, Spoelstra said, "Gehringer may decide the club cannot pay so handsomely for nine victories." The next month Gehringer showed that he would not hesitate in moving out the storied names of recent Tiger history. With Trout, Wertz, Evers, and Kell sent away during the season, he traded Virgil Trucks, Johnny Groth, and Hal White to the Browns in December. Harold Newhouser was conspicuous as the only Tiger who remained from the club's winning seasons.

Still, there were high hopes. Bob Swift, now the bullpen coach, said the pitching would be much better in 1953. "I'm especially sold on Hal Newhouser," Swift said. "With a chance to pitch regularly, he could win 15 games without much trouble." Gehringer met with his lefthander for an hour's contract discussion in early February and then told reporters, "Hal has recently made a fine business connection . . . He wants one big year before he quits and somehow I have the idea he will get it." He added, "Newhouser isn't as fast as he once was, but his arm is sound and he knows how to pitch." The business connection referred to by the general manager was what the reporter called "administrative duties in a machine-shop operation."

Hal left for Florida two weeks before the Tigers opened training camp. He played golf in Lakeland and Miami, fished in Lake Okeechobee, and talked long-distance to Gehringer in Detroit to try to settle on a contract. He was the last one on the team to sign, but he said it was a "contract that shows they want me with the club" – no maximum pay cut this time, no bonuses, no incentives, just a straight salary. "With an even break in luck," Hal said, "I should have one of my best years."

Early in spring training, Newhouser suffered from an infected leg, but the rest of the stay in Lakeland was fine for him. He and Garver were the best pitchers in camp, and Newhouser's control was superb. A reporter wrote that "Hal has been much faster and sharper than last spring, raising the hope that he can contribute 12 to 15 victories this season."

That hope was a bit high.

When the season opened, Newhouser was still feeling the effects of the leg trouble, and he did not make his first appearance until April 25, when he was knocked out in the seventh inning by Cleveland, giving up successive home runs to Harry "Suitcase" Simpson and Jim Hegan. The Tigers lost, 4–3, but Newhouser was not involved in the decision. A bad omen was that his pitching arm started hurting. He opened against the Yankees on May 4 but came out after four innings. He pitched effectively, but his arm and shoulder were paining him. His next effort was on May 20, in New York. Staked to an early 7–2 lead, he gave up five runs in five innings and saw his teammates lose the game after he departed. Again, his arm hurt.

On June 4, Newhouser pitched one and two-thirds innings in relief of Ted Gray in an 11–2 loss to the A's. Nine days later, Hutchinson called him in to relieve Garver with a 7–6 lead over Washington, two outs in the ninth, and two men on. He retired Carmen Mauro on a fly ball to record a save. This performance earned him a start on Sunday, June 21, in the first game of a doubleheader against the Yankees. He lost, 6–3, to Whitey Ford, giving up home runs to Mantle and Berra in his three and a third innings of work. After the game, a New York reporter asked Prince Hal about Mantle. "That boy may become one of the great hitters," Newhouser said. Then, more wistfully, "I would like to have pitched against him, though, when I had my good stuff."

On July 1, the Detroit club signed a bonus-baby outfielder from Baltimore, a young man named Albert Kaline. The Tigers' past and future were crossing paths. Newhouser pitched one and a third innings of relief against the Browns on July 5, giving up four runs and five hits in that time. It was the last game he ever pitched in a Detroit uniform.

For two more weeks, Gehringer tried to decide what to do about the great lefthander. The club was not in the pennant race, so there was no pressure in that direction. On the other hand, there was now little realistic prospect that Newhouser's arm would come back, so he certainly did not figure in plans for rebuilding the team.

Finally, on July 22, as Newhouser was driving infielder Jerry Priddy (still recovering from his broken leg) to his home, he received word that Gehringer wanted to talk with him. At that point he had little doubt what it was. He met with the general manager for a long talk, and then

Gehringer announced to the press that the Detroit club had released pitcher Harold Newhouser unconditionally.
Hal talked to the reporters as well:

> I'm through as a pitcher. For a long time I had hoped my arm would come around. I worked in the bullpen. I pitched in batting practice. I did everything I could and now I'm convinced that I haven't got it anymore.

Asked about the release, he said,

> I've been expecting it. It's still something of a shock but I'll get over it. I don't hold any grudge against anybody. The Tigers always treated me fine. I mean both the players and the front office. Sure, I had a few heartaches along the route, as we all do, but I also had my share of success and with it a lot of fun.

He said he had no intention of trying to sign with anyone else. "I'd rather pitch for Detroit than any other team in the world," he said. "I'd like to finish out the season with the rest of the boys. I feel like I'm being taken out in the ninth inning with two men out."

Hal Newhouser was 32 years old.

Finally, he said that he hoped to stay in baseball with the Tigers' organization, but Gehringer squelched that hope. "At the moment, I don't see where we can place him," he said. "Maybe in the wintertime, if we have some openings in our organization, we can find a spot for him. But there's nothing now."

The Associated Press headed its story on the release by saying that "one of the most colorful pages in the history book of baseball was closed today."

The Detroit front office had no plans to do anything

for Hal Newhouser, but the players on the club, led by Jerry Priddy, chipped in to buy a large silver loving cup as a token of esteem for the left-handed pitcher who had won 200 games in a Detroit uniform. They made the presentation to Hal at a team dinner.

That was the end of his career as a Detroit Tiger.

17

AN INDIAN AT LAST

With Newhouser out of baseball, his critics were able to start in on him again. In February 1954, Williams in the *New York World Telegram & Sun* produced a classic of the type:

> Beyond the vague and conventional sore arm explanation, no specific reason was ever advanced for his gradual decline. It could have been, as harsher critics contend, his record was deceptive. They did seem to have a point.
>
> Most of the good hitters were off to war or in a state of readjustment during Newhouser's period of dominance ... yet in '48, when they were all back, he had another big year, winning 21, which was the league's best. But his strikeouts diminished from a peak of 275 to 143, which was significant.
>
> Whether the absence of the big bats made Newhouser look better than he really was may be debatable but is a point that can't be dismissed altogether. At the same time it seems evident he did suffer some sort of setback. A sore arm, in fact, or mental distress because he no longer could get the hitters out ...

So it was not really a sore arm which troubled Hal Newhouser; it was "mental distress" at being unable to get batters out. It was amazing that Newhouser was able to average more than 19 wins a year over five seasons while suffering mental distress at his inability to pitch well anymore.

Unfortunately for Joe Williams and his kind, Hal Newhouser had a surprise in store for them. One day during the winter, Dick Wakefield stopped in to see Hal. Wakefield, one of the great disappointments of the post-war years, had been traded by the Tigers to the Yankees after the 1949 season, and in the time since then had had brief and (he thought) unfair trials with the Yanks and Giants. He felt he should try once more and he urged Newhouser to give it one more shot as well. "You know," he said, "maybe we're quitting one year too soon. Why don't we give it another try?"

Newhouser demurred, and that was that. Except that, a few days later, he came across a couple of baseballs in the cellar of his house, picked them up, and began to throw them against the wall. "This was the first time I had even touched a baseball since last July," he said. "My arm felt so good that I began playing catch with my wife's brothers. I was throwing hard and there was no pain." With his arm feeling better, he remembered what he had once heard an old-time ballplayer say, that everyone quits a year too soon, and then spends the rest of his life looking back on that lost year.

Hal recalled that Hank Greenberg, now general manager of the Indians, had contacted him after his release by the Tigers, offering him a job in Cleveland. Now he called Hank and told his old friend that he was considering a comeback. He planned to go down south to see whether his arm was up to the effort, and, when he had determined what he could do, he would get back to Greenberg. Hank, who had played with Newhouser both before and after the war, had no doubts about the quality of

Hal's pitching skills, his determination and will to win; he said he would wait to hear.

Newhouser and Wakefield went down to Anna Marie Key, near Bradenton, Florida, to work out. There were a number of ballplayers living near there – Hutchinson, the Detroit manager, Hoot Evers, Earl Torgeson and Vern Bickford of the Braves – and the two old Tigers were able to plan a conditioning routine with the players in Bradenton. Newhouser and Wakefield rented a place on the beach, and they worked out. The whole program cost them about $2,000 each. Hal got Torgeson and Evers to come out and hit against him. He pitched every other day, fishing in the Gulf on the days in between. "I wanted to see if my arm would start hurting me again," Newhouser recalled. But his arm felt good. He called home and told Beryl, "I think I can do something. I don't think I can start but I think I can relieve."

Hal returned to Detroit for his wife's birthday on February 11 and talked over his prospects. Beryl was no doubt ready to start the rest of their lives, but Hal wanted to go back to baseball. When a telegram arrived from Greenberg, asking what he intended to do, Hal Newhouser decided to go to Tucson, to the Indians' training camp, to hook on once again with the comfortable life of a big league ballplayer.

Before he left home, he said, "My wife and I agreed that this would be my last whirl. If I make it all the way back and help this Cleveland team, fine. But if I find out that I can't pitch, or if the arm goes haywire again, well, that will be the windup."

Newhouser told Greenberg that he would report to Tucson on a trial basis. Greenberg said, "He told me he didn't want to sign a contract unless he felt he could help us . . . He is a great competitor. If his arm is all right, he'll be a tremendous help to us." In the meantime, Newhouser suffered through some strange sensations: "It'll seem funny to be wearing the uniform of another club." He thought about his situation with the Indians: "I'll be just like a rookie trying to make good ... If I can't make the grade with the Indians, I'll quit baseball for good and go into some other business."

Going after a job with the Cleveland Indians in 1954 was not like trying out with any old team. The Indians, under manager Al Lopez, had finished in second place, behind the Yankees, each of the past three seasons. This record of being not quite good enough produced some malicious talk around the league that the Indians could not take the pressures of a tight pennant race. The club had three top starters in Bob Lemon, Mike Garcia, and Early Wynn. They had Feller, who was not what he had been but was still a major league-calibre pitcher, and Art Houtteman, plagued with bad luck in Detroit but still in the prime of his career. For 1954 they had two top minor league pitchers in Ray Narleski and lefty Don Mossi, both bringing good records up from Tulsa, but untried in major league combat. What particularly struck Greenberg and Lopez was that the Indians were woefully short on left-handed pitching. Hal Newhouser could help to remedy that deficiency. When he reported, Newhouser was very pleased to be given uniform number 16, the same numerals he had worn for 15 years in Detroit. When Lopez called a squad meeting, though, Hal was reluctant to attend, because he was not even signed to a contract. Lopez insisted that he wanted Newhouser present at all such meetings; he considered the lefthander a part of the team. *The Sporting News* in mid-March reported that "Hal Newhouser looks better at each workout."

The Indians used Newhouser in a game against the New York Giants in March, and, since it was the spring debut of both Newhouser and Feller in the same game, the city of Tucson put up temporary bleachers to accommodate the crowd of nearly 6,000 people. The Giants pounded both great pitchers and won, 16–6. They got six runs off Feller, six off Newhouser, and, for good measure, four off Wynn. Newhouser gave up 10 hits in three innings. With a lot of clubs such a performance on the part of a marginal pitcher would have resulted in an instant ticket home. Greenberg, Lopez, and pitching coach Mel Harder watched closely and were not all that unhappy with what they saw. Harder, the longtime Cleveland pitching star, said, "I saw some encouraging signs. He threw overhand and the more he pitched the more he used his shoulder instead of his arm . . . You must remember he hadn't thrown under game conditions since last July."

All Lopez said was, "The important thing is to see how the arm feels after a day or two." Newhouser himself said, "I wasn't elated by all those runs. But I was elated with the way my arm felt. No matter how I threw, there was no pain." When his former teammate Vic Wertz, now with the newly-minted Baltimore Orioles, saw Newhouser pitch, he said, "Look, he's not throwing sidearm any more."

Lopez used Hal three more times in spring games, for a total of 13 innings, and the lefty yielded only one earned run. When the team broke camp and headed north and east, Newhouser left the club at Chattanooga and returned to Detroit, where he would talk over his progress with Beryl and discuss his future as an Indian with Greenberg.

Meanwhile Al Lopez left no doubt about his position. "I'm going to tell Greenberg by telephone today that I'd like to have Hal," he told reporters on April 8, "but it's up to them to work out the terms." He pointed out that general manager Frank Lane of the White Sox had been following Newhouser's progress closely; "I'm sure the Chicago White Sox will sign Newhouser if we don't."

Hal and Hank Greenberg spoke over the phone and quickly came to terms on a contract for $18,000. Newhouser, relieved that his arm was giving him no pain, said he was "happy as a kid" to sign with the Indians

(16 years after Cy Slapnicka showed up five minutes late), and Greenberg called Newhouser "a fine pitcher, a wonderful guy and a great competitor."

As the major leagues prepared for the 1954 season, they faced a new rule passed over the winter, requiring players to take their gloves into the dugout with them while their team was at bat, rather than simply leaving them on the field of play. American League officials at first threatened to disobey the new rule, on the grounds that it would cause slower games and stalling and would somehow reduce "dramatic interest in play." They eventually complied, and baseball survived.

In Cleveland, preparation for the baseball season included the annual luncheon of the Cleveland Advertising Club, honoring the Indians on April 12 in 1954. Bob Feller drew a big round of applause when he introduced the newest member of the Tribe, saying, "I'd like to welcome Hal Newhouser to our team. Personally, I'm very happy to have him with us."

When the season got underway, Newhouser sat, on the bench or in the bullpen, until the club visited Detroit. Greenberg instructed Lopez to start Newhouser against the Tigers on April 24. Perhaps it was to help the Tigers boost their lagging attendance; the game attracted a crowd of 25,445. Steve Gromek, the former Indians' pitcher, started for Detroit. Newhouser appeared shaky, but he had a 3–2 lead in the fifth inning when shortstop George Strickland booted a ground ball that should have been the third out. Ray Boone, another ex-Indian, blasted a three-run home run, and, when Newhouser was then hit by a line drive on his left foot, his day was over. The ball hit a tendon, resulting only in a bad bruise; it might have broken his foot, which would have ended the comeback attempt very abruptly.

Newhouser later said, "I wish to hell that I never pitched that game." He points out that he had a win-

ning career record against every other club, but he stands
0–1 lifetime against the Detroit Tigers.

The Indians started the season winning, and they kept
winning. The American League was very unbalanced in
1954. It was the first season for the Baltimore Orioles,
who were the old St. Louis Browns in new garb, and the
last season for Connie Mack's Philadelphia A's. Both
teams were very bad, finishing 57 and 60 games out of
first place, respectively, but the Senators, Tigers, and
Red Sox all finished more than 40 games back as well.
The White Sox won 94 games, the most for that franchise since 1920, and the Yankees won 103, the most in
any one of Casey Stengel's years at the helm in the Bronx,
but neither club even came close. The Indians of Al Lopez won 111 games, and no American League team in
history has ever won as many.

The '54 Indians had Vic Wertz (obtained from Baltimore) and Bill Glynn at first base; Bobby Avila, who
hit .341 to lead the league, at second; steady George
Strickland at short; and the powerful Al Rosen at third.
In the outfield were Larry Doby, who paced all hitters
in home runs and runs batted in, Al Smith, Dave Philley,
and Wally Westlake. Jim Hegan, a fine catcher, was
behind the plate. Hank Majeski, Hal Naragon, and Sam
Dente led a strong bench. Most of all, though, the Indians had pitching. Both Wynn and Lemon won 23 games,
and Garcia won 19 and the ERA title. Houtteman picked
up 15, and Feller won 13. Mossi and Narleski, the rookie
relievers, pitched sensationally, and Hal Newhouser, in
the bullpen for good after the lone start at Detroit, won
seven and lost only two. Houtteman and Feller were the
only ones of that number whose earned run averages were
over three, and Cleveland easily won the league ERA
crown.

Newhouser's first relief appearance for Lopez came on
May 2. Narleski was holding onto a 6–4 lead over Wash-

ington when, with two out in the eighth, Jim Busby singled and Roy Sievers doubled. Newhouser came in and fanned Tom Wright for the final out. He retired the side in order in the ninth to pick up a save.

After a brief appearance in Baltimore on the 8th, Hal pitched two scoreless innings to get the win, 8–7, over the Senators on May 13. "I waited two years for that baby," he said after the game, recalling his last win near the close of the 1952 season.

On May 18, Newhouser pitched one and two-thirds perfect innings against the Red Sox for another save. Eight days later, Hal relieved Art Houtteman at Chicago in the relief pitcher's nightmare. With the score tied in the ninth, the home team had the bases loaded with none out. The infield played in; the outfield played in. Newhouser got the first batter, Ferris Fain, to hit an infield grounder for a forceout at the plate, but Cass Michaels, the next hitter, lofted a ball over the shallow Doby's head for a single that ended the game.

As the season wore on, Lopez and Mel Harder worked out their method for using Newhouser. Lopez said that Newhouser, with his arm problems, "would not know until he loosened up whether he would be able to pitch to a couple of hitters or go for two or three innings." Lopez would ask Harder how he was, Harder would ask Newhouser, and Hal would pass the word back. Lopez, Newhouser said, "never once ever questioned my judgment." The results showed it, and Newhouser today calls Al Lopez "probably the greatest manager I ever played for." Lopez said that Hal "was a great guy on the club," and Harder commented that "he certainly was a winner and you could feel it when you were with him."

Part of what Greenberg, Lopez, and Harder were counting on was Newhouser's savvy, his knowledge of pitching and hitters after 14 big league seasons. He and Hegan, the Indians' fine catcher, tried to work out a pattern that would help him get hitters out. He told Hegan, "Jim, it's not Hal Newhouser anymore; he doesn't throw hard anymore, and the curve ball is not there any more . . . By the fast ball not being there, the change of pace is no good anymore . . . I came up with a little slider, and it doesn't hurt my arm so much." As he got into the season, though, Newhouser worked out a pattern. "Very simple," he called it. "Uncomplicated. Why the hitters didn't pick it up, I don't know." What he told Hegan to do was, when he got ahead in the count, to call for a fastball.

Hegan said, "Hal, I don't think that's going to work for you."

Newhouser answered, "Say, for instance, you're a hitter, Jim, and you know you've got a pitcher out there who can't throw hard, but he has still a fairly decent breaking ball and has a fair slider. What would you think if you were up there hitting and I had you two strikes and you know that I can't strike you out on a fastball? What would you look for?"

"Yeah," Hegan replied, "I'd be looking for an off-speed curveball or something."

As a result, Newhouser recalls, "That's how I pitched the whole season: to get ahead of the hitter and throw nothing but fastballs. When I got behind, the same way. They'd say, well, you're not going to throw me a fastball, you're gonna throw me a breaking ball." He laughs at the memory: "I threw more fastballs after I hurt my arm and lost my zip than I did when I had it." And the system worked.

On June 2, Hal won his second game of the year. The Yankees battered Early Wynn for seven runs in the first inning, but the Indians came back. Newhouser pitched three hitless innings to end the game, and Cleveland won, 8-7. One wonders if Joe Williams was watching. On the 6th, Newhouser pitched to one batter in each game of a doubleheader sweep at Philadelphia. He retired the last man to save Feller's 2-1 win in the opener, and in the nightcap he got a force-out for the next-to-last out in the ninth before Lemon came in to wrap it up.

After brief appearances on June 15 and 26, Hal picked up another win on the 27th. After the Indians had lost two games to the Yankees at home, they needed to win the series finale to avoid a sweep. Facing Whitey Ford before a crowd of 47,782, Bob Lemon had to leave after two innings with an injury. Newhouser came in without a warm-up, pitched six innings, and yielded but two runs and four hits. Philley and Westlake hit home runs, and the Indians won a big one, 4–3. As June came to a close, they led the White Sox by three games and the Yankees by three and a half.

On July 3, Hal pitched another six innings of relief and won his fourth game of the year. Coming in behind Houtteman and Mossi against the White Sox, with the score tied at three at the end of nine innings, Newhouser won it on a bases-loaded single by Hank Majeski in the 15th. Six days later, at Chicago, Newhouser lost to the Sox. He pitched to two batters, walked both, and saw both score against later relievers Bob Hooper and Mossi. Two days after that, he had another ineffective outing at Chicago — what he recalls as "the worst game that I pitched the whole year" — just before the All-Star break. Cleveland led the Yankees by a half game at the break.

After resting his arm for a week, Newhouser threw three scoreless innings at Washington on July 18 to save a game for Don Mossi. He had two more brief appearances in July and then opened August with three perfect innings and a win over the Senators. The frosting on Hal's cake was his single in the seventh inning which drove in the winning run. Newhouser's arm was a little achy after this game, however, and Lopez did not use him again until the 20th, when he pitched three scoreless innings in relief of Houtteman in a 7–2 win at Baltimore.

Ten days later, Newhouser came in to pitch in the sixth inning of a game at Fenway Park, behind Narleski, Dave

Hoskins, and Hooper. The Red Sox led, 4–0, but the Tribe scored five in the seventh inning, capped by Majeski's three-run homer; Newhouser pitched two and a third scoreless innings, and Mike Garcia finished. The Indians won, 5–4, and Hal Newhouser had his sixth win. As August came to an end, Cleveland led the Yankees by five and a half games, and the pesky White Sox had faded out of the picture.

Newhouser had a couple of scoreless appearances in early September, and on September 9 he picked up his seventh win of the year in an 11-inning win over the Athletics. Hal pitched the 10th and 11th innings, yielding just one base on balls, and won when A's pitcher Ed Burtschy walked Hal Naragon with the bases loaded. It was the Tribe's 100th win of the season, and the lead over New York stood at five and a half games.

After adding another game to their lead, the Indians prepared to host the Yankees in a doubleheader on September 12. The Cleveland players knew their reputation for having choked in September the prior three years, and they knew people were expecting the still-dangerous Yankees to come from behind to win their sixth straight pennant. The twin bill attracted 86,563 people, the largest crowd in baseball history, and the Indians were ready. Lemon won the opener, 4–1, and Early Wynn won the second game, 3–2, and the pennant race was effectively over. The Cleveland players came whooping and shouting into their clubhouse, and Hal Newhouser, who had not been involved in the failures of the past three seasons, was the first to shout, "So we're the choke-up champs!" The other players took up the cry, and Al Lopez, acknowledging that his team probably would have won even if they had lost that day, said, "To win it without beating the Yanks would have left something to be desired."

Newhouser had two more brief appearances as the club rolled on to the pennant and the record 111 victories.

When the regular season came to an end, he could look at a sparkling record: 7–2 wins and losses, an excellent 2.51 earned run average, 46 2/3 innings pitched in 26 games, and seven saves. It was not bad for a pitcher with a dead arm, who was only supposed to be able to pitch to wartime batters. Cleveland writer Hal Lebovitz summed things up succinctly: "'Nuff said about Newhouser's value? His is the comeback story of 1954."

The World Series, against the New York Giants, of course, was a disaster for the Indians. The first game in the Polo Grounds set the tone, with Willie Mays saving the game in the eighth inning with an incredible catch of Vic Wertz's long drive and Dusty Rhodes winning it in the 10th with a routine fly ball down the right-field line that turned into a three-run home run. Lemon lost the first game, Wynn the second, and Garcia the third, this one in Cleveland. For the fourth game, Lemon started again, gave up three early runs, and was knocked out in the fifth inning. Hal Newhouser came on to make his first World Series appearance since 1945. He pitched to two men, gave up a walk to Henry Thompson and a Monte Irvin single, and departed. The Indians lost, 7–4, and the Giants were world champions. The sudden demise of the record-setting Indians left Cleveland and the American League in a state of shock.

After the disappointing end to the year, Newhouser considered retiring. Pointing out that he had lost 15 pounds over the course of the season, he said, "Relieving is very hard. To get in shape for next season I'd have to start loosening up early in January. That's a long hard grind." He said he would talk it over with Beryl before coming to a decision. But Hal remembered a promise he had made to Greenberg, to stay around and help out young Herb Score, the brilliant lefthander the Indians were bringing up from their Indianapolis farm. So when the club sent him a contract calling for the same salary as the year before, he quickly signed it and sent it back.

Newhouser did not prepare for the 1955 season as he had the year before. There would be no more Florida workouts; he stayed in Detroit. "I figured that as long as I had no hopes of becoming a starter again," he said, "the Florida conditioning was needless." The lack of it, however, showed when he got to Tucson for spring training. He did not have the sharpness of the previous year, and he was hit hard in several spring games.

In 1955, too, the Indians had a lot more left-handed pitching in camp than they had had the year before. Then it was only Newhouser and the rookie Mossi. The defending league champs now had, along with those two, five others including Score, Hank Aguirre, and Bill Wight. Lebovitz wrote that, in 1954, Newhouser "was a big help to Mossi . . . schooling him in the wiles of lefthanded pitching. Now he has five others under his southpaw wing, and he often takes them aside for instruction."

Nevertheless, heading into the season, Hal Newhouser was still on the Cleveland roster. He pitched two-thirds of an inning against the Tigers on April 5, walking two but allowing no runs. Then, on May 3, before 24,813 at Municipal Stadium, he pitched one and two-thirds innings in relief of Mike Garcia in a 7–4 win over the Yankees. He gave up a hit and two walks, but no runs. It was, though he did not know it at the time, the last baseball game that Hal Newhouser would pitch.

As the mid-May deadline for cutting rosters to 25 players approached, Hank Greenberg had a problem, made no easier by the fact that he knew what he had to do. The club was in New York, so Greenberg went there and called Newhouser, telling him he had to see him. When he got to the pitcher's room, he said, "Hal, you're the 26th man on the club." Newhouser said he knew it. Greenberg suggested that Newhouser go on the inactive list, and he could be put back on the active roster on September 1, when clubs could carry 40 men once again. He would pitch batting practice, travel with the club, and draw his salary; he would not be in uniform during games. Newhouser declined: "I'd just be a bad penny," he said.

On May 11, the Indians announced that Hal Newhouser had been given his unconditional release. Hal told the press, "I had a nice time in Cleveland. It's a topnotch outfit." Then he flew back to Cleveland, gathered all his belongings together, and drove home to Detroit.

18
AFTERWARDS

When Newhouser arrived back at his residence in Franklin Village, in suburban Detroit, he sent off a telegram to his former Cleveland teammates:

> Sorry I didn't have time to say goodbye. I'll be pulling for all of you for another pennant. When you get into the World Series, I'll be ready for the eighth and ninth innings. God speed.

The Indians, in first place when Newhouser left them, eventually finished three games behind the New York Yankees.

For the pitcher, it was a time of waiting. He felt that he could still win in the major leagues, and he hoped to be offered a job. After a week or so, he was quoted in *The Sporting News*: "I've had several pitching offers. One minor league job is a honey, but I don't know about going back down. It has been a long time." Newhouser was exaggerating his prospects a little. There was apparently an offer made by the Toronto Maple Leafs of the International League, but Newhouser turned it down. Even though he would have been close to home, he really did not care to go to the minors. No big league

clubs broke down his door with job offers, so Prince Hal
Newhouser was forced to the conclusion that he was
through as an active player.

He considered a number of possibilities. He was 34
years old, and, in the anomaly that the nature of baseball forces upon its participants, a "washed-up old-
timer" in his chosen profession at the same time that
he was a healthy young man to the outside world. He
thought of going into what he had been trained for
many years earlier, tool designing or wood pattern-
making. He had worked during several off-seasons for
County Judge Arthur Moore, helping with juvenile de-
linquents in the county detention center; he was good
at that work and he considered a full-time position
there. Indeed, one of the things he did on a volunteer
basis in the next few years was to set up a sports program for the juvenile home. But when it came to making a career decision, Hal Newhouser knew he wanted
to stay with baseball.

The Tigers had made it all too clear in 1953 that they
had no intention of offering Newhouser a place in their
organization. But in 1955 his old catcher Paul Richards
was both general manager and field boss of the Baltimore Orioles. The Baltimore organization was alive
with purpose and direction. Under the imaginative leadership of Richards, it was quickly erasing all memory
of its woeful Brownie forebears. Hal called Richards.
He felt that he did not want to manage or coach, but
he hoped to get into an office position. He knew that
he would have to start at a low level since he had no experience. He asked Richards if anything was available,
and Richards said, "Why don't you start off scouting?"

And so Newhouser became a scout for Baltimore.
His territory was the Detroit area, which translated
into Michigan and northern Ohio. He sat down with
Jim McLaughlin, the Orioles' farm director, to talk over
what he would be looking for. Obviously, Hal had never

scouted talent before, and he had not seen much except major league players for years. But he knew what it took to play in the big leagues, and it was potential big league ballplayers he was after. Initially, it was decided, he would work with another scout named Lou D'Annunzio — the same Lou D'Annunzio who had, as a Tiger birddog, tipped off Wish Egan many years earlier to a teenage flame-thrower named Hal Newhouser.

It was not long before Newhouser was able to work on his own, with no help needed. The Baltimore front office was soon commenting on the high quality of his scouting reports, and he signed a number of prospects, among them two young pitchers named Milt Pappas and Dean Chance, who between them won 337 major league games. Newhouser was promoted to the position of scout-supervisor, in which job he toured the country to look at players other scouts had turned up and to recommend whether the Orioles should sign them and for how much. Newhouser was instrumental in Baltimore's signing of Jack Fisher, Ron Moeller, and Willie Tasby, among others, and in the Orioles' purchase of first baseman Jim Gentile from the Dodgers' organization at St. Paul.

In February 1961, after five years with the Orioles, he resigned, in part because of all the travel. "I just thought I'd drop out for a year and stay around the house," he recalls.

Soon, however, Newhouser became itchy to get back into baseball, and when he ran into another old Tiger, Hoot Evers, it was not long before he was employed again. Evers was the player personnel director for Cleveland, and he asked Hal to join the Indians. After talking it over with Gabe Paul, the Cleveland president, Newhouser signed a three-year contract on October 24, 1961. He was designated scout and minor league pitching coach, but within a couple of months he was being referred to as Cleveland's chief scout, Evers' right-hand man, and supervisor of the minor league spring training camp at Tucson.

Newhouser soon found himself traveling all over the United States again, living from motel room to motel room, looking at young ballplayers, and seeing his wife and daughters on a hit-and-miss basis. He loved the baseball part of it, but he did not love the travel. So it was that he was receptive after a year or so when a friend talked to him about a job in a wholly different area. Community National Bank, in Pontiac, Michigan, not far from his home, was opening up a new business development department, and the directors of the bank approached Newhouser about heading it. Once he satisfied himself that it was not just his name the banking people were after, he looked further into the position and what it could offer and found the idea intriguing. Still, he told the Community National people, he had a contract with the Cleveland Indians which had another year to run. Fine, they said, we can wait.

When Newhouser spoke with Evers and Paul, they urged him to take the banking job if he was interested in it; the Indians would continue to pay him until the end of his contract. If he were able to do some scouting, that would be welcome. And if he found out that banking was not for him, the Cleveland organization would have a job waiting. As a result of all this, in October 1964 Prince Hal Newhouser became Harold Newhouser of Community National Bank.

After a few months, the bank promoted Newhouser to assistant vice president and raised his pay, and he told Evers and the Indians that he was in the banking business to stay. In fact, he stayed for 20 years, as vice president in charge of business development, public relations, advertising, and community relations. Hal Newhouser was not a man with a great deal of formal education, but he was intelligent, had acquired a good bit of polish in his years in the big leagues, and was a quick learner. Although somewhat reserved by nature, he worked well with people, something which his pre-war Tiger teammates never would have believed. The banking business, it turned out, was just right for him. The years passed, the Newhousers moved to a new home in Bloomfield Hills, closer to Pontiac than to De-troit, and Beryl and Harold became grandparents. Beryl told a reporter that, with Hal out of baseball, they had a "less excitable life, but [did] the more enjoyable things as average citizen and businessman." As the 1970s passed by and the 1980s moved along, though, and Hal could see his bank retirement and pension coming closer, the old itch started again. In 1983, Hal, as a member of six or more All-Star teams, was invited to the 50th anniversary All-Star Game in Chicago. He and Beryl went and "had a barrel of fun . . . seeing all the guys that I pitched against and played against and hung around with."

As Hal was preparing to check out of the Hyatt Re-gency in Chicago, he encountered his old teammate Al Rosen, at the time the president and general manager of the Houston Astros. Rosen said he had heard New-houser was considering retiring from the bank, and, if that was true, would he be interested in a job? Hal said he was thinking of getting back into scouting, just in the Michigan and southern Ontario area, but that he was still a year and a half away from his retirement. Rosen said, "When you're ready, give me a call."

As a result, when Newhouser reached his 20-year milestone and retired from Community National Bank, he stepped into a job scouting for the Astros, the first National League club with which he was ever associated. He quickly proved that he had not lost his touch; Rosen said, "His reports on players were much like his career— precision plus; no nonsense and the straightforwardness about players he had seen."

From Hal Newhouser's point of view, the difference

this time around was that Beryl could accompany him on all his trips. "Sometimes she . . . watches the games and sometimes . . . she goes shopping," he says, but "every night we have dinner together. We have breakfast together. We have lunch together." Hal watches ball games all spring and summer, writes up his reports for the home office in Houston, and never strays far from home. From mid-September until the end of March, there is no baseball to cover, and he can do all the painting, patching, and scraping around the house that he wants. "Talk about a happy retirement," Hal Newhouser says, "it's the retirement I have."

19
PRINCE HAL'S BURDEN

In 1960, Hal Newhouser became eligible for election to the Hall of Fame by the baseball writers. As the years went by, he always had some votes, but he never came close to the 75 percent necessary for election. As his final year of eligibility approached, *The Sporting News* on December 28, 1974, ran an editorial addressed to those who would soon be voting for the Hall. "Four are worthy of the voters' close scrutiny, we think" and it identified the four as Ralph Kiner, George Kell, Bob Lemon, and Hal Newhouser.

Kiner was elected on that ballot, and Lemon went in the following year. Kell was selected by the Veterans' Committee in 1983, but Hal Newhouser remains on the outside. His only avenue of selection for the Hall now is the Veterans' Committee.

"I'm not bitter about the Hall of Fame," Newhouser says, but the tone of voice and the torrent of words that follows make it clear that his non-election is a source of great disappointment to the lefthander. One writer asked him which players should go into the Hall; Newhouser answered, "You're talking to one." That he should feel this way is certainly not surprising. For a man who has devoted a great part of his life to baseball and who rose to the very top of his profession, the desire for recognition as one of the best of all time is a natural feeling.

Many of Newhouser's peers agree that he should be in the red-brick shrine at Cooperstown. The late Hank Greenberg said, "I definitely feel that he should be in the Hall of Fame." Charlie Metro, long active in the game as a player, coach, and manager, said Newhouser's election "is long past due." Al Rosen said his exclusion "is a rank injustice" to "one of the game's greatest left-handers." Ray Boone, Red Borom, the late George Case, Dave "Boo" Ferriss, Ned Garver, Steve Gromek, George Kell, the late Ted Lyons, Johnny Pesky, Nelson Potter, and Ted Williams are just some of his contemporaries who have stated that Newhouser should be in the Hall.

Ted Lyons is one whose opinion ought to carry some weight. He pitched in the big leagues from 1923 to 1946 (with three years out for the war), all with the Chicago White Sox. He managed the White Sox for three years, and he served as a pitching coach in the majors for many years after that. He won 260 games for the Sox, lost 230, and was himself elected to Cooperstown in 1955. Lyons saw a great many pitchers during his long career. Interestingly, he did not see Hal Newhouser pitch in his wartime years, 1943, 1944, and 1945. But he did see him pitch before and after the war, and Lyons said that Hal Newhouser deserved election to the Hall of Fame.

In 1986, Nick Acocella and Donald Dewey published a little book they called *The "All-Stars" All-Star Baseball Book*, in which they asked big leaguers from many eras to pick, from their contemporaries, a 10-man team, eight position players and a right- and left-handed pitcher, for one crucial game. Of the respondents who could be said to have had careers in the American League which overlapped Newhouser's, 13 named him as their choice for a left-handed pitcher. Twenty-two selected Whitey Ford, the league's top lefty for the generation after Newhouser, and 18 picked Lefty Grove, the best in the prior generation. No other American League lefthander of the era received more than three picks (Lefty Gomez and Herb Score). Leading pitchers of the day – Spud Chandler, Tex Hughson, Ferriss, Garver and Gromek – wanted Newhouser as their man on the mound for a pressure game. And Lou Boudreau, though he went outside his time to pick Sandy Koufax as his left-handed pitcher, said that Newhouser and Red Ruffing were the toughest pitchers for him: "I could never follow their pitches."

The following year, 1987, Eugene V. and Roger A. McCaffrey came out with a book entitled *Players' Choice,* the compilation of the results of a survey *they* took among every living big league ballplayer, coach, and manager they could find. The McCaffreys received 645 responses from participants in every era of the 20th century. In the category of "best lefthanded pitcher," Newhouser was rated eighth, trailing Koufax, Grove, Warren Spahn, Steve Carlton, Carl Hubbell, Ford, and Gomez. After Newhouser there was a big dropoff to Score, Herb Pennock, and Rube Waddell. Hal Newhouser was also included among those possessing the best curveball and the best change-up.

If Hal Newhouser was the eighth-best left-handed pitcher of all time, or if he was the best lefty of his own time, as the Acocella and Dewey poll would indicate he was, then there can be little justification for excluding him from the Hall of Fame.

But the recollections and judgments of the men who played the game make up just one form of measurement. His peers believe that Newhouser belongs in Cooperstown – but do the statistics say so as well?

A look at Newhouser's record reveals that he led his league in various pitching departments numerous times. Four times he led the league in victories, twice in earned run average. He led twice in complete games and in strikeouts. Newhouser is the last pitcher to win

25 or more games in three consecutive seasons and the last American League pitcher to lead in earned run average two straight years. He is one of only seven pitchers in baseball history to have won the pitching triple crown (winning percentage, earned run average, and strikeouts in a single season).

In 1946 – when all the stars had returned from the service – Hal Newhouser struck out 275 batters. To put this in perspective, note that only nine pitchers have ever topped that mark in the history of the American League, and in the more than 50 years between 1912 and 1965 only one man (Feller) in either league struck out more in a season. Since 1920, only three men have recorded more victories than Newhouser's 29 in 1944.

Newhouser's lifetime statistics can be compared with those of the 46 pitchers who are in the Hall of Fame. Even with the career-shortening arm trouble, he has more victories than nine of them, more shutouts (while pitching in a hitter's park) than 12 of them, including Lyons and Dazzy Vance, and a higher winning percentage than 15, including Early Wynn and Robin Roberts. Newhouser's earned run average is better than 19 of those in the shrine, including Spahn and Catfish Hunter. Even counting Newhouser's early wild years, he allowed fewer walks per game than Hall of Famers Gomez, Feller, and Lemon. And he struck out more batters than 20 of the 46.

Newhouser's dominance over hitters is illustrated in three categories in which he leads more than half of the pitchers considered the best of all time. Opposing batters hit just .239 against Prince Hal in his career, a lower mark than that for 26 Hall of Famers, including Christy Mathewson, Grover Cleveland Alexander, and Cy Young, all of whom pitched in the deadball era. Newhouser gave up fewer hits per inning than 30 of those in Cooperstown, and he struck out more hitters per game than 35 of them, including Grove and Walter Johnson.

In addition to such relatively traditional statistical standards, there have recently been developed increasingly sophisticated methods of objective statistical analysis, driven by computers, and named by writer Bill James "sabermetrics," after the growing Society for American Baseball Research (SABR). How does Hal Newhouser measure up with these analysts?

Two major works have been published recently using "sabermetrics" to compare and analyze players' performances throughout baseball history. One is the exhaustive *Total Baseball* (1989), edited by John Thorn and Pete Palmer, while the other is *The Bill James Historical Baseball Abstract*, published by that popular author in 1986.

These writers use complex, sometimes arcane methods, often confusing to readers without a mathematical bent, to evaluate players. Their sophisticated formulas attempt to take into account the team, era, ball park and league for each player. Thorn and Palmer are pure baseball scientists, following where their formulas and methodology take them, while James often interjects his personal feelings and opinions into his ranking of players, using his formulas as a guide.

Thorn and Palmer rank every pitcher in major league history—from the first one to throw a pitch in 1876 through the last pitcher used in 1988. By their rankings, Harold Newhouser was the 15th best pitcher of all time, the 15th best pitcher who ever lived. The 14 ahead of him are all in the Hall of Fame, as are, obviously, 32 of those behind him. The fifth best left-handed pitcher of all time, according to Thorn and Palmer, is Newhouser, just behind Grove, Spahn, Ford and Hubbell.

When these writers consider every player who ever

played the game, regardless of position, Newhouser is rated the 51st best – *the 51st best player ever to walk onto a major league ballfield!* (There are 204 members in the Hall of Fame.) Thorn and Palmer also ranked players by era, and for the period from 1942 through 1960, Newhouser is the third best pitcher (ahead of Lemon, Feller, and Hoyt Wilhelm) and the eighth best player overall.

Obviously one can argue with Thorn and Palmer's formulas; a slight change of weight to this factor or that can make a difference in rankings. Nevertheless, these respected writers have fine-tuned their analytical tools over a period of years and have determined to their own satisfaction that they are as accurate and fair as possible.

James, in his book, rates Newhouser ninth among left-handed pitchers in peak value, defined as "the value of a player to his team at his highest clearly established level of performance," but not in his top 10 in "career value," covering his entire career. The problem James had with Prince Hal in both categories was the usual one: wartime baseball. James writes, "I cut him quite a bit because of the calibre of competition that he was facing," but then admits that "his performance in 1946 and 1948 would put one through some fairly hefty contortions to show that he was not a worthy pitcher."

In February 1975, after the Hall of Fame vote was announced in Newhouser's last year of eligibility with the baseball writers, Hal tried to explain to an Associated Press reporter why he had failed to secure enough votes. "Most of the writers who saw me have either retired or passed on," he said. "I don't know whether the writers today would know that I was the only pitcher in the history of baseball to win the Most Valuable Player award two years in a row, 1944 and 1945. I don't know if they would recall that I won 80 games over three seasons."

He was kidding himself. It was not the two MVP awards that were a problem: it was the years when he won them. As time passed, and Hal Newhouser's career receded into the gray yesterdays, it was the label "wartime player" which was fastened to him. The "with-it" writers of the '60s and '70s were not about to elect a wartime player to the Hall of Fame; they had heard enough about Pete Gray and Snuffy Stirnweiss and 15-year-old Joe Nuxhall and the Browns. So they withheld their votes from a pitcher who had dominated wartime baseball, when the stars were away. It was a burden which would not be lifted from Harold Newhouser.

Perhaps we should look at wartime baseball a little more closely.

There were four baseball seasons played between Pearl Harbor and V-J Day, although the 1945 campaign lasted a month or so beyond the end of the war. Each of those seasons presents a slightly different picture. In 1942, for example, there was really very little impact of the war on baseball. Most of the big names were still around—Ted Williams won the triple crown in the American League, Musial and Slaughter led the Cardinals to the National League pennant, and Mort Cooper, Johnny Beazley, Tex Hughson and Ernie Bonham were 20-game winners. The Yankees, with Gordon, Rizzuto, Henrich, DiMaggio, Keller, and Dickey, easily won the junior league crown. The biggest name missing was Hank Greenberg, and his absence from the Detroit lineup certainly did not help Newhouser.

In 1943 the bite of Selective Service was a little deeper, and there were fewer pre-war starters still playing. Keller, Chandler, Gordon, Bonham, Crosetti, Borowy and Dickey were still around for the Yanks, leading them to another pennant. Hall of Famer Luke Appling won the batting title with a relatively modest .328. Joe Gordon, who many believe should be in Cooperstown, pounded wartime pitching to the tune of just .249. Bobby Doerr and Lou Boudreau, who *are* in the Hall, hit .270 and .286 respectively. Indian Bob Johnson batted .265, Mickey Vernon .268, and Joe Kuhel of the White Sox .213. Obviously, some of those wartime fill-ins must have been getting some pretty good hitters out. In the National League, where Billy Southworth's Cardinals won another flag, there were still people such as the Cooper brothers, Musial, Frank McCormick, Ernie Lombardi, Mel Ott, Stan Hack, Phil Cavarretta, Joe Medwick, Arky Vaughan, Kirby Higbe, Johnny VanderMeer, and Schoolboy Rowe suiting up on a regular basis.

Of course, 1944 was the year of the Browns, and everyone knows what that means. Never mind that Kramer, Potter, Muncrief, and Denny Galehouse were all legitimate big league pitchers, or that McQuinn, Kreevich, Gene Moore, Gutteridge and Laabs were all established major league players. American League teams were happy to give Vern Stephens and Al Zarilla steady employment for years after the war. Never mind; this was the year of the Browns. The two leading hitters in the league were Boudreau and Doerr, at .327 and .325, followed closely by Bob Johnson at .324. These were all quality hitters having good, but not great, seasons. George Kell came up to the A's as a rookie and hit .268, and his fellow Hall of Famer, Rick Ferrell, hit .277 for Washington. If the pitching was so awful, it seems strange that no one hit any higher.

In the other league the victorious Cards still had Walker Cooper and his brother Mort, Marion, Kurowski, Musial, Hopp, Litwhiler, Lanier, and Brecheen. Rip Sewell and Preacher Roe led the Pittsburgh staff, while Bucky Walters, Claude Passeau, Paul Derringer, Ken Raffensberger, and Big Bill Lee were among the other National League pitchers. McCormick, Cavarretta, Bob Elliott, Hack, Ott, young Andy Pafko, Medwick, Tommy Holmes, Bill Nicholson, Eddie Stanky, Dixie Walker, Mickey Owen, Augie Galan, and Ron Northey were regulars. There was obviously not the depth of pre-war years, but there were still a lot of good players in the lineup. This was the season, of course, in which young Joe Nuxhall, not quite 16 years old, pitched two-thirds of an inning for Cincinnati; much has been made of that. But if 1944 is to be judged by one very brief appearance by a teenaged Nuxhall, is 1951 to be judged by the successful pinch-hitting appearance of Bill Veeck's midget?

The last of the wartime years, and in many ways the most difficult, was 1945. The unrelenting manpower demands of the armed services and the munitions industry cut deeper than ever into the bone and sinew of baseball, carrying off players like Musial, Northey, Wakefield, Early Wynn, Walker Cooper, and others. It was the season that Pete Gray played for the Browns and the one in which Stirnweiss won his batting title. Bert Shepard, a war veteran with a wooden leg, pitched for Washington. And Tony Cuccinello was released by the White Sox after finishing second in the league in hitting.

But Tony Cuccinello was a pretty good ballplayer. He had hit over .300 four times earlier in his career; he was nothing to be ashamed of. Shepard, like Nuxhall before him, pitched in only one game; we can bring out the Eddie Gaedel test again. Gray, the one-armed outfielder, hit but .218; there were still standards of competence for big league play in 1945, and Pete Gray could not meet them. Besides, all through the season there was a trickle of discharged veterans who rejoined their old teams. Greenberg, of course, was the most prominent, along with Feller, who started nine games. Dave Ferriss of the Red Sox, a pre-war minor leaguer, was another valuable returnee, as was Charlie Keller, who played in 44 games, with 10 home runs and a .301 average. Buddy Lewis came back after three and a half years, played in 69 games, hit .333, and almost put the Senators in the World Series. Al Benton, Red Ruffing, and, over in the National League, a young redhead named Albert Schoendienst were among the discharged servicemen who made meaningful contributions in 1945. So it is well to keep in mind that, while 1945 was certainly the last of the wartime seasons, it was also, to some degree, the first of the post-war seasons.

For a little further perspective on wartime ball, let us look, not at the Pete Grays or even the Snuffy Stirnweisses, but at some players who were – and are – recognized as stars. Start with Stan Musial, acknowledged from his first appearances with the Cardinals to be a superstar. During three full wartime seasons, Musial averaged .341 – pretty good hitting, but not far off his lifetime average of .331, which was pulled down by some low years at the end of his career. Hall of Famer Joe Medwick played four full wartime seasons and hit .302, well under his lifetime mark. Mel Ott averaged .284 and almost 24 home runs over the four years – not bad, but a bit under his career figures. Bob Elliott of the Pirates played all four years and averaged 101 runs batted in a season – again, not bad, but not spectacular. Elliott would do much better in his MVP season two years after the war.

In the American League, Indian Bob Johnson averaged .291 for the four years, very close to his lifetime average, and Lou Boudreau averaged .301, six points over his career mark. Wally Moses played four wartime years with the White Sox and put up a .272 average, well under his lifetime .291 record. George McQuinn of the Browns played through the war and averaged 18 points under his lifetime mark and far below the .304 he would record as a Yankee regular in 1947. Early Wynn of the Senators averaged 12 victories a year over three full wartime seasons. Bobby Doerr of the Red Sox, playing nearly three full years, compiled a wartime batting average of .293, a shade over his lifetime average.

The point here is not to denigrate these fine ball-players. Rather, it is to emphasize that if baseball was so much weaker during the war years that fact does not show up in the records of these legitimate baseball stars. Dixie Walker of the Dodgers had a year when he hit .357, but his overall wartime average was .313, not that far above his career .306. Tommy Holmes had one big season, hitting .352, but his wartime average of .303 matches almost exactly his career average. Phil Cavarretta hit .355 in 1945 and .309 for his four wartime seasons; this is substantially over his lifetime .293, but it is the big average in '45 that pulls him up. Cavarretta's appears to be the only figure which is considerably skewed, and without the batting championship of '45 included his three-year average is .296, very close to his career norm.

If these stars, and others who could be mentioned such as Frank McCormick, Stan Hack, Ernie Lombardi, Rudy York, and Joe Kuhel, could not take advantage of wartime ball to pile up big numbers, then perhaps World War II baseball has taken a bum rap. Granted, many of the big names were gone, but their replacements were able to keep the quality of the game at a respectable level. Superstars such as Williams, Feller, DiMaggio, and Greenberg were irreplaceable, but other superstars such as Musial and Ott, and players nearly in that category such as Boudreau, Medwick, Wynn, and Doerr, were around for all or most of the war. Many of the other players who went off to the service were just average ballplayers, and the men who replaced these drafted journeymen were only marginally inferior, if at all, to those for whom they were filling in. This is the fact that is overlooked in all the attention given to the Pete Grays and Joe Nuxhalls.

Much the same point is made by David Nemec in *The Ultimate Baseball Book*. He points out that a large improvement in the records of those big league stars who were not drafted simply did not occur, and accordingly, taking the case of the one player who *did* show such improvement, he concludes that "the neglect into which Newhouser has fallen seems sad and unfair." If Newhouser were simply an average pitcher taking advantage of poor competition, then high win totals comparable with his should have been compiled by any number of other average pitchers. And this did not happen. The only other pitcher to achieve a number of victories close to what Newhouser had in 1944 and 1945 was Trout, who won 27 in 1944 before falling off to 18 the next year. An interesting factor which comes into play here is that influence to which Harold Newhouser gives so much credit for making him a winning pitcher: the tutelage of Paul Richards. Trout suddenly came into his own in 1943, the first year Richards was with Detroit, and Newhouser did so the next season. It may very well be, as Newhouser has said all along, and as many observers noted at the time, that it was the presence of Richards — and not wartime baseball *per se* — that accounts for the Detroit Tigers having the only big winning pitchers of the period.

Another point to be made is that in 1941 and 1942 observers all around the American League predicted that young Newhouser, when he learned control, would blossom into a great left-handed pitcher. He learned control and he did blossom, just as predicted, so it seems nonsensical to say that his blossoming was because of the war, especially when he kept on pitching well after the war.

If it can fairly be said, then, that major league baseball suffered some but not significant weakening during World War II — perhaps comparable to that which the big leagues inflicted upon themselves with the series of expansions of the 1960s and 1970s — then Hal Newhouser's career should be re-examined — his entire career.

And yet, the exact opposite seems to be happening. A writer named Donald Honig has filled the last decade with several books, mainly picture books with incidental text, which, by their sheer number, threaten to define baseball history in the popular mind. Honig appears to bear Hal Newhouser some sort of undying grudge. He wrote a history of the American League in which Newhouser's name never appears, even though there is a full chapter on the 1940s, when the Tiger lefthander won more games than any other pitcher. Honig published a history of the World Series, and his game-by-game description of the 1945 classic never mentions Newhouser, who started three games, won two, and was the dominant player in the Series. Finally, though, in the spring of 1989 Honig published a paperback book on the American League's Most Valuable Player award winners. He could not just leave two pages blank, so he had to mention Hal Newhouser. What he did, of course, was damn the Detroit lefthander with the faintest praise imaginable. Newhouser's '44 season, he wrote, was that of "a lion with a carcass," and Trout should have won the MVP award. In 1945, "again, he was a flashlight in a roomful of glittering candles." Honig quotes an *unnamed* teammate as saying, "He wasn't a bad pitcher, but he . . . was as irritating a player as I have ever known." Honig concludes that Newhouser's current reputation is simply that of "a wartime player . . . a cactus among the cornstalks." Obviously, Donald Honig would prefer that Newhouser sink into oblivion.

But Hal Newhouser's career must be addressed. And it must be addressed in context. Certainly a part of his career took place during wartime, but it is terribly unfair to criticize a player for the era in which he performs—something over which he has no control. Cy Young won 511 games at a time when pitchers started 50 or more games a season, but he is still recognized as an all-time great because no other pitcher of his day approached his totals despite having the same "advantages." Burleigh Grimes won more games than any other pitcher in the 1920s, but some discount his accomplishments because he was allowed to continue throwing the spitball after the pitch was outlawed. Bill James disagrees: "Grimes took the advantages that he had and used them to win." He went on: "Do you penalize Walter Johnson because he could throw harder than anyone else of his time? That's what the game is all about: you all start out unequal, and you use what you've been given to try and win." And nobody was better than Hal Newhouser in his era, winning more games than anybody in the 1940s. For a five-year stretch after the war, Newhouser *averaged* over 19 wins a season—and that does *not* include 1944 or 1945.

On the testimony of the numbers and of his contemporaries, Newhouser is one of the top left-handed pitchers of all time—certainly within the top 10—and the dominant southpaw of his era. His career was curtailed at a relatively early age by the affliction in his left arm and shoulder, but in his prime he had blinding speed, an awesome curveball, and a baffling change of pace. Once he learned control, of his pitches and of himself, he was a master on the mound. As he once told Ned Garver, he never threw two pitches in a row the same speed—even two fastballs. He became a crafty veteran who could retire hitters on guile and deception when he no longer had his great stuff. Most of all, Hal Newhouser is remembered as a great competitor, a pitcher who hated to lose and who had the tools to avoid doing so most of the time.

Metro, who played with him on the Tigers and against him for the Athletics, said, "Hal Newhouser was the most fierce pitching competitor that I have ever seen in my lifetime of baseball . . . If you hit a ball good off him in batting practice, the next one was chest high and in. The first time I faced him after leaving the Ti-

gers he knocked me down with three straight pitches —
and me a .200 hitter. He had that overpowering competitive arrogance that all great athletes have."

Metro went on to say, "What an absolute delight it
was to watch him pitch a ball game, pitch for pitch, out
for out, inning by inning, a true pitching masterpiece
unfolding."

Another Tiger teammate, Edward "Red" Borom, said
that "every time he went to that mound it was with the
idea of pitching a complete game." Dickey mentioned
the way Newhouser "took charge on the mound." Dave
Ferriss, the Boston righthander, said that when he
thinks of Newhouser, "I think of great poise, concentration, and a fierce competitor. He had a smooth and
stylish motion and it was a real treat to watch him
pitch and challenge the hitters."

Newhouser hated to give up an important hit. Rosen
recalls the time "when I hit a home run off of him in
1950; he followed me around the bases calling me every
name that he could think of." Ted Williams said Newhouser "had the attitude that if you got a hit, you were
a lucky sonofabitch, and he would eye you as you went
around the bases." Mike Garbark, who hit .244 in two
wartime seasons catching for the Yankees, recalls a
game when Newhouser walked the hitter in front of
him to load the bases, then broke off a curveball to him
that he hit on the fists, a dying quail pop that eluded
the first baseman and landed just inside the right-field
foul line for a two-run double. Newhouser glared at Garbark, standing on second, and said, "it's the chickenshit
hitters that'll beat you every time."

Interestingly, both Paul Richards and Bob Kennedy,
the longtime American League outfielder who is now
vice-president for baseball operations of the San Francisco Giants, stress Newhouser's closing ability. "You
better get him early in the game," Kennedy said, "because if he went into the seventh inning with a one-run

lead, forget it, you didn't beat him and he didn't need bullpen help." Richards said the same thing: "When he took a lead into the 7th inning, he was unbeatable." In a statistical exercise, based on the assumption that one of the major aims of a starting pitcher is to pitch well enough to be around at the end, we find that Newhouser's record of completing 56.7 per cent of his starts is far superior to that of such pitchers as Gomez, Gibson, Wynn, Lemon, Ford, Koufax, and Drysdale, and just marginally behind that of Spahn and Feller.

Perhaps Sid Hudson, the fine pitcher for so many years for the Senators, summed up Newhouser the best. Hudson talked about Hal's fastball, curve, and change-up, his method of pitching, his competitive drive, and then said simply, "He was a complete pitcher."

Election to the Hall of Fame is supposed to be based upon a "player's record, playing ability, integrity, sportsmanship, character [and] contribution to the team(s) on which the player played." Given these criteria, it is hard to understand why Hal Newhouser has not been selected. His record and playing ability are attested to by his contemporaries, by the raw statistics, and by the unbiased formulas of the sabermetricians. His contributions to his teams are evidenced by his MVP awards, the world's championship of 1945, the near-miss the year before, his years as the Tigers' staff leader, and the valuable work he did for the '54 Indians. His integrity and character are unquestioned, and his sportsmanship was of the highest quality: he never let up in his determination to win — fairly and honestly. Hal Newhouser came at his opponents with everything he had and expected them to do the same in return.

With everything else, with the contentions about his place in baseball history, with the burden of wartime ball, the successes, the failures, the arm and shoulder problems, Hal Newhouser always remained a gentleman. So many of the old ballplayers who responded to questions about Newhouser went out of their way to make that point. "A class guy," George Vico called him; "a person I felt privileged to have known," Don Ross said. The young man who came out of an ethnic neighborhood in Detroit to make his mark in life with a strong left arm and a fiery spirit on the ball field was a quiet, reserved family man off the field, a man of whom both friend and foe spoke well, and a successful businessman after his playing days were over.

As it turns out, Hal Newhouser does not need Cooperstown to validate the quality and accomplishments of his life; the Hall of Fame is perhaps a lesser place for his absence.

A NOTE ON SOURCES AND BIBLIOGRAPHY

The first source, obviously, for a work like this is one's own memory. I was fortunate enough to see Hal Newhouser pitch on numerous occasions, during and after the war. The first big league game I ever saw was one in which Newhouser, on May 31, 1943, pitched a two-hit shutout against the Athletics in Shibe Park. And I followed baseball closely during the period covered by Newhouser's later career.

Still, it is surprising how much is blurred in one's memory and how much becomes clearer when contemporaneous sources are consulted. The best of these sources, of course, is *The Sporting News*, known at the time as "Baseball's Bible," which printed a full column on each team every week of the year, carried the boxscore of every game, and added feature articles on many players and games of special interest. *The Sporting News* is simply indispensable for baseball research.

Other newspapers I have consulted have been the *Detroit News* and *Detroit Free Press*, obviously very important for the career of a man who grew up and spent most of his baseball career in the Motor City, *The New York Times*, *New York Herald Tribune*, *New York World-Telegram*, and (later) the *World Telegram and Sun*, the

Philadelphia Inquirer, the *Philadelphia Evening Bulletin*, the *Washington Post*, and the *Wilmington Journal Every Evening*. Also used were *Baseball Digest*, *Baseball Magazine* (now defunct, but very valuable in its time), and *Sportfolio*. In addition, I used many editions of the *Official Baseball Guide* and the *Baseball Register*, both published by *The Sporting News*.

There were many former ballplayers who were most helpful, men, some of them now dead, with whom I met in person, with whom I talked on the telephone, or from whom I received letters containing reminiscences or comments. Foremost among these, of course, was Newhouser himself. Others included Joe Astroth, John Berardino, Ray Boone, Red Borom, Tommy Byrne, George Case, Roger "Doc" Cramer, Frank Crosetti, Bill Dickey, Bob Dillinger, Dominic DiMaggio, Bobby Doerr, Charles "Red" Embree, Bob Feller, Dave "Boo" Ferriss, Denny Galehouse, Mike Garbark, Ford Garrison, Ned Garver, Charlie Gehringer, Hank Greenberg, Don Gutteridge, Mickey Haefner, Mel Harder, Al Hollingsworth, Sid Hudson, Eddie Joost, George Kell, Charlie Keller, Ken Keltner, Bob Kennedy, Lou Kretlow, Eddie Lake, John Lazor, Johnny Lindell, Eddie Lopat, Al Lopez, Tony Lupien, Frank Mancuso, Walter Masterson, Tom McBride, George Metkovich, Charlie Metro, Lambert "Dutch" Meyer, Les Mueller, George Myatt, Lamar "Skeeter" Newsome, Bill Nicholson, Irv Noren, Joe Orengo, Roy Partee, Hal Peck, Johnny Pesky, Nelson Potter, Allie Reynolds, Paul Richards, Al Rosen, Don Ross, Carl Scheib, Frank "Spec" Shea, Tex Shirley, Roy Sievers, Tuck Stainback, Chuck Stevens, Ed Stewart, Billy Sullivan, John Sullivan, Elmer Valo, George Vico, Al Vincent, Jim "Skeeter" Webb, Al Widmar, Ted Williams, and Al Zarilla.

Books, articles, and other publications which were helpful included the following:

Acocella, Nick, and Donald Dewey, *The "All*

Stars" All Star Baseball Book (New York, 1986).

Amman, Larry, "Newhouser and Trout in 1944: 56 Wins and A Near Miss," *Baseball Research Journal* (1983).

Angelo, Frank, *Yesterday's Detroit* (Miami, FL, 1974).

Bartell, Dick, with Norman L. Macht, *Rowdy Richard* (Berkeley, CA, 1987).

Boudreau, Lou, with Ed Fitzgerald, *Player-Manager* (Boston, 1949).

Conot, Robert, *American Odyssey* (New York, 1974).

Crissey, Harrington E., Jr., *Teenagers, Graybeards and 4-Fs*, v. 2: The American League (Trenton, NJ, 1982).

Feller, Bob, *Strikeout Story* (New York, 1947).

Greenberg, Hank, *The Story of My Life*, ed. Ira Berkow (New York and Toronto, 1989).

James, Bill, *The Bill James Historical Baseball Abstract* (New York, 1986).

Masterson, Dave, and Timm Boyle, *Baseball's Best: The MVPs* (Chicago, 1985).

McCaffrey, Eugene V., and Roger A. McCaffrey, *Players' Choice* (New York and Oxford, U.K., 1987).

Mead, William B., *Even the Browns* (Chicago, 1978).

Newhouser, Harold, *Pitching to Win* (Chicago, 1948).

Okrent, Daniel, and Harris Lewine, eds., *The Ultimate Baseball Book* (Boston, 1979).

Reichler, Joseph L., ed., *The Baseball Encyclopedia*, seventh ed. (New York and London, 1988).

Smith, Red, "Doghouse to Let: Apply Newhouser & Trout," *Saturday Evening Post*, March 31, 1945.

Speer, Renwick W., "Wartime Baseball — Not That Bad," *Baseball Research Journal* (1983).

Sullivan, George, and David Cataneo, *Detroit Tigers: The Complete Record of Detroit Tigers Baseball* (New York and London, 1985).

Thorn, John, & Pete Palmer, *The Hidden Game of Baseball: A Revolutionary Approach to Baseball and Its Statistics* (Garden City, NY, 1985).

Thorn, John, & Pete Palmer, eds., *Total Baseball*, (New York, 1989).

Williams, Ted, as told to John Underwood, *My Turn At Bat: The Story of My Life* (New York, 1969).

Three other works which were checked but were hardly of use were by Donald Honig, *The American League: An Illustrated History* (New York, 1983), and *The World Series: An Illustrated History* (New York, 1986), both notable primarily for their pointed omission of any mention of Hal Newhouser, and *American League Most Valuable Players* (Toronto, New York, London, Sydney and Auckland, 1989).

INDEX

276